Mathematics

The Creative Curriculum® Approach

Juanita V. Copley

Candy Jones

Judith Dighe

Toni S. Bickart and Cate Heroman, Contributing Authors

Teaching Strategies Inc.
Washington, DC

Editors: Toni S. Bickart, Judith F. Wohlberg, and Laurie Taub
Cover, book design, and computer illustrations: Carla Uriona
Illustrations: Jennifer Barrett O'Connell
Layout/production: Jennifer Love King, Kristina W. Lowe, and Jeff Cross

Teaching Strategies, Inc.
P.O. Box 42243
Washington, DC 20015
www.TeachingStrategies.com
ISBN: 978-1-879537-88-0

Library of Congress Cataloging-in-Publication Data

Copley, Juanita V., 1951-
  Mathematics : the creative curriculum approach / Juanita V. Copley,
Candy Jones, Judith Dighe.
    p. cm.
  Summary: "Shows teachers how to create a mathematically-rich
physical environment and guide children's mathematics learning
through focused lessons and integrated learning throughout the day.
Supplements The Creative Curriculum for Preschool, a comprehensive
curriculum for children ages 3-5. Discusses the components of
mathematics, mathematical process skills, mathematics learning in
interest areas, and mathematics activities"--Provided by publisher.
  Includes bibliographical references.
  ISBN-13: 978-1-879537-88-0 (alk. paper)
  1. Mathematics--Study and teaching (Primary)--United States. 2.
Mathematics--Study and teaching (Early childhood)--Activity programs.
3. Curriculum planning--United States--Handbooks, manuals, etc. 4.
Child development--United States--Handbooks, manuals, etc. I. Jones,
Candy, 1956- II. Dighe, Judith, 1938- III. Title.

  QA135.6.C665 2007
  372.7'044--dc22

                        2007001078

Printed and bound in the United States of America
2011   2010   2009   2008   2007
10 9 8 7 6 5 4 3 2 1

Acknowledgments

We received lots of help from many talented people. We want to thank our expert panel for their work in reviewing our drafts and providing specific feedback and suggestions:

Rosalind Charlesworth, Ph.D., Professor and Chair, Department of Child and Family Studies, Weber State University, Ogden, UT

Laura Colker, Ph.D., early childhood education consultant and co-author of *The Creative Curriculum for Preschool*, Washington, DC

Nell W. McAnelly, M.Ed., Associate Director, Gordon A. Cain Center for Scientific, Technological, Engineering, and Mathematical Literacy, Louisiana State University

Roberta McHardy, Ph.D., Assistant Professor, Department of Educational Theory, Policy, and Practice, Louisiana State University, Baton Rouge, LA

Lois Rector, M.Ed., early childhood education consultant, member of the Teaching Strategies Staff Development Network, Slaughter, LA

Walter Rosenkrantz, Ph.D., Professor Emeritas, Department of Mathematics and Statistics, University of Massachusetts (Amherst), Amherst, MA

Toni S. Bickart and Cate Heroman of Teaching Strategies provided so much help that we are delighted to list them as contributing authors. We thank Sue Mistrett, who gave us particular guidance about adaptations to the Computers Interest Area and helped us make modifications to the activities to better meet the needs of all children.

Thanks to Carla Uriona, Creative Director, for her excellent work on the management of the design and production process; Jennifer Love King, Kristina W. Lowe, and Jeff Cross for their cheerful work (and good humor) on production and layout. We thank Judy Wohlberg and Laurie Taub for their editing skills and Rachel Friedlander Tickner for her diligent copy editing. Thanks to Jan Greenberg for reviewing the activities and Maha Jafri for helping with the review process.

Over the last three years we have introduced the concepts in this book to hundreds of teachers who have used them with many groups of children. We thank all of them for their commitment and hard work.

We thank Diane Trister Dodge, president of Teaching Strategies, for her continuing support and encouragement.

Table of Contents

Chapter 5–Mathematics Activities 169

Foreword

Children are eager to explore mathematical concepts and are capable learners of mathematical ideas. As researchers learn more about the skill development of young children, early childhood mathematics has become an important focus of the educational community. The National Council of Teachers of Mathematics (NCTM) included prekindergarten in its published *Principles and Standards* (2000) and its new publication, *Curriculum Focal Points for Prekindergarten through Grade 8 Mathematics* (2006), and it added a series of books about early childhood mathematics to its list of publications. At the same time, the National Association for the Education of Young Children (NAEYC) published several books about mathematics, co-published books with NCTM, and initiated the development of a position statement that was widely disseminated by both organizations. In addition, as state education departments and Head Start have developed standards for mathematics, they have also included mathematical objectives for prekindergarten children.

As expectations for children and mandates for programs have changed, more researchers have focused on mathematics and young children. Their findings confirm that teachers must be intentional about the way they talk with children and the kinds of activities and experiences they plan to help children acquire important attitudes, skills, and knowledge about mathematics.

In *The Creative Curriculum® for Preschool*, we included information about teaching mathematics in the preschool classroom that is based on research findings about how children develop mathematical skills. *Mathematics: The Creative Curriculum® Approach* offers more detailed guidance, including up-to-date, research-based teaching strategies. The book is intended for programs using *The Creative Curriculum for Preschool*, but the content can be applied by all programs for preschool children.

Mathematics instruction is most effective when it is part of a comprehensive approach that pays equal attention to all aspects of a child's development: social/emotional, physical, cognitive, and language. There must be opportunities for children to explore independently and times for direct teaching in small groups, in large groups, and one-on-one. In addition, children practice and use mathematical skills during daily routines and during the active learning that takes place in interest areas. The curriculum goals and objectives must link directly to an assessment system so that teachers can pinpoint each child's progress in developing skills, plan instruction on the basis of that information, and ensure that every child is learning. This is the approach explained in *The Creative Curriculum*.

Mathematics Instruction in *The Creative Curriculum*

Two principles are central to understanding our approach to mathematics instruction.

- **The child is the focus of mathematics instruction.** Good mathematics teaching begins with knowing children, that is, their developmental levels as well as their unique characteristics, skills, interests, and learning styles. Teachers must combine their knowledge of children and their knowledge of mathematics to plan instruction that is mathematically rich, age-appropriate, and individualized.

- **The child also teaches you.** As teachers observe children at play during choice-time and group-time experiences, they learn much about children's knowledge of mathematics. With this information, they plan what, when, and how to teach.

A distinguishing feature of *The Creative Curriculum* is its organizational structure, which includes five components and rests on a solid foundation of theory and research. Here are brief explanations of how each component of *The Creative Curriculum* helps teachers make decisions about teaching mathematics in a preschool program.

How Children Develop and Learn: Teachers must know what preschool children are like, developmentally and individually, as well as the ways in which culture influences children's learning. They use this knowledge to make decisions about daily and weekly practices, including routine experiences, instructional activities, and interactions with children.

The Learning Environment: The learning environment influences what is learned and how. In *The Creative Curriculum* classroom, the physical space is arranged in interest areas: Blocks, Dramatic Play, Toys & Games, Art, Library, Discovery, Sand & Water, Music & Movement, Cooking, Computers, and Outdoors. Children make choices about where to work, what to do, and whether to engage in activities independently or with a few other children. By including mathematical materials in every interest area, children can explore mathematical ideas on their own and develop important skills such as reasoning, problem solving, and communicating. They explore mathematical ideas and represent their thinking and learning. Daily routines and activities offer more opportunities to involve children in meaningful mathematical experiences. Children are able to connect concepts in mathematics with everyday experiences.

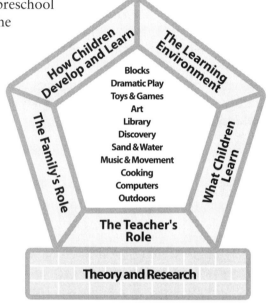

What Children Learn: This component identifies the knowledge and skills that are essential for children to learn in all content areas: literacy, mathematics, science, social studies, the arts, and technology. In order for teachers to be intentional about mathematics instruction, they must know the components of mathematics and the process skills that are identified in the research literature. This book expands the discussion of mathematics that is offered in chapter 3 of *The Creative Curriculum for Preschool*.

The Teacher's Role: After families, teachers are the single most important influence on children's learning. To address the learning needs of every child, teachers must know how to observe children intentionally. They observe children with the goals and objectives of *The Creative Curriculum* in mind as well as the skills and concepts that are related to each component of mathematics. Then they document their observations so they can think about their meaning and plan instruction that will be appropriate for each child.

Teachers plan instruction for individual children, for large and small groups, and for interest areas. As they involve children in long-term studies, children explore science and social studies topics and use literacy and mathematics skills as they investigate. The strong link between systematic assessment and curriculum enables teachers to scaffold children's learning, including the learning of mathematics.

The Family's Role: Mathematics is an integral part of children's everyday lives. They use it in their play and when they participate in family activities such as cooking dinner, shopping, and playing games. Sometimes family members have difficulty recognizing the important role of mathematics in their lives because they often use mathematical skills unconsciously. *The Creative Curriculum* encourages teachers to build on what families already know and do in relation to mathematics, to expand the way families think about mathematics, and to suggest ways in which families can support their children's understanding and use of math skills during everyday experiences.

What This Book Offers

Building on the comprehensive approach of *The Creative Curriculum for Preschool*, this book offers teachers practical ideas and strategies for teaching mathematics in the preschool classroom. Its clear, practical format makes it easy for teachers to find and understand information and to incorporate ideas into their programs. Research is described in practical terms, so teachers learn not only *what* to do but *why* particular strategies and activities are important and effective.

Mathematics Content, Process Skills, and Effective Strategies

This book includes a detailed description of mathematics content and process skills for preschool programs and offers explicit guidance about how to teach these skills effectively. In addition to an explanation of the research about how and when children develop understanding, you will find detailed scenarios that describe teacher-guided instruction in small groups, in large groups, and as part of studies.

Purposeful Use of Interest Areas

Central to *The Creative Curriculum for Preschool* is the knowledge that children need time, opportunity, and materials to construct their own understandings about the world. When mathematics is integrated into interest areas, children have opportunities to explore mathematical ideas on their own. They learn to think logically, solve meaningful problems, and see connections between mathematics and real-life experiences. *Mathematics: The Creative Curriculum Approach* shows how to incorporate mathematical materials into interest areas and gives examples of what teachers say and do to encourage critical thinking skills and scaffold children's learning.

Mathematics Activities

The final chapter of the book offers activities that help children learn, practice, and master the content and process skills described earlier. It explains activities related to each component and offers guidance about ways to extend the activities to make them more (or less) challenging and meet children's individual needs.

We hope that teachers are inspired and empowered by the many ideas presented in this book and that they come to enjoy teaching mathematics. Children who sense that their teachers enjoy and value mathematics will learn to love it, themselves. Children are likely to become competent mathematicians when their early mathematical experiences are meaningful and satisfying.

Diane T. Dodge

Diane Trister Dodge
Founder and President, Teaching Strategies, Inc.

How to Use This Book

Mathematics: The Creative Curriculum® Approach is an important part of Teaching Strategies' mathematics program. While teachers can use the book by itself, it is a valuable part of a comprehensive curriculum and assessment system for children ages 3–5. This supplement expands on the information in *The Creative Curriculum® for Preschool*, showing how and why mathematics can and should be part of children's everyday experiences and activities. It explains early mathematics learning and describes when and how to teach directly the skills and concepts children need to become successful mathematical thinkers.

Chapter 1, The Components of Mathematics, describes the mathematics content for preschool including: 1) number and operations, 2) geometry and spatial sense, 3) measurement, 4) patterns [algebra], and 5) data analysis. There is a description of the concepts involved, a summary of related research, explicit guidance about ways in which teachers intentionally promote children's understanding of the concepts, and suggestions for assessing children's learning. The section includes "Tips to Share With Families," ideas for ways to support children's understanding of the concepts at home.

Chapter 2, Mathematical Process Skills, describes the five process skills of mathematics: 1) problem solving, 2) reasoning, 3) communicating, 4) connecting, and 5) representing. The chapter shows how teachers can intentionally promote the development of each skill. A sample classroom activity illustrates ways to encourage children to use each process skill presented, to help teachers clearly understand how to teach the skill.

Chapter 3, Planning Your Mathematics Program, helps you get started. To plan, you have to know what you want children to learn. This chapter therefore begins with *The Creative Curriculum* cognitive objectives that address mathematics. Throughout the book, references to these objectives will guide your observation and planning. Because the physical environment is a powerful influence, the next step is to create a mathematics-rich classroom, including a wide range of materials that encourage children to engage in mathematical experiences. We show how every event in the day, from children's arrival to their departure, is an opportunity to promote mathematical skills. Teachers have to plan a variety of learning experiences for children. The next section of this chapter describes how teachers offer learning opportunities for large and small groups during planned, teacher-guided instructional experiences. We show how studies can be used to give children meaningful opportunities to use mathematical thinking. Because some children have special needs, this chapter offers guidance about meeting the specific needs of English language learners, advanced mathematics learners, and children with disabilities.

Chapter 4, Mathematics Learning in Interest Areas, invites you to reconsider your interest areas as the context for mathematics learning. The chapter begins with a discussion of the Toys and Games Area, the hub of mathematics learning in *The Creative Curriculum* classroom. The discussions of the remaining ten interest areas are formatted in the same way. The first section of each discussion looks at everyday experiences that typically occur in the area and shows the relationship to mathematics. As you evaluate your interest areas, use the suggestions from this chapter to include mathematics-related materials and books. There are suggestions about how to scaffold children's learning as they engage in everyday experiences in the area. A final section helps you observe children's progress while working in the area.

Chapter 5, Mathematics Activities, includes specific instructions for activities for large groups, small groups, or individual children. The activities are organized by component and designed so that teachers can easily identify the targeted concepts. Single activities often address multiple concepts and sometimes multiple components. The directions for each activity include a list of materials, instructions for preparing the activity and guiding children's learning, the recommended setting, and the expected duration of the activity. Adaptations are suggested for a range of learners.

First, look at your daily schedule and think about the best opportunities to include the activities. Next, think about the children's developmental levels related to mathematics and the specific skills and concepts you want to teach. With this information in mind, select activities that meet the particular needs of the children.

The Appendix includes tools to help you with various aspects of your mathematics program. There are blackline masters for some of the activities in chapter 5. The "Matrix of Activities" lists all the activities, shows which components of mathematics they address, and suggests the interest areas in which you might choose to do them. The "Scope of Instruction" and the cognitive goals from *The Creative Curriculum Developmental Continuum for Ages 3–5* will be helpful in your planning. We prepared two observation checklist forms ("Number and Operations Observation Form" and "Geometry and Spatial Sense Observation Form") as reproducible forms for tracking aspects of each child's learning and development. We hope the "Mathematics Implementation Checklist" will help you evaluate your classroom environment and they way you interact with children. Finally, the "Glossary" is a helpful resource to make sure you are using mathematical language correctly.

Mathematics: The Creative Curriculum Approach can be used in a variety of ways. Teachers can use it independently to learn more about mathematics learning for young children and to plan instruction. It can also serve as the content for focused professional development, either in study groups or learning teams, or as part of ongoing training. Teachers could learn about a specific component and related activities and then practice them in the classroom. These classroom experiences can be discussed at future sessions with colleagues.

inside this chapter

Components of Mathematics

Through observation of young children, we have come to know and understand that mathematics is already a part of their world—and they love it! A 1-year-old asks for more cookies and cries when someone takes one away. Two-year-olds display two fingers to tell how old they are. Three-year-olds use geometric skills as they rotate and stack blocks to form tall towers. Four-year-olds identify patterns on the floor tile and predict what will happen when they turn the corner. Five-year-olds are fascinated with how tall they are and how their height compares to that of the *Tyrannosaurus rex*.

Research supports the notion that young children have an intuitive sense of informal mathematics. It can be seen during play when they use mathematics to make sense of their world. Numerically, young children count coins as they shop at the store, write numbers to help them remember how many orders of flowers a pretend customer wants, and use a number sequence as they exercise in a pretend aerobics class. Geometrically, children manipulate puzzle pieces, use positional words when they enact the *Three Billy Goats Gruff*, and investigate shapes as they build a city in the Block Area. Algebraically, children create patterns in their art work and march in rhythm to a song. From a measurement perspective, they build tall structures and compare them to friends' structures, or they weigh fruit at the class supermarket. Indeed, the skills children learn and use during creative, imaginative play easily involve mathematical concepts.

As an early childhood teacher, you play an important role in bridging children's informal understanding of mathematics with more formal, school-based mathematics. That is, you design the learning environment by purposely placing mathematics materials in interest areas for child-initiated explorations and by intentionally introducing activities with a mathematics focus. You observe and listen as children interact with materials and their peers, and then you use mathematical vocabulary to describe their actions and thinking. You ask questions as children investigate. You play logic games, create mathematical problem-solving stories, and include numerical and algebraic activities as part of the daily routine.

The National Council of Teachers of Mathematics crafted content standards in five areas for the prekindergarten child:

- number and operations

- geometry and spatial sense

- measurement

- patterns (algebra)

- data analysis

These standards are described in *Principles and Standards for School Mathematics* (NCTM, 2000) and were used to organize the content information in *The Creative Curriculum for Preschool* (2001). The latest NCTM publication, *Curriculum Focal Points* (2006), confirms that number and operations, geometry, and measurement are the areas that should receive the most emphasis in preschool.

This chapter discusses each component in more detail, relating research to the teacher's role and assessment strategies. With a clear understanding of the components of mathematics, teachers will be able to observe children, analyze and evaluate their mathematical learning and development, and plan instruction to help each child progress.

Number and Operations

Number concepts are the most easily identifiable mathematical content in early childhood classrooms. In fact, young children will often say, when asked about math, "It's about numbers and counting." Without doubt, number is the most important and usable concept for young children and is the concept that should receive the most emphasis in the preschool classroom. At the preschool level, number and operations concepts involve nine different ideas.

Counting

To count well, children must learn three things: the number sequence, one-to-one correspondence, and that the last number named when counting a set of objects tells *how many* are in the set. The first 20 numbers in the *counting sequence* are usually learned by rote. Young preschoolers first learn to understand the words *one, two, three, four* and to identify collections of objects that represent those numbers. Older preschoolers may count to 10 and beyond, but they may not do so consistently or in the correct order. When children encounter the larger decades such as the 30s, 40s, or 50s, they begin to understand the pattern of number names and counting becomes easier. Because number names like *eleven, twelve,* and *thirteen* do not follow a typical pattern like *twenty-one, twenty-two,* and *twenty-three,* they can be especially troublesome.

One-to-one correspondence means that one number name is given or matched to one and only one object in a set being counted. One-to-one correspondence is important in helping children to keep track of the objects they have or have not counted in a set. Finally, children must realize that the last number named when all objects in a set have been counted is the number that tells *how many.* This is called the *cardinal* number. For example, after a child counts four pennies, he says, "I have four pennies," and does not start the counting sequence again.

Quantity (Sense of Number)

Understanding how many are in a set is one of the first number ideas a child demonstrates. When asked how old she is, a young child may incorrectly show two fingers and say, "Three," or extend three fingers and say, "Two." With experience, children easily develop a sense of number about objects in small sets, that is, sets with two, three, or four objects. Children often can look at a group of objects or fingers extended on one hand and identify the quantity without even counting. This is referred to as *subitizing.* In most instances, however, young children develop an understanding of quantity by counting the objects in a set or making a specific set of objects.

Comparisons (More/Fewer or Less)

When comparing two sets, children often can tell which set has more or less by simply looking. They also can match the individual items in the sets to determine which set has more or which set has fewer. At an early age, children should be able to use words like *one more* or *two more*. The words *fewer* or *less* are seldom part of children's everyday vocabulary; however, they often use words that have the same meaning, such as *littler* or *not as much* to talk about the set containing fewer items.

Order

Ordinal numbers—*first*, *second*, *third*, and so forth—indicate sequence. Common uses of these words indicate where someone is in line or the position of items in a row of objects. Most young children have no problem understanding *first*; the other ordinal numbers are more difficult.

Numerals

Just as young children need to learn about alphabet letters and how to write them, they also need time to investigate the use of numerals. Writing numerals is not an important skill at the preschool level, but children should see numerals displayed, begin to develop an understanding of what they represent, and investigate their use.

Combining Operations (Adding)

While young children are not adding with symbols in the traditional sense, they often combine sets of objects to find out *how many in all*. Common word problems for children involve getting more of something and then finding out how many they have all together. They also combine sets of objects to make a larger set.

Separating Operations (Subtracting)

The operation of *take away* is a common separating operation and one that young children understand. A common separating problem is one that involves a child's having a set amount of objects and some objects being removed; they then find out how many *are left*.

Sharing Operations (Dividing)

Young children grow up *sharing* snacks, coins, and small toys. When they begin with a set of objects and *share* them with friends, they are beginning to understand the operation of dividing, or forming groups. In working with young children, the concept of a *fair share* will need to be taught and emphasized.

Set-Making Operations (Multiplying)

Children begin to develop an understanding of multiplication when they engage in activities such as distributing birthday treats or passing out materials. For example, they make equal sets when they give everyone two cookies or four crayons, or when they place three pieces of plastic eating utensils at each place setting in the Dramatic Play Area.

What Does Research Say?

Children develop counting skills at very early ages. The easiest collections for a 3-year-old to count are those in a straight line. From 3 to 5 years of age, children learn to count objects in larger sets and in different arrangements (Baroody, 2005).

Many 3-year-old children believe that two sets of objects have the same number if the objects are close to each other. By age 4, many children can develop a matching process so that they can compare the sets (Piaget & Szeminska, 1952).

Three- and 4-year-old children can often solve subtraction problems before they can solve addition problems (Copley & Hawkins, 2005).

Three-year-olds can divide small collections into equal subsets; many 4- and 5-year-olds can divide larger collections using specific sharing strategies (Clements, 2004).

To solve combining or separating problems, young children use counting strategies and typically model the activity directly using objects or fingers. Later they develop rather complicated counting strategies (Baroody, 2005).

Most preschoolers have developed a counting schema for the numbers 1–5, a quantity schema that allows them to think of small quantities in comparison to one another, and can use words to talk about changes that can be made. However, they do not connect the ideas until later. (Starkey, 1992; Siegler & Robinson, 1982; Gelman, 1978).

Young children can think about small numbers without having the physical objects (Steffe & Cobb, 1988).

Children often do not understand mathematical words in a problem situation and require modeling with concrete objects and words to develop an "operation sense" (Copley & Hawkins, 2005).

What Is the Teacher's Role in Developing an Understanding of Number and Operations?

Although young children naturally begin to develop some informal mathematical understandings, many more opportunities to learn more school-based or formal mathematics need to be provided. The teacher's role is critical to that development. Generally, teachers should identify everyday situations that involve numbers and operations and intentionally teach those concepts to children through daily routines, choice-time activities, and large- and small-group instruction. There are many teaching strategies that can contribute to children's development of numerical understanding.

Practice counting using a variety of learning styles and representations.
Count using rhymes and verses and in ways that involve children physically. For example, children can touch their heads, shoulders, waists, knees, and toes as they count so that they can practice one-to-one correspondence. On occasion, point to the numbers on a number chart as children count aloud. The numbers have a visual pattern, and the auditory and visual clues used together are helpful.

Provide a variety of materials to help children develop an understanding of quantity.
Introduce children to many different number representations, for example, pips on a domino or number cube, tally marks, footsteps, fingers, counters of all kinds, and a wide variety of art materials. Ask them to create sets of two, three, four, or five using concrete materials. After they have created many concrete sets, children can draw pictures or paste cutouts on paper to represent specific quantities.

Model counting strategies.
Model correct counting. As you count, demonstrate how to keep track of objects you have counted and respond with one number to tell *how many* are in a set. Label what you counted (e.g., five boys or three fingers) and record the answer using numerals and words.

Model comparing the number of objects in two sets.
Compare two lines of children by having them join hands with a partner. Then emphasize that the people who do not have a partner are in the line with *more* people and the people who have a partner are in the line with *fewer* or *less* people. Do the same task with objects showing how the objects are individually matched to compare.

Identify everyday situations to use ordinal numbers.

As children participate in routine activities such as taking turns to wash hands, working in interest areas, or listening to their favorite stories, use ordinal numbers to describe people or objects. For example, you could say, "The first person to run the obstacle course is Dallas," or "I think the second block in your tower is the biggest one," or "The third goat had the hardest time getting over the bridge." You can also play hiding games in which you hide a particular object under one of four cups. A child must figure out if the object is under the first, second, third, or fourth cup. Emphasizing the words for ordinal numbers is critical to children's understanding.

Make obvious mistakes so that children can identify the errors.

Using a favorite puppet, pretend to count incorrectly, forget number names, mix up terms like *more* and *fewer*, and give wrong answers. Encourage children to correct the puppet and respond correctly. After the children are secure in their number understanding, you can make mistakes as well; however, make them very obvious and talk aloud to indicate that you might make a mistake. "I can't remember…" and "I wonder what comes next…" are two good beginning phrases.

Illustrate and model a variety of problems that involve combining, separating, sharing, or set-making.

Use everyday situations to model the use of operations. Helpers can pass out materials so everyone gets the same number, class treats can be shared, and the total number of children in the class or an interest area can be constantly changed as children leave or enter during the school year.

Act out operation stories.

Pose story problems that involve adding, subtracting, multiplying, or dividing. Have the children act out the stories themselves or with objects. Then count to solve the problems. Use the numbers (1–5) and remember to emphasize the vocabulary that indicates the actions (e.g., *take away*).

Use books to encourage numerical reasoning.

Many books that you share with your class include number questions or problems. After reading a book several times, add numbers to some of the sentences. Write the numbers on an adhesive note and put it on the page. Ask the children to tell *how many* or to solve a problem created with the numbers.

Encourage children to tell *how many* stories.

Ask children questions that prompt them to tell *how many*. For example, they can tell how many rode in the car during outdoor time, how many played at the water table, how many footsteps it took to walk across the room, or how many cookies they had after their friend gave them more.

Publish number books.

Share a variety of number books. Cover some pages and then ask the children to tell what pages are missing. Help them create the missing pages. Have children write, illustrate, and publish class number books. Some possible titles for these books could be *All the Animals We Saw at the Zoo* or *The Purple Things We Found at School* or *The Eyes in Our Class.*

Create a numerically-rich environment.

Include numerals in every area of your classroom. Display them in written or cutout forms and include them as manipulatives where appropriate (e.g., magnetic numerals in the Toys and Games Area, stamps in the Library Area, sponges in the Art Area). Include a variety of collections for counting and sorting activities. Number books as well as number stories should be included in the Library Area. A calendar, attendance chart, lunch or snack numbers, and any other management tool with numbers should be displayed. Counters of every kind should be easily available as well as number lines, a hundred chart, and a well-written list of numerals (1–20). Props that include numbers for the Dramatic Play Area should be prominently displayed so students can use them as they play (e.g., grocery receipts, old checkbooks, price lists). Games that include dice and require children to move spaces also contribute to children's counting skills.

How Do You Assess Children's Progress?

To assess children's progress with number and operations, observe children consistently and regularly. Observe children in interest areas and in group settings as they

- count sets of objects

- solve number problems

- play games that require them to move one, two, or three spaces

- compare the number in two sets of objects

- "see" small groups of numbers

- write symbols for number quantities

As children complete activities or work in small groups, ask the following questions:

How many are there? How did you find out?

Which set has more? How do you know?

How many do you see? Why do you think so?

I have three counters. John gives me two more. How many do I have now?

Jeffrey has four cookies. The dog ate two of them. How many cookies does Jeffrey have left?

Amy's mom made 30 cookies. Do we have enough for everyone to get two cookies?

How far can you count? What number comes before 10? After 30?

Why are you adding one more spoon to that place?

How many balloons do you think we should have for the party? Why do you think so?

Tips to Share With Families

- Count everything! Touch the objects as you say the corresponding numbers.

- Count incorrectly or lose track of which objects you have already counted. Encourage children to help you find your errors.

- Read counting books with your child frequently. Together, check each page to see whether the number of pictured objects matches the numeral on the page. After the objects on a page are counted, hide some of them with a small piece of paper or your hand. Ask children to decide how many objects are hidden.

- Ask children to help set the table, distributing the same number of each object to each place, or ask them to tell how many more they need of something to have a particular number.

- Concentrate on either the number 5 or 10. Ask children to use their fingers to talk about parts of 5 (2 fingers on one hand and 3 fingers on the other hand, or 1 finger on one hand and 4 fingers on the other). In a similar manner, ask children to talk about the parts of 10 (for example, 3 fingers have rings and 7 fingers do not, or 2 thumbs and 8 other fingers).

- Play games with 5 objects and 10 objects. For example, suggest that children toss 5 or 10 pennies, or 5 or 10 puffballs. They should count and tell how many pennies land "heads-up" and how many land "heads-down." They can identify how many puffballs land in a plastic cup target and how many land outside of the cup.

Geometry and Spatial Sense

Young children find geometry an exciting topic. Unfortunately, many early childhood teachers only focus children's attention on learning about four shapes: square, rectangle, triangle, and circle. There is so much more to investigate! In preschool, there are four important geometry concepts young children need to explore and develop.

Shape

Both two- and three-dimensional shapes are important to the understanding of geometry. Young children need to recognize shapes, build with them, illustrate them in their own way, describe shapes' attributes, compare shapes, and sort them by their characteristics. Naming shapes is not the most important aspect of this topic. However, children should be exposed to the correct geometric terms for shapes, and they should be given opportunities to identify shapes by both name and what they look like. (See the Glossary.) Finally, young children should be encouraged to predict what will happen when they build and create with shapes or put together two- or three-dimensional shapes.

Some three-dimensional shapes that preschool children can easily identify include

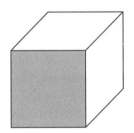

cube
"Like a box"

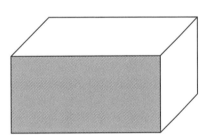

rectangular prism
"Like a box"

cylinder
"Like a can"

sphere
"Like a ball"

Space

Children should describe shapes and other objects using relationship words like *near, under, by, on top of, right,* and *left.* They should be able to locate and find shapes or other objects when given simple verbal directions or when using maps with pictures and diagrams. Shapes should be positioned in a variety of ways and orientations in space so that children can identify them regardless of how they "look."

Transformations

Moving shapes by sliding them to a new position, flipping them over, turning, or combining them are important geometric skills. Notice how children use these skills when they work puzzles, attempt to fit blocks on a shelf, or mold clay to make a model of a three-dimensional shape. Young children also can create shapes that are symmetrical, as shown in the following illustration.

Symmetrical Block Picture

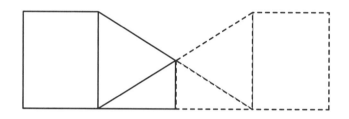

Visualization

Young children should be able to picture geometric shapes mentally after seeing them and then represent what they visualized using the same geometric shapes or drawings. Also give children opportunities to see pictures or drawings from different orientations (e.g., portrait or landscape) and block creations from different perspectives, (e.g., from the top, side, and underneath).

Children do not develop their ideas about shapes from simply looking at them. They must manipulate, draw, or represent the shapes in a variety of ways (Clements, 1999).

Three- and 4-year-old children typically recognize shapes in a variety of orientations. As children get older, they identify particular shapes only if they are in one orientation. That is, a triangle is a triangle only if it is "flat on a side" (Copley, 2000).

Typically, young children judge shapes by appearance as a whole; that is, a triangle is a triangle because it "looks like one" (Van Hiele, 1986).

Children learn about shapes during their preschool years, and their concepts of shapes stabilize as early as age 6 (Clements, 1999).

Three-year-olds can build simple, yet meaningful maps with landscape toys such as houses, cars, and trees. Older preschoolers can learn the relative distances between landmarks (Clements, 2000).

With experience, preschool children can develop visualization. They can observe a shape picture using five shapes, remember it by visualizing what they just saw, and then make the picture accurately using the appropriate shapes in the correct relationship to each other (Copley, 2004).

Four- and 5-year-old children can move shapes to determine if they are identical to other shapes; they slide, rotate, and sometimes flip the shapes to determine whether they match (Clements, 2003).

Children in an environment where they investigated shapes by combining, folding, cutting, drawing, and copying them were able to select examples of specific shapes much more accurately than children who had not been provided the rich, investigative environment (Clements, 1999).

Visualization and spatial reasoning are improved with interaction with computer animations and in other technological settings (Clements et al., 1997).

What Is the Teacher's Role in Developing an Understanding of Geometry?

Geometry is a topic that young children naturally explore and enjoy. They build amazing constructions with blocks, create pictures with shapes, and view objects from a variety of perspectives as a result of their constant movement. The teacher's role is to encourage children to reflect on these activities, to use appropriate vocabulary to describe shapes or the orientation of objects, to scaffold children's understanding as they explore, and to encourage children who are not playing with geometry to investigate the ideas. Specific teaching strategies can be used to support young learners of geometry.

Provide opportunities for *all* children to use the Block Area.

The Block Area is the perfect place for children to explore the attributes of three-dimensional shapes. For example, when children stack blocks, they naturally investigate the surface to see if it is flat and can stack easily or if it is curved and cannot stack. All children should have access to this important area, so accommodations may have to be made to enable children with disabilities to use the area easily.

Label shapes with correct names as the children use them.

Use the geometrically correct names for shapes. This can be done by simply adding vocabulary to the child's descriptions or manipulations. For example, when a child says, "I got a round one," when describing a sphere, you can say, "Yes, it is round. It looks like a ball. I call it a *sphere*." When a child identifies a square correctly, you can say, "Yes, it is a square. I call it a *square-rectangle,* because it is a special kind of rectangle." Refer to the Appendix for a list of common two- and three-dimensional shapes and their descriptions.

Provide a rich variety of shapes for investigation.

Unit blocks are essential for teaching and learning geometric concepts. A variety of other three-dimensional shapes are important as well. Hemispheres, triangular prisms, triangular pyramids, rectangular prisms, square pyramids, and spheres provide many other contrasting experiences for children. The same is true for two-dimensional shapes. Often children are only introduced to shapes that have sides of equal lengths. To develop a real understanding of shape, children need to see *squashed* triangles, *really long* rectangles, *funny-shaped* pentagons, and other shapes with unusual configurations.

Ask children to predict and investigate what will happen when two shapes are combined.

Introduce activities that require children to match sides or surfaces of two shapes. Asking children to make a *tall, smooth tower* out of unit blocks encourages them to predict and then investigate how to accomplish that task. Similarly, giving children a set of identical right triangles and asking them to match sides to create shapes encourages a discovery of new squares, triangles, or quadrilaterals.

Shapes Made From Two Congruent Triangles

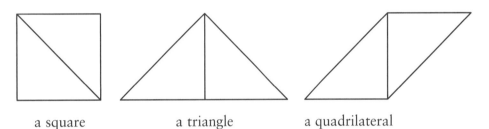

a square   a triangle   a quadrilateral

Model and describe how to make two- and three-dimensional shapes.

Create a particular shape using clay, paper, or another flexible material and describe it as you work. For example, as you transform a clay ball unto a cylinder, you can say, "I am rolling the clay to make the sides smooth. Now I am patting it on the ends so that it will have flat circles on the top and bottom." As you cut paper to make a triangle, you might say, "I need to cut off this corner so I have a straight side. Now I need two more straight sides to make a triangle."

Guide children to act out stories that use positional and spatial words.

Many familiar stories use positional words to describe the motions of a character or an object. *The Three Billy Goats Gruff* and *Goldilocks and the Three Bears* are just two favorites that provide opportunities for children to explore concepts such as *near, inside, outside, far, under, over, next to, between,* and *on top of.*

Begin with three-dimensional shapes.

Children need to hold and manipulate objects before they work with paper representations of objects. The same is true as children explore geometric shapes. Building with three-dimensional shapes, rolling them down ramps, tossing them at targets, and modeling three-dimensional shapes with clay are all good beginning activities for children. Three-dimensional shapes should be used to introduce the two-dimensional shapes, for example, by making block prints in water, paint, or clay. The resulting prints can then be identified as the more common two-dimensional shapes (e.g., a cube makes six square prints, a square pyramid makes four triangle prints and one square print.)

Provide activities that ask children to visualize and represent particular shapes.

Show children photos, models, or sketches of particular shapes or combinations of shapes. Ask children to look and remember what they have seen; then hide the representation. Have children recreate the photo, model, or sketch by using their own shapes. As children develop this skill and have more frequent practice, the models and shape orientations can become more complex and more difficult to visualize and remember.

Use technology to help children visualize geometric ideas.

Computer technology allows children to manipulate shapes and visualize the results quickly and frequently. Often, preschool children's less developed fine motor skills make it difficult for them to move particular blocks so that the others remain in place. Computer technology allows children easily to make the movements piece by piece, see errors, and then correct their actions.

Use the word *not* to introduce non-examples of specific shapes.

To fully understand the attributes of particular shapes, it is critical that young children know what shapes are *not* classified as a particular shape. Create many opportunities for children to sort shapes into two groups, those that are the shape and those that are *not* the shape.

Make class maps and have children use them to find particular objects.

Children love a mystery! Hide or select a particular classroom object. Give the children a map of the classroom with identifiable landmarks and specific clues about the object's location. Have the children search for the hidden object by using the map. For example, if the object is hidden *under* a box-like wastebasket, there could be a sketch of a rectangular prism with an arrow indicating *under*. With older preschoolers, try giving clues that involve relative distances, that is, clues that tell how far an object is from a landmark.

Suggest that children sketch their building plans so that they can be remembered.
Encourage children to represent their constructions in a variety of ways.
They can create sketches or blueprints using black crayons on white or
blue rolled paper or on newsprint. Take photos of the buildings and attach
them to the representation. Do not forget to have the builders sign the
representation. Then place it in the Block Area for future architects and
builders to use.

Encourage the discovery of shape attributes.
Rather than telling children about a shape's attributes, plan experiences
that allow them to experiment with shapes and discover them on their own.
Ramps allow children to discover which three-dimensional shapes roll,
slide, and stand; targets invite them to toss shapes; and feely bags allow
children to discover the attributes through touch. Cutting and folding,
collage, and printing activities are all vehicles for exploring the attributes
of two-dimensional shapes. The discoveries children make on their own
are much more important than anything you can tell them. You guide and
extend learning when you label their discoveries by using their words and
incorporating geometric terminology.

**As children work puzzles, use words like *turn, flip,* or *slide* to explain how the
pieces might fit.**
Transformational language for young children includes the words *turn, flip,*
and *slide*. As teachers interact with children who are working puzzles, they
can teach transformational words by stating how a child should manipulate
a puzzle piece, by describing what the child does—turn, flip, or slide—or
by helping to work a puzzle while describing their own movements. Both
commercial and teacher-made puzzles can be used to help young children
learn to transform shapes from one orientation to another. Teachers can
also create other opportunities for children to fit shapes together by having
them fill in a quilt square or a particular size piece of paper so that there is
no space showing.

Have children clean up by placing shapes on a shelf or in a box so they can easily fit.
Opportunities for cleanup abound in an early childhood classroom.
When shelves in the Block Area are labeled as described in *The Creative
Curriculum for Preschool,* children can match the blocks with their
two-dimensional representations. In the Toys and Games Area, containers
can be labeled so that children can place all the triangles together, all the
circles together, or all the squares together.

How Do You Assess Children's Progress?

To assess children's progress with geometry, observe students regularly. Observe children in interest areas and in other group settings as they

- manipulate shapes

- create structures or make pictures using shapes

- name or label shapes during class activities and in their environments

- experiment with shape attributes

- describe the attributes of shapes

- work puzzles

- use geometric vocabulary appropriately

- work in the Block Area

- move shapes to fit into a confined space

As children complete activities or work in small groups, ask the following questions about shapes:

How is this shape like this one? How is it different?

What would happen if I moved this shape here?

Why isn't this shape a _____? Why is it called a _____?

What if I turned this shape? What would it look like if I flipped it? What would happen if I slid it from your paper to mine?

Where have you seen this shape before?

Can you make a picture out of shapes?

Do you think this would roll?.... slide?.... stack?

How could you cut this paper to make another shape?

What shape could you make out of these two shapes?

What would happen if I dropped this block and it broke?

What would happen if I cut off an end of this shape? What would it look like?

Can you make a square? A triangle? A rectangle with pipe cleaners? How about a ball? A box? Or a cone?

Ask the following types of questions related to spatial sense:

How can I get to the cafeteria from here? To the office from our classroom?

Tell me about the city you have made in the Block Area. Pretend I cannot see it. What does it look like?

Tips to Share With Families

- Encourage children to build towers with blocks. Talk about the blocks that make the best towers and the specific shapes that do not work well.

- Help your child understand geometric vocabulary by using objects. For example, *A cylinder is like a can. A sphere is like a ball, and a square is like the side of this box.*

- Invite children to make particular three-dimensional shapes (cubes, cylinders, or spheres) with playdough or clay.

- Take photos of block constructions that children have made. Ask them to rebuild the constructions by using the photo as a guide.

- Play "Look, Draw, and Fix." Draw a picture using squares, circles, and triangles. Ask children to look at it. Then hide the picture and ask the children to draw it from memory. Then uncover yours and ask the children to fix their pictures if they do not match the one you drew.

- Encourage children to work puzzles. Use words like *turn, slide,* or *flip* to help them decide where to place their puzzle pieces.

Measurement

Measurement is an important, practical mathematical concept that you often hear children discussing with their peers.

I'm bigger than you!

Wow, that giraffe can really stretch his neck huge!

This rock is fat...I can't move it.

I'm four years old...I just had my birthday party!

As these few examples illustrate, children naturally use measurement and comparing language to discuss their surroundings and their relationships to other children. Although the language they use is often incorrect or general, they still love to compare objects using size as an attribute. Young children watch adults use measurement tools and use measurement to solve problems in their world. Children begin to model measurement behaviors and frequently experiment with both standard and nonstandard tools. There are three measurement topics that should be explored by preschool children.

Measurement Attributes

Young children are aware that there are different ways of describing measurements. They begin to recognize the attributes of *length* (how long or tall something is), *capacity* (how much something holds), *weight* (how heavy something is), *area* (how much space is covered), and *time*. However, they often are unable to use the correct vocabulary to describe a particular attribute. They frequently over-use the words *big* or *little* when describing length, volume, weight, area, and even time. Before children learn how to measure, they must first be able to describe and differentiate the attributes of an object by length, capacity, weight, and area.

Comparing and Ordering

Comparison is a fundamental concept that enables children fully to develop an understanding and use of measurement. They begin by comparing two objects by specific attributes: describing one object as taller or shorter than the other, holding more or holding less than the other, heavier or lighter than the other, or covering more or less space than the other. They also can describe an event as taking more or less time than another. Next, children compare three or more objects or events and place them in order. This is a much more difficult task and one that requires many problem-solving, experimental experiences.

Measurement Behaviors and Processes

Actual measurement involves assigning a number to an attribute of an object, such as the length of a crayon or the capacity of a jar. Understanding how to measure accurately is a skill that takes many years to learn. The process of measuring is based on three fundamental concepts:

- **conservation**—a set maintains the same quantity no matter how its parts are arranged or rearranged; an object maintains the same length if it is bent; an amount of liquid poured from one container into a differently sized container retains the same quantity

- **transitivity**—if length A is less than length B, and length B is less than length C, then length A is less than length C

- **unit**—the number and size of units is used consistently for the measurement of one object

To learn these three concepts, young children first experiment with nonstandard measurement tools (e.g., straws or yarn to measure their height, rice or sand in plastic tubs to measure how much "cookie dough" they need for their party, and rocks or marbles to measure the weight of the class gerbil). Experimenting with nonstandard units is a preliminary step to understanding why the use of standard tools is important for accurate measurement. In preschool, experimentation with measurement behaviors is essential to mathematical understanding. Children will learn how to *conserve*, to reason with *transitivity*, to select appropriate *units* or tools for the attribute being measured, and measure with multiple copies of units of the same size (e.g., using teddy bears laid end to end to measure the length of a classroom rug).

What Does Research Say?

Young children know that attributes of length, weight, capacity, and time exist, but they do not know how to reason about them or measure them accurately (Clements, 2003).

Preschool children are interested in measuring and begin to develop important measurement concepts during the ages 3–5 (Clements, 2003).

Children's initial ideas about the size or quantity of an object are based on perception. They judge that one object is bigger than another because it looks bigger (Piaget & Inhelder, 1967).

Preschool children can learn significant ideas about measuring. They can arrange objects side by side to compare their lengths. They can hold one object in each hand to compare their weights if the weights are significantly different. They can lay one leaf on top of another to see which has the greater area if the smaller shape fits within the boundary of the larger leaf (Clements, 2003).

Four-year-old children can begin to learn the process of measuring with nonstandard units. They can lay identical plastic chains end to end across the length of a room and count the number of chains. They can cover a sheet of paper with sticky notes to measure the area of the sheet of paper. They can use teddy bear counters to measure the weight of a toy (Copley, 2004).

Current thinking and research suggests that children can benefit from using rulers along with concrete models of units, even during beginning activities with measurement (Clements, 2003).

What Is the Teacher's Role in Developing an Understanding of Measurement?

The goal of measurement activities in preschool is to encourage exploration, not mastery. Teachers should introduce measurement concepts through a variety of experiences while using the appropriate vocabulary to describe the process. Most importantly, teachers should not limit their expectations of young children when it comes to measurement. Providing a variety of experiences along with reflection and communication about those experiences will likely produce some surprising results.

Provide many standard measurement tools for children to use.
While measurement with standard units is not emphasized at the preschool level, standard measuring tools should be a part of the classroom environment. Rulers, yardsticks, meter sticks, measuring tapes, balance scales, centimeter grid paper, and marked measuring cups are tools that should be accessible to children in the classroom. Children should be encouraged to use them as they want for their measuring experiences. Similarly, teachers and other adults should use them as intended during appropriate class activities.

Model measuring behaviors frequently.
Many measurement opportunities occur throughout the day in preschool. Measuring the length of the Library Area when you need a new rug, using a clock to judge how many more minutes you have until lunch, deciding if a stack of books is too heavy to carry, or deciding if a piece of butcher paper is big enough to cover a table are all measurement activities. To help children develop an understanding of measurement, these activities need to be modeled explicitly for children. Thinking aloud, or describing what you are doing, as you measure will likely prompt children to explore measurement on their own.

Talk about what you are doing as you measure.
An important aspect of any modeling activity is the oral language that is used to describe the activity. Talk aloud as you model the measurement activity, to help children focus on the activity and the particular measurement strategy that is being used.

Encourage measurement problem-solving activities.

Many problem-solving activities also involve measurement. Car races between the teacher's car and the class's car provide good opportunities to explore *measuring fairly*— especially when the distance the teacher's car travels is measured with tiny sticks and the distance the class's car travels is measured with long sticks. Having children completely cover a paper quilt with different rectangular shapes requires them to experiment with area. Making a straw bridge for the *Three Billy Goats Gruff* creates an opportunity for understanding the concept of weight. Preparing cookies for the entire class requires measuring capacity, counting, and addition operations.

Take advantage of daily experiences to discuss measurement concepts.

Many daily experiences lead to a discussion about measurement concepts, particularly time. Almost every day, children ask and teachers answer questions like these: "How much time is left for choice time?...How much longer until outdoor time?...When is snack time?...Is it time for clean-up?" They are also perfect opportunities to introduce a timer. Using a timer allows children to see time passing and, when used along with comparison words to describe the time, children begin to develop an understanding of time measurement.

Use estimation vocabulary.

Most measurements do not need to be exact. Often, only rough estimates are required for length, weight, or capacity measures. Children need to hear estimation vocabulary such as *about*, *close to*, and *almost* in the context of real-life situations.

How Do You Assess Children's Progress?

To assess children's progress with measurement, observe students consistently and regularly. Observe children in interest areas and in group settings as they

- use measurement tools

- try to fit objects into specific spaces

- compare the size of objects

- use measurement vocabulary

- pour water or rice into containers

- use the term *bigger* to describe something

As children complete activities or work in small-group settings, ask the following questions:

About length

Which one is longer? Shorter?

Can you find something that is longer than this? Shorter? How can you show me?

How much ribbon will you need to go around this? How can you figure it out just by looking?

Can you put these three straws in order from the shortest to the longest? How can you show me that your answer is right? Where would you put the fourth straw? How did you know?

About area

Which shape can be covered with the most number of blocks? The least?

Will it take more blocks to cover the table or the book? How can you show that your answer is right?

What if you used cubes to cover the book? Would it take more cubes or blocks to cover it?

About weight

Which is heavier? Lighter? How do you know?

How can you show which person weighs more? Less?

Put these three rocks on the balance, one at a time. How can you tell which rock is the heaviest? The lightest?

About capacity

Which container holds the most? The least? Why do you think so?

How can you find out which container holds the most water?

What if you had three containers? How would you find out which one holds the most water if you could only fill one container at a time?

About time

> *Will it take longer to walk to the door or to write your name?*
>
> *Will it take longer than a minute to walk home? Why do you think so?*
>
> *What do we do when we come to school? What do we do after that? Before lunch? What do we spend the most time doing in our class?*
>
> *What do you think took longer? Shorter?*

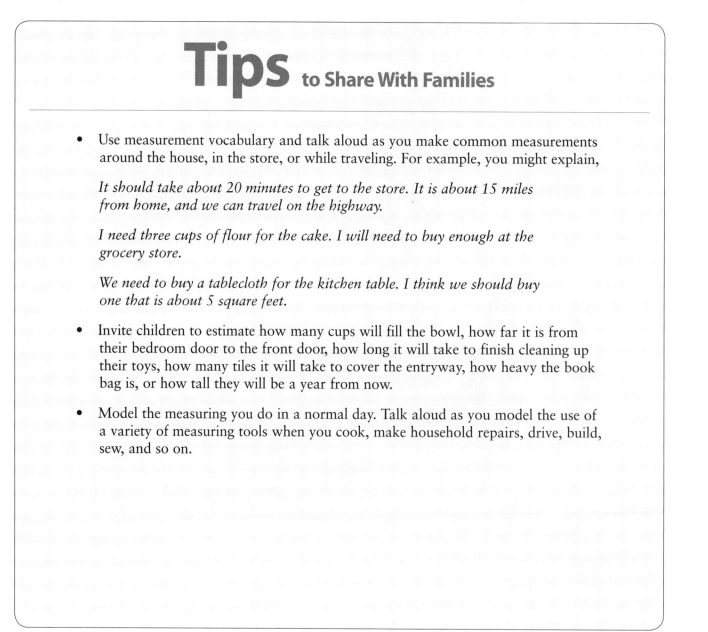

Tips to Share With Families

- Use measurement vocabulary and talk aloud as you make common measurements around the house, in the store, or while traveling. For example, you might explain,

  It should take about 20 minutes to get to the store. It is about 15 miles from home, and we can travel on the highway.

  I need three cups of flour for the cake. I will need to buy enough at the grocery store.

  We need to buy a tablecloth for the kitchen table. I think we should buy one that is about 5 square feet.

- Invite children to estimate how many cups will fill the bowl, how far it is from their bedroom door to the front door, how long it will take to finish cleaning up their toys, how many tiles it will take to cover the entryway, how heavy the book bag is, or how tall they will be a year from now.

- Model the measuring you do in a normal day. Talk aloud as you model the use of a variety of measuring tools when you cook, make household repairs, drive, build, sew, and so on.

Patterns (Algebra)

Algebraic concepts are key to a good basic understanding of mathematics. The recognition, creation, and extension of patterns and the analysis of change are important pre-algebraic concepts for preschool children. The study of patterns and change are exciting topics for young children and can be a strong motivation for discovery and creative thinking.

Patterns

Children begin to identify patterns in their environment at an early age. A consistent daily schedule, the phrases in a song or verse, or the repeated colors of the wall tiles are all patterns that can be easily recognized and described by young children. Extending those patterns in a consistent way is a skill that can be taught to young children and, with practice, transferred from one representation to another. Patterns in sequences of sounds and movement (e.g., stomp, clap, clap; stomp, clap, clap; stomp, clap, clap...), colors in a striped shirt (e.g., blue, red; blue, red; blue, red...) and shapes and positions in a block wall (e.g., block up, down; up, down; up, down...)

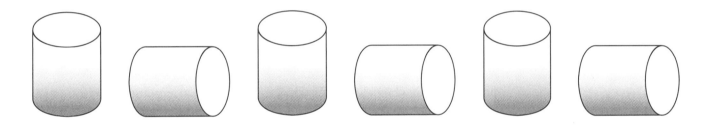

are examples of *repeating* patterns because each unit is repeated in a consistent way. To translate one pattern representation to another, a child must be able to read the pattern using her own words and then read it another way. For example, the cylinder block pattern shown above could be read, "block like a can standing tall, block like a can on its side; block like a can standing tall, block like a can on its side." Then it could be translated to the sound pattern of "stomp, clap; stomp, clap; stomp, clap."

Growing patterns also are important as children's algebraic thinking increases. They become critical to children's understanding of number operations. The plus-one pattern is a growing number pattern because one is added to each number and therefore increases by one each term of the pattern. The following picture of a block staircase is an example of a plus-one pattern.

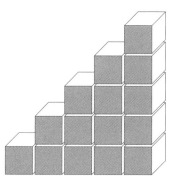

Many rhymes and songs used in early childhood classrooms are examples of growing patterns. In the familiar song "My Aunt Came Back," children add one phrase and action to each verse until they reach the tenth verse with ten actions and phrases. The song is a perfect example of a growing pattern—and one that is hard to perform all at one time!

Change

Young children love to talk about how they have grown or how tall they are. Analyzing change is an important algebraic concept and one that can begin at a young age. To analyze change, children can talk about it qualitatively.

I am bigger than my brother 'cause I growed!

When I was little, I drank milk from a bottle.
Now that I am big, I drink from a glass.

Our eggs have hatched! Look at the chickens!

Children can also describe change quantitatively by using numbers. The growth of the pet gerbil, the change in the height of the bean plants after winter break, or the change from one day to the next in the number of children who drink milk are all examples that young children can relate to about quantitative change.

Very young children are interested in patterns and can learn to copy simple patterns made with objects. Subsequently, they can learn to extend and create their own patterns (Clements, 2004).

Young children can determine the unit of a repeating pattern and can use this skill to determine that two perceptually different patterns actually have the same structure (e.g., red, blue; red, blue; red, blue and stomp, clap; stomp, clap; stomp, clap) (Clements, 2004).

Children will often identify an incomplete unit to repeat or grow. They do not see the part or unit that is being repeated or growing as a whole (Copley, 2005).

Before age 5, children can learn to copy simple patterns made with objects and subsequently, can learn to extend patterns and create their own patterns (Clements, 2003).

Children often believe that something is a pattern simply because a color or shape is repeated once. They do not see that it must be repeated or grow many times before a pattern is established (Copley, 2005).

From the earliest age, children can be learning the basic rudiments of algebra, particularly its representational aspects. When both patterns and their representations are emphasized, the basic ideas of algebra are introduced (Kilpatrick, Swafford, & Findell, 2001).

As young children extend patterns, they are making conjectures that are logical and make sense from their perspective (Carpenter & Levi, 1999).

What Is the Teacher's Role in Developing an Understanding of Patterns?

Many young children naturally search for patterns, but their discoveries need to be labeled and extended. The teacher's role is to challenge children to identify patterns in many settings, represent those patterns auditorially and with objects, and extend those patterns in consistent ways. In addition, the teacher should provide many opportunities for children to create their own patterns with objects, sounds, or words and purposefully teach children different representations for the patterns they identify. Teachers also need to guide children to analyze the changes that occur in their everyday lives by asking them to use words or numbers to talk about the changes they observe. Several specific teaching strategies can contribute to children's development of algebraic concepts.

Identify different patterns in daily routines.

Job assignments, the class schedule, and other daily procedures can be identified and labeled as patterns. If outdoor time is always after snack, the pattern can be written on colored paper and identified as a class pattern (e.g., on Monday, snack [red paper], outdoors [blue paper]; on Tuesday, snack [red paper], outdoors [blue paper]; on Wednesday, snack [red paper], outdoors [blue paper]; and so on.) In any preschool classroom, patterns in daily routines abound and teachers should consistently help children to identify them.

Encourage pattern "talk" and identification.

"Look, it's a pattern!" should be a common expression in a preschool classroom. Initially, teachers model patterns and "think out loud" when seeing patterns (e.g., "Let's walk like an elephant, swaying back and forth and moving our trunks: right, left; right, left; right, left. Oh, it's a pattern!" "Jonathan, you have a pattern on your shirt: blue stripe, red stripe; blue stripe, red stripe."). As children become pattern "detectives," encourage them to describe the patterns they identify and represent them (e.g., in a class book titled, *Patterns Discovered by Our Class*).

Point to numerals as you count out loud.

Rote counting is a familiar pattern. The number sequence of 1, 2, 3, 4, 5, 6, 7, 8, and 9 repeats as children count higher and higher. Because some of the words used to name numbers are unusual (e.g., *eleven* rather than *ten-one* or *twelve* rather than *ten-two* or *fifteen* rather than *ten-five*), the auditory patterns are not as obvious as the visual patterns. The numbers 11, 12, 13, 14, and 15 have an easily recognizable visual pattern and, if pointed out, can be identified by children.

Begin with color patterns and progress to shape and size patterns.
Color patterns are the easiest patterns for young children to identify. Help children create patterns by isolating one attribute at a time. For example, encourage children to use objects that are identical except for color to help them create color patterns. Next, have them use objects that are the same color but different shapes. Continue the sequence with same-colored, same-shaped, and differently sized objects.

Describe positional patterns.
Positional patterns are not the typical patterns described in preschool classrooms. However, they provide a good opportunity to take spatial terms that are critical to geometric understanding and connect them to algebraic ideas. Block or object patterns can be described using words like *up*, *down*, *right*, *left*, *high*, *low*, *crooked*, or *straight*. To encourage the use of positional patterns, provide children with identical blocks or objects. This will help them to focus on the attribute of position rather than color, shape, or size.

Focus on the unit that is to be repeated in a pattern.
To help children focus on the pattern unit, children can "become" part of the unit. For example, to make sidewalk chalk patterns, one child can use the green chalk to make a squiggly line, another child can use the pink chalk to make a squiggly line, and still another child can use the pink chalk to make a squiggly line. The pattern unit—green squiggly, pink squiggly, pink squiggly—would be emphasized, because each child would need to take a turn in order to make the pattern. The pattern unit could then be recorded on a piece of black paper to emphasize the repetition of the unit written on the sidewalk.

Use patterned stories and verses.
Many stories and verses repeat events or phrases in a patterned, consistent manner. These patterns can be illustrated and extended by writing additional parts for the verses or stories. Similarly, many stories include growing patterns. *Mrs. McTats and Her Houseful of Cats* (Alyssa S. Capucilli), *The Napping House* (Audrey Wood), and *The Relatives Came* (Cynthia Rylant) are books that include growing patterns that easily can be acted out by children. This is a wonderful way to connect mathematics and literacy.

Create pattern and change books.
Encourage children to represent patterns they have discovered or created by making books with illustrations of the patterns. Photos of patterns combined with children's illustrations of the same patterns provide children with both two-dimensional, real representations and more abstract representations. Similarly, class stories that represent change can be illustrated with children's drawings or photos. Books such as *When I Was Little: A Four-Year-Old's Memoir of Her Youth* (Jamie Lee Curtis) can be used as models for children's creations. Children can complete phrases like, "When I was little, I could…. Now that I am big, I can…."

Provide opportunities to observe change.

By including plants and animals in the classroom, children are presented with natural opportunities to observe change. They also have a chance to learn that change does not always occur in predictable ways, for example, as indicated by the rapid expansion of the class gerbil population. As changes occur, teachers should describe them by using both words and numbers (e.g., "We had just two gerbils, and now we have lots!" "In our gerbil cage, we had 2 gerbils. Then we had 8, and now we have 17!")

Use a variety of representations for patterns.

Patterns should be described with sounds, words, movements, and objects rather than letters (e.g., ab, abb, abc patterns). Because children are learning letters and the sounds each represent, the use of letters to represent patterns can be confusing and should be avoided.

Extend pattern units for at least five units before a pattern is established.

A pattern is a pattern *only if* it consistently repeats or grows. A pattern cannot be established if a unit is only used one or two times. To encourage children to recognize and extend patterns, they must first be introduced to a well-established pattern.

How Do You Assess Children's Progress?

To assess children's progress with algebraic understanding, observe children consistently and regularly. Observe children in interest areas, during transitions, and in group settings as they

- create patterns using objects

- identify patterns in their environment

- follow movement patterns

- see patterns in stories or verses

- can begin to use more complex patterns

- add to patterns created or discovered by other students

- predict what will happen next in the class schedule

- suggest unusual patterns

- use words to describe patterns or changes

- observe changes in classmates, classroom animals, or classroom plants

As children complete activities or work in small-group settings, ask the following questions:

What do you think we should do next? What do we do normally do after choice time? What happens after snack time?

Would blue or yellow be next? Why do you think so? What if it were green instead?

Oh, I ripped my new striped sweater! What color of yarn should I get to fill in the tear?

What shape should go here to finish this quilt? Would that fit the pattern? How?

How does your block wall look like the playground gate in this photo?

Can you read your pattern? Can you read it a different way? What if you started here? How would your pattern be different?

What if I hid part of your pattern? Could you figure out what part is missing?

What movements do you want us to make today during dance time? What patterns do you want us to follow?

Should this go next...or this? Why?

Let's go on a pattern trip around the school. What patterns do you see? Why should we take a picture of that pattern? How would you use words to describe the pattern?

What will happen on the next page of this story? Why do you think so? What pattern do you see in the story?

How did you change from the beginning of the year to the end of the year? How have you grown? What can you do now that you couldn't do when you began school?

Tips to Share With Families

- Identify patterns everywhere:

  clothing—plaids or repeated stripes, colors, and shapes

  tiles—repeated or growing squares in the kitchen, bathroom, or hall

  books—repeated or growing patterns on the cover or pages, repeated words or phrases

  behavior—repetitions in daily routines; clothing worn in various types of weather; walking, exercise, dance, or marching patterns.

- Encourage children to create and extend patterns with blocks or other toys. After they make a pattern, ask them to describe it (for example, a child could make a pattern of colored blocks and describe it as *orange, blue; orange, blue; orange, blue.* A staircase growing pattern can be described as *one block, two blocks, three blocks, four blocks,* and so on or as *one block, one more, one more, one more,* and so on.

- Algebra includes the concept of change. Create books with your child about how much he or she has grown. A variety of titles can be used, for example, *I Was Two, but Now I Am Three* or *I Used to Be a Baby, but Now I Am Big!*

Data Analysis

Many preschool classrooms contain teacher-made graphs and pictures of data collected by children. An apple graph showing "Our Favorite Apples," pictures of "Things That Are Red," or a chart containing pictures of classroom activities and labeled "Our Schedule" are often posted on the walls around the classroom. These are important tools for data analysis and, if used appropriately, can facilitate children's mathematical understanding. In preschool, there are three important ideas that involve concepts of data analysis.

Sorting and Classifying

Using the attributes of objects to sort and classify is an important skill for young children in many content areas. Initially, children sort objects by separating a group of objects from a larger collection. Their sorting rule is often based on an arbitrary attribute such as "I like this one" or "These are my favorites." With more practice, children begin sorting more consistently, using one attribute to describe the objects in a set. They may label objects as *red* or *big* or *balls* and place all objects that have that attribute to one side. Typically, children begin sorting by color, then by size, and then by shape. Other attributes, such as texture, sound, and function, are also used as sorting rules by young children but often inconsistently. After the objects are sorted and classified, the data needs to be organized so it can be represented and communicated to others.

Representing Data

In preschool classrooms, data is normally represented by using concrete objects, pictures, and graphs. The goal of graphing with young children is to provide a way of showing data about a child or his surroundings so it can be seen and understood. If displayed and labeled properly, children can make comparisons and describe what they see. Young children can often "become" the data in graphs, for example, by standing in a line with others who "like cheese crackers" or by sitting next to a friend who "drinks chocolate milk." Afterwards, children can draw pictures to represent their preferences and place them in a bar graph or inside a circle to represent the organized data. Samples of data representation follow:

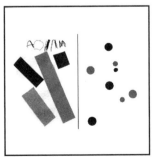 

Describing Data

Vocabulary like *more, fewer, the same number as, larger than, smaller than,* and *not* can be used to describe data displayed on a graph or picture. These terms help connect the topic of number with data analysis. To describe data, it is important that young children separate sets of objects into two groups: one group that has a particular attribute and another group that does *not* have the attribute. Children who can describe and identify objects that are *not* red or *not* circles demonstrate an ability to describe data.

What Does Research Say?

Initially, children sort before they count the number of items in each group (Clements, 2003).

Children sort objects into groups before they can describe them with a label (Russell, 1991).

Typically, young children can only sort a set of objects by one attribute. Normally, it is difficult for 4- and 5-year-olds to classify a set of objects in more than one way (Copley, 2003).

The normal developmental progression of graphic representation is concrete (i.e., using physical objects, like toys, to make the graphs) to pictorial (i.e., using pictures of objects, like drawings of toys) to symbolic (i.e., using letters to represent the color of toys, like *b* for a blue car and *r* for a red car) (Friel, Curio, & Bright, 2001).

With a variety of experiences, young children can read the data displayed in pictures and graphs (Kilpatrick, Swafford, & Findell, 2001).

What Is the Teacher's Role in Developing an Understanding of Data Analysis?

A rich variety of experiences, particularly those involving sorting and classifying, help children to develop the concepts and skills that underlie data analysis. Experiences that help children pose questions, collect data, organize data, represent data, and describe data are all very important aspects of this topic.

Use classroom routines to represent data.

Attendance, bus riders, and snack choices are examples of data that are accumulated in a typical preschool classroom. These data can be shown graphically or pictorially and described and counted using children's own words. Picture and name cards can be placed in a column labeled "bus rider" or "apple juice." When the cards are placed one above another, they form a bar graph that shows the number of people who will be riding the bus home or drinking apple juice at snack time.

Encourage children to organize objects using their own rules.

Young children naturally sort objects. Observe them as they sort and encourage them to explain why things are in particular piles or groups. Use their words to label their graphs or pictures and model appropriate vocabulary to describe the data.

Purposely describe collections in more than one way.

Work with small groups of children to organize collections of objects. Ask them to tell how they organized the objects. To give them experience classifying objects in more than one way, facilitate a variety of descriptions and model how they can all be methods.

Ask children to line up in classification groups.

Create three-dimensional graphs by asking children to form two lines: one line that has children with a particular attribute or preference and the other line with children who do not have that particular attribute or preference. For example, children in one line could have tie shoes, and children in the other line could *not* have tie shoes; children in one line could be wearing red clothes, and children in the other line could *not* be wearing red clothes.

Use two groups to organize data.

Rather than sorting objects into many groups, use two groups to sort: one group for objects that have the attribute and the other group for objects that do *not* have the attribute. This method allows children to classify objects easily and gives them an opportunity to understand the word *not*. For example, a can rolls when it is placed on its side on a ramp. It would fall into the category of objects that *roll*. A rectangular box will not roll no matter how it is placed on a ramp, so it would be classified as an object that does *not roll*.

Use paper of the same size to create bar graphs.

Give each child paper of the same size and have each draw a picture of his or her snack or toy preference. When they are finished drawing, place each piece of paper in line, one above the other, to create bars for a graph (e.g., all the apples in one column, all the bananas in another column). Because the bars are made of paper of the same size, children can easily make comparisons and describe the data pictured.

Demonstrate classification and ask children to "guess" the describing words.

Select a set of objects and ask the children to observe as you separate them into two groups. Model the classification process, slowly and thoughtfully considering each object as you place it in a group. When the sorting is complete, ask the children to describe each group using their own words. Check each child's "guess" by seeing if the objects fit their rule.

Use symbols to represent data.

Label graphs or other representations, using symbols that are easily understood by children. Color words can be written with matching colored crayons; pictures can be drawn and labeled with words; *not* can be indicated by writing or drawing a picture of the attribute and then drawing a large X across it. In the following example, the things that are red would be placed on the left side, and things that are *not* red would be placed on the right side.

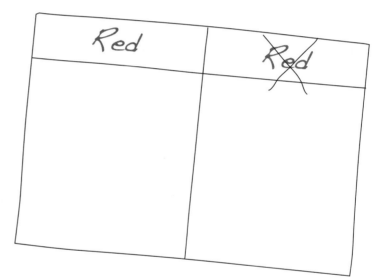

How Do You Assess Children's Progress?

To assess children's progress in understanding data analysis, observe children consistently and regularly. Observe children in interest areas and in group settings as they

- put objects in piles or groups

- talk about the class charts or graphs

- create art projects

- play classification games

- identify objects by color, size, or shape

- participate in class routines

As children complete activities or work in small groups, ask the following questions:

Which group has more? Which group has fewer?

How would you describe this group?

How are these two, three, four, or five objects alike? How are they different?

Why did you put that object here? Why did you put that object next to this one?

You have said these are all red. Can you find something that is not red?

Is there another name for these objects? Anything else?

Could this object go in your group? Why? Why not?

Tips to Share With Families

- Ask children to sort their toys, clothes, or shoes into two groups according to a common attribute like color (for example, red and not red), shape (for example, box and not box), or size (for example, big and not big) or according to another attribute (for example, laces or not laces, or stripes and not stripes). Decide which group has the most objects by matching an item from one group with an item from the other group.

- Make charts that show family job responsibilities, practice sessions, or homework assignments. Use checks or color coding to show when a job is complete.

- Invite children to put their drawings on a bulletin board or on the refrigerator in an organized way. Label the different sections (for example, *Jennifer's pictures about winter, Jennifer's pictures about our family, Jennifer's pictures about our dog,* and so on.)

- Make grocery lists together. Organize the items by groups (for example, cereals, dairy products, breads, meats, and so on).

- Make a photo album together. Label and organize the pictures as your child suggests.

- Organize a coin, stamp, or trading card collection.

- Help your child survey relatives or friends to find out what they like to eat, want for birthday presents, or wish. Report the findings to interested relatives or friends.

inside this chapter

2

Mathematical Process Skills

In *The Creative Curriculum* classroom where children are actively learning mathematics, there is an air of excitement and sounds of learning abound. Children in the Dramatic Play Area sell flowers in the class "flower shop," **communicating** the prices of arrangements with handmade signs that say *20 pennies* or *lots of dollars*. In the Block Area, children discuss blueprints or **representations** of earlier constructions, comparing them to attached photos. Nearby, two children discuss whether there will be enough cupcakes for everyone in the class to have two during an afternoon birthday celebration. They try to **solve the problem** by using a cupcake pan having spaces for a dozen cupcakes as well as the picture and word label for the pan. They wonder aloud as they begin to count, "How many will that make? Is that more cupcakes than children?"

In the Library Area, three children **connect** what they have learned about patterns and books by creating a patterned border around each page of the class book, *Our Favorite Animals*. Finally, two children study a poster with a large circle in the middle. Some of the children's photos and names are *inside* the circle, while others are *outside* the circle. The children discuss why their pictures and names are inside the circle and explain their **reasoning**, "I'm in the circle 'cause I have glasses!" "No, I'm in the circle 'cause my name starts with *J* like *John* and *Jennifer*!"

The examples above illustrate five mathematical process skills identified by NCTM as important for children's learning. These five process skills— **problem solving, reasoning, communicating, connecting,** and **representing**— are the means by which children learn the content described in chapter 1. They are an important part of mathematics instruction in *The Creative Curriculum* classroom and should be emphasized throughout the day. In this chapter, we describe each process skill, discuss how to teach and encourage skill development, and describe a routine example that focuses on that particular skill. While each process skill is discussed separately and individually, in reality, they are neither separate nor inclusive of all processes, and they are part of each and every learning activity related to the components of mathematics.

Problem Solving

A problem is a question that prompts someone to find a solution, and young children love to solve problems! In fact, they spend much of their time solving problems that occur naturally in their everyday world. Some problems involve number; others are more geometric or spatial in nature. The questions young children pose often generate new mathematical questions or problems to solve. The teacher's role in the preschool classroom is to expand upon children's natural disposition to solve problems and ask new questions. Teachers also model an attitude of wonder and investigation.

Teaching and Encouraging Problem Solving

Problem solving is key to helping children develop mathematical understandings. Through problem-solving experiences, children learn that there is a variety of ways to solve a problem and that a problem can have more than one answer or solution. Over time and with consistent nurturing, children develop into mature problem solvers. To teach problem solving, a teacher

- identifies routine problem-solving opportunities

- uses daily activities to teach problem solving

- uses open-ended questions and comments

- models problem-solving behavior

Identify routine problem-solving opportunities.

Problem-solving opportunities occur naturally during the day. For example, finding a place to store additional blocks in the Block Area can be a geometric problem; determining if there are enough snacks for the field trip is a number problem; deciding which of two rugs fits best in the large-group area is a measurement problem, and taking attendance and counting the children who are absent is a routine number activity that requires children to problem solve. These are just a few examples of how everyday routine situations become problem-solving opportunities. Teachers may overlook these problem-solving opportunities or solve the problems themselves. By doing so, they miss rich teaching and learning opportunities.

Use daily activities to teach problem solving.

Problems also present themselves during daily activities, for example, story time. Books and stories are perfect beginnings for problem-solving situations. Characters can be added to a story, numerical situations can be improvised, mathematical vocabulary can be introduced, and story patterns can be extended. From these initial experiences, new stories or mathematical word problems can be created, acted out, and written. Other activities that occur during outdoor time and group times are perfect for teaching problem solving.

Use open-ended questions and comments.

Naturally, problem solving is encouraged when teachers ask questions and pose problems for children to solve. Questions like "Do we have enough?" or "What if there were 10 more apples?" prompt numerical solutions. Other questions, such as "What would you predict comes next in the pattern?" or "What shapes do you see in the block tower?" require word or pictorial solutions. Teachers' responses can further encourage problem solving. For example, if a teacher actively listens to children's solutions or responds to a possible solution with a neutral response, children continue to think and design solutions.

Model problem-solving behavior.

The most important way a teacher can encourage problem solving is to model problem-solving behavior to show a desire to solve problems, appear excited about solving problems, think aloud during the problem-solving process, and demonstrate the belief that children can solve problems in many ways.

A Routine Example of Problem Solving: "How Many Are Missing?"

During the spring, a playground situation led to a relevant problem-solving activity in one preschool classroom. Children were not responding to the teacher's signal that outdoor play was over and that it was time to return to the classroom. In fact, several children were often missing when the teacher was ready to lead them inside. She was continually solving the problem, "How many are missing?" Deciding this would be a perfect time to enlist children's help, the teacher introduced the problem to children during their weekly theater time, which occurred each Friday. During theater time, the teacher usually read or told a story and invited some of the children to act out the events of the story while the others participated as the audience. Many of the stories were math-related stories that required children to find answers to particular problems. Children enjoyed acting out the stories, and they especially enjoyed the applause of their peers.

For the first "How Many Are Missing?" story, the teacher invited five children to act out a playground situation. When she signaled that it was time to return to the classroom, three children joined her while the others hid. The teacher asked the audience, "How many are missing?" The teacher invited several children to share their answers and their strategies for solving the problem. When the two missing children were revealed, the audience was delighted to see that they had indeed solved the problem. The children requested many more "How Many Are Missing?" stories during Friday theater time. Each situation prompted new subtraction problems for the children to solve.

The teacher then decided to translate this problem-solving situation to other concrete experiences. She had children form pairs. Then she gave each pair a large piece of construction paper to represent the playground, a smaller piece of green paper to represent a bush, and counters to represent children. To begin, one child told a playground story using the counters and then hid some of the counters under the bush. The other child listened to the story and then tried to solve the "How Many Are Missing?" problem. The storyteller lifted the bush to reveal the answer. The children reversed roles and new story problems were told and solved.

Problem-solving experiences often prompt other activities. In this instance, the class suggested making a book of *How Many Are Missing?* stories. Each child drew a playground scene with a chosen number of children. Then they attached a construction paper bush to hide some of the children and dictated their story problem to the teacher. The individual stories were combined to form a class book that was titled *How Many Are Missing?* and placed in the Library Area. At choice time, the children could read a problem, solve it, and check their answer simply by lifting the construction paper bush.

Not only did this experience offer children continued opportunities for problem solving, it helped them to see the connection among their own playground experiences, mathematics, and literacy. One 4-year-old child commented to the teacher after returning from outdoor play, "It is a good thing you have us around, 'cause you have so many problems! You really need our help!" These children are becoming powerful problem solvers!

Reasoning

Reasoning is the heart of mathematics. It means thinking through a question or a problem to arrive at an answer. Young children can and do reason. When presented with a problem or question, they make conjectures or guesses and then, in their own way, justify them. Their justifications often seem illogical, and they are not always aware of how they arrived at their answers. Because preschool children are just beginning to make sense of mathematical situations. As they experience more and more mathematics, their understanding and reasoning skills develop.

Teaching and Encouraging Reasoning

Preschool children need experiences to help them develop and clarify their thinking. To teach reasoning, teachers

- observe, listen, and interact with children

- plan experiences that promote children's reasoning

Observe and listen to children in order to interact in ways that promote reasoning.
Begin by observing children and listening to them talk as they work and interact with peers. As children make predictions, classify objects, or identify patterns, ask them to explain why they think as they do or why they made a choice between one assumption or another. Listen thoughtfully to their responses. Their initial response may be, "Because," or they may simply shrug their shoulders. Regardless of the responses, persist in encouraging children's justifications and reasoning. With continued experience, children will learn to verbalize their reasoning and justify their ideas more clearly and concisely.

Children know that you value their ideas by the way you respond, including the way you listen to them. Listening to each child's reasoning, encouraging children to listen to one another's justifications, asking relevant questions, and sharing your reasoning are ways to show children that you value reasoning.

Plan reasoning experiences.

Reasoning can be encouraged by offering activities that invite children to make conjectures, to explore and investigate their ideas, and to explain or justify their beliefs. Examples of such activities include classification activities that require children to look for similarities and differences among objects, or prediction activities that require children to identify and extend patterns.

Not is an important word that is essential to the process of reasoning. Classification systems require a child to understand what *is*, as well as what *is not*. For example, children who are wearing jackets with hoods can be identified as well as children who are *not* wearing jackets with hoods. Objects that are red can be identified as well as objects that are *not* red. It is important to use the word *not* in daily conversation and to introduce other words that are important to reasoning, such as *or, if, then, because, none, some, all, never,* and *probably.*

A Routine Example of Reasoning: "In the Circle"

Classification activities require the use of reasoning and are routinely enjoyed by children. Initially, young children classify sets of objects randomly, seemingly with no reasoning at all. They simply put things together in a group because they *like them* or the things *are special.* Children then begin to group objects by using one attribute for classification (e.g., they are all blue; they all have three corners; they all have wheels). They later realize that an object may be classified in more than one way (e.g., an object can have corners and be blue and have wheels). Finally, children can view objects that have already been classified and identify the rule that places them in a particular group.

A favorite classification activity or game of preschool children is called "In the Circle." To play, the teacher classifies a group of objects by one "secret" attribute. She forms a circle on the floor with a piece of yarn and then places the objects that have the secret attribute *inside* the circle. The objects that do not have the secret attribute are placed *outside* or *not in* the circle. The children's task is to identify the secret attribute by using the objects as clues. To do this, the children must use their reasoning skills, identify similarities and differences between objects *in* the circle and *not in* the circle, and verbalize the classification rule.

Consider what happens one day when a group of 4-year-old children play "Inside the Circle." It is midyear, and the children have played "Inside the Circle" many times, using color as the sorting rule. They also played once when the three-dimensional shape *sphere*, or *ball*, was the sorting rule.

Ms. Tory, the teacher, places a poster with a large circle drawn in the middle of it on the floor where all of the children can see it.

Ms. Tory:	*Today we will play our game with shapes. Remember, your job is to be a detective and figure out what shapes go inside the circle. Then, if you are really a good detective, you can use words to tell me what those shapes are called. Remember, a good detective doesn't guess until he gets some clues. Here are the first clues.* (Ms. Tory places a red triangle inside the circle and a red circle outside the circle. Children begin talking to each other and quietly saying answers. After a minute, Ms. Tory places a thin blue triangle inside the circle and a blue octagon outside the circle. She is quiet as children begin talking.)
Ms. Tory:	*Now, talk to a partner and see if you can tell me what my word or rule might be.*

There is a buzz in the room as most children discuss what the sorting rule could be. Some children sit silently.

Children:	*It's red. It's blue. It's a rectangle. It's not a circle. It has points. It only has three points.*
Ms. Tory:	*Now let me give you some more clues. Watch carefully.* (Ms. Tory places two green triangles inside the circle in a rather random position. They are not equilateral triangles; one is long and thin, and the other is short and thick. She then places another green shape that is not a triangle outside the circle.) *Talk to your partner again and see if you can figure out what my word might be.*

The children talk among themselves. Some try to get Ms. Tory's attention to tell her what they think. She listens but does not respond to their ideas. She simply points to other children, indicating that they should explain their reasoning to their friends.

Ms. Tory:	*Now we are ready to test your answers. Remember, we listen to everyone's answer. There may be more than one way to tell about the shapes that are inside the circle! What do you think?*
Setsuko:	*It's pointy.*
Ms. Tory:	*You're really thinking. Can you show us the points on the shapes?* (Setsuko touches the shapes' points.) *Now, what about the shapes outside the circle? Remember, they can't have any points! Do you see any points there?*
Setsuko:	(Shrugs and looks puzzled. Ms. Tory pretends to be puzzled also.)
Dallas:	*I think it is green.*
Ms. Tory:	*Another idea! Can you point out the shapes that are green and inside the circle?* (Dallas points to the two green triangles inside the circle. He looks at the other green shape outside the circle and points to it as well.) *Hmmm. There are two green shapes inside the circle, but there is also a green shape outside the circle. Let's look at all the shapes inside the circle. How are they all alike? What do they have that is the same?* (Again, Ms. Tory allows time for children to talk to their peers.)
Crystal:	*There are three points.*
Leo:	*And three sides.*
Ms. Tory:	*Oh, some other ideas! Let's check!* (Children check each shape inside the circle and identify the ones that have three points and three sides.) *Now we must check the shapes outside the circle. They must not have three points, and they must not have three sides.* (Children check each shape, and the teacher makes sure she uses the word *not*.)

Ms. Tory:	*Any other ideas?* (The process is repeated for the other guesses. All answers are checked and demonstrated, with children explaining their answers each time.)
Ms. Tory:	*Now we need many more shapes on our poster.* (She distributes many paper shapes to the children, and they use glue sticks to place the triangles inside the circle and the other shapes outside the circle.)
Sonya:	*Can we do more?*
Ms. Tory:	*Absolutely! Where should we put the poster so you can add more shapes?*
Leo:	*How about the Art Area? There is paper and glue there already!*
Children:	*Yeah! The Art Area is a good place.*
Ms. Tory:	*Okay, we'll put the poster in the Art Area. Your job is to add more shapes to our poster. If a shape fits our rule, glue it inside the circle. If it does not fit our rule, glue it outside the circle. Remember to check your reasons before you glue a shape.*

The poster is then placed in the Art Area, where children can draw or trace their own shapes, cut them out, and glue them on the poster. At the end of the day, the class reviews the shapes on the poster. The descriptive labels—*triangles, 3 points, 3 lines*—are written on the poster.

Note that not all of the children were able to identify the common attribute of the shapes inside the circle. However, after working with many shapes and classifying them using the children's terms, they have a much better understanding of the geometric concept of *triangle*, and they have begun to develop their reasoning skills. With repeated experiences such as this one, children's reasoning skills will develop.

Communication

Communication is the sharing of thoughts, ideas, and feelings with others. We communicate in many ways: through gestures, facial expressions, drawings, writing, and speaking. Children are often adept at communicating, but, when they begin communicating about mathematics, their ideas and thoughts are often unorganized and undeveloped. This is because they do not have the language of mathematics or an understanding of the symbols that represent particular ideas or concepts.

Teachers can help children learn to communicate mathematically by encouraging them to share their ideas orally, visually, and symbolically. Teachers also clarify or restate children's ideas with mathematical language or symbols. The more opportunities children have to share their ideas as well as listen to other children's ideas and strategies, the better they will become at verbalizing their mathematical understandings and connecting their informal understanding with more formal, school-based mathematics.

Teaching and Encouraging Communication

Teaching for communication involves equipping the children with the tools and skills they need to communicate their mathematical ideas. Teachers promote communication when they

- provide communication tools

- interact with children to promote communication

- provide time and opportunities for children to communicate

- encourage the use of a variety of communication resources

- emphasize the communication of mathematical ideas

Provide tools for communication.

Writing and drawing tools and a variety of paper and other writing surfaces should be a part of every interest area. In addition, resources that include numbers, symbols, measurements, and spatial drawings should be displayed and incorporated into the environment as well as integrated with topics of study. Include such items as newspaper or magazine ads, signs, blueprints, phone books, catalogs, size labels, and receipt pads. Both real and toy oral communication tools, such as tape recorders, phones, and microphones, should also be included because they prompt speaking and listening. Finally, technological tools such as computers, e-mail, or cameras can be made available for children to explore. All of these items can encourage children's mathematical communication.

Interact in ways that promote communication among children and between the teacher and children.

Tools alone will not teach children how to communicate mathematically. Teachers must interact with children as they use these tools, listening attentively, asking questions, restating concepts, and describing processes. Suggestions for ways in which teachers can prepare the environment and interact with children to encourage communication can be found in chapter 4, "Mathematics in Interest Areas."

Provide time and opportunity for children to communicate.

Children will learn to communicate only if time and opportunities to do so are available. In a child's early years, family members and others encourage communication and express great delight when children say their first recognizable words. As children enter more organized or formal school settings, their opportunities to communicate freely are often restricted or limited. If children are to develop communication skills, teachers must honor communication by listening attentively to children, encouraging conversations and peer interactions, and creating an environment that conveys the message, "Your ideas and thoughts are important."

Encourage the use of a variety of communication resources.

Teachers must introduce and encourage the use of a variety of communication resources: visual (e.g., pictures, drawings, photos, sketches, diagrams, computer software programs, and stamps); oral (e.g., tape and audio recordings, children's voices, dramatic productions, phone conversations); and kinesthetic (e.g., mime, playdough, objects, sculptures, and blocks).

Emphasize the communication of mathematical ideas.

Teachers must specifically emphasize the communication of mathematical ideas. To encourage mathematical communication, numerical and spatial tools as well as standard (e.g., measuring tapes, rulers and meter sticks, balancing scales, number lines, charts, and graphs) and nonstandard tools (e.g., blocks, counters, links, and yarn) must be evident and accessible to children. When teachers model the use of these materials and children have opportunities to experiment with these tools, children learn to communicate mathematically.

A Routine Example of Communication: "Calling Houston Central"

An inexpensive cordless microphone became a unique communication instrument for one group of preschool children. Every day, a child would pretend to be an astronaut calling the classroom from the "space station," which was an area behind a file cabinet. Using the microphone, the child would say, "Calling Houston Central! Calling Houston Central!" The astronaut would then give oral instructions to other children about how to use a particular item or material. For example, one week the astronaut directed the children to use playdough to create the three-dimensional objects he described. Another week, the astronaut had children create pictures with attribute blocks. Still other children told stories involving the use of counters and particular mathematical operations.

Initially, the teacher played the role of the Mission Control agent, interpreting and clarifying some of the astronaut's communication. Later, children became quite good at communicating the details necessary for success. The children who participated in this activity over the course of the year, as an astronaut or as part of Houston Central, showed marked improvement in both their listening and speaking skills, and they learned important mathematical concepts.

Connections

Connections involve linking new learning to previous experience. According to NCTM, "The most important connection for early mathematics development is between the intuitive, informal mathematics that students have learned through their own experiences and the mathematics they are learning in school" (NCTM, 2000, p. 132). Several types of connections can be made:

- connections between math at home and math at school (e.g., counting in Spanish at home and counting in English at school, homework questions that involve the use of numbers at home, using recipes from home in the Cooking Area)

- connections between content areas (e.g., introducing mathematical concepts by using a story or a book, measuring the results of a science experiment, identifying patterns in a song, using circular shapes in an art picture)

- connections between the components of mathematics (e.g., number and pattern—children create patterns using numerals; geometry and measurement—three-dimensional shapes are placed in a box that is just the right size; geometry and data—identifying all the triangular shapes on a class scavenger hunt and making a graph to show the results)

Teaching and Encouraging Connections

To teach and encourage connections, teachers must first be aware of the many connections that are possible between mathematics at home and at school, between mathematics and other content areas, and among the components and process skills of mathematics.

Teachers also should know that young children rarely, if ever, see their learning as "mathematics." Instead, their experiences are categorized as "home stuff" or "school work" or "choice time" or "outdoor time." Teachers must intentionally and explicitly call attention to the connections. Phrases like these can be used frequently to help children make connections: "This is like…," "Do you remember when we…?," "I think we did something like this…," or "How do you do this at home?"

Although a teacher's language highlights connections for the child, the most important connection words are the child's. When a child says, "Look, there's a pattern on the wall!" or "I see a triangle on top of the trash can!" or "Our house has more windows than the school 'cause I counted!" we know that connections are beginning to form. To help children see connections between mathematics and their world, teachers

- use mathematical vocabulary to label ideas and activities

- include and highlight mathematics in activities across a variety of contexts

Label ideas and activities by using mathematical vocabulary.
Connections can be made quite naturally, particularly during choice time when children are free to choose where, with what, and with whom they want to play. During choice time, a teacher thoughtfully observes children and then determines whether, how, and when to interact with them. A skillful teacher uses this time as an opportunity to label situations using mathematical vocabulary (e.g., "We will need to use numbers to tell how many cupcakes we need for the party," or "I see you've sorted and folded the laundry. Do you help your mom do that at home?") or highlight the use of mathematical tools such as the timer or measuring cups in the Cooking Area, the balance scale in the Discovery Area, or the calendar in the Dramatic Play Area.

Include and highlight mathematics in activities across a variety of contexts.
Teachers also pay attention during choice time to materials and activities that are relevant to mathematics, and they explicitly identify and expand upon them. For example, after noticing that several children are deeply engaged in block building and will probably not want to dismantle their construction, the teacher suggests that they draw a sketch of their building similar to the blueprints architects and builders use. She also offers to take a digital photograph of their construction as another way to preserve their work. She reminds them that they can use the sketch and photograph to rebuild their structure at another time. Not only are these suggestions satisfying to the children, the teacher has helped them make a connection between their work, the real world, and representation, which is an important process skill.

Teachers also help children understand the connections between mathematics and other content areas, for example, science. As children pour liquids for an experiment, observe their bean plants, or feed the class pet, teachers can encourage them to measure and record their ideas and findings in journals, on chart, or on graphs. Similarly, the teacher who hears children singing *The Ants Go Marching* and encourages them to act out the number song will help children make the connection between music and math (e.g., "There's a pattern in our song!") Adding the book *The Ants Go Marching* (Sandra D'Antonio) connects math and literacy.

A Routine Example of Connections: The "Snake Game"

Games that facilitate connections are important in the early childhood classroom. One of the children's favorite games is the "Snake Game." Children play this game as partners, and the communication process is emphasized as children help each other remember the rules and how to count correctly. Mathematically, the "Snake Game" facilitates connections between many different number and operation topics. As children play this game, they discover properties of zero, practice one-to-one correspondence, begin to estimate, and identify specific numerical patterns.

The "Snake Game" was originally played in South America using easily obtained pea pods as snakes and the peas as counters and tokens. In classrooms, the snake is outlined on a game board and divided into about 25 sections. It looks something like this:

The "Snake Game" is played by two children at a time. Each child receives a token and three counters. To play the game, the children place their tokens on the snake's tail with the goal of reaching the snake's head. To begin the game, the first player puts zero, one, two, or three counters in his hand and hides the remaining counters. The second player tries to guess the number of counters that are in her partner's hand. If she guesses correctly, she moves that number of spaces. For example, if the first player is holding three counters and the second player guesses three, the second player gets to move three spaces. If the second player guesses incorrectly, the first player (the one holding the counters) gets to move that number of spaces (in this case, three). The game continues, with players taking turns until one reaches the head of the snake.

Initially, preschool children play this game with a teacher, an adult volunteer, or an older child. As they play, they learn the rules and become experts at following them consistently. Later, when they begin to play with peers, their reasoning becomes amazingly logical. After watching young children play the "Snake Game" many times, the following generalizations were made:

- After just a few plays, children begin consistently to put three counters in their hands. They quickly realize that, if their partners guess wrong, they will get to move three spaces.

- Almost as quickly, children recognize that their partners are going to put three counters in their hands, and they begin consistently to guess three. Thus, the guessers are always correct, and they get to move three spaces. Play goes back and forth, with each player moving three spaces.

- After the children recognize the pattern of three moves, they begin to try to fool each other by putting different numbers of counters into their hands. Play continues for many moves, with children changing the number of counters at each turn as they try to fool each other.

- Eventually (normally after three or four games), one child decides to put zero counters in his hand. The other child never guesses zero, and the first child gets very excited because his partner has been fooled. However, the excitement quickly ends when he realizes that zero means no moves. When zero is used in other classroom experiences, children often connect it to their experience in the "Snake Game".

Children love to play the "Snake Game" at school and at home with family members. They especially enjoy fooling their partners. Each time they play, they are not only having fun, they are learning important mathematical skills and concepts: one-to-one correspondence; identifying sets of one, two, and three without counting; guessing the number of counters held; and, of course, making connections.

Representation

Young children represent, or show their thoughts about, mathematical ideas in different ways and with a variety of tools. Sometimes they draw or use tally marks or other symbols to explain or represent their ideas. Other times, they use blocks, counters, cutouts, or even their own fingers. Some representations require that children also give a verbal explanation so others can understand their meaning. Representations are essential to young children's understanding of mathematics. They help children solve problems and are useful to children when explaining their reasoning. Representations also make mathematical relationships more apparent to children. When combined with an explanation, representations offer teachers a window into a child's way of thinking mathematically.

Teaching and Encouraging Representation

Teachers set the stage for children to represent their mathematical ideas when they expose them to a variety of representations, including materials they can manipulate (e.g., advertisements illustrating various monetary amounts; maps; house plans; graphs; and toy cars, planes, or dinosaurs). Teachers also observe children as they work to represent their understandings, listen attentively to their explanations, and take photos when possible. Children need to know that you value their ideas and that it helps others to understand when they see a representation of some sort. To promote representation, teachers

- model the use of a variety of representations

- use questions, comments, and suggestions to encourage representation

Model the use of a variety of representations.
The most important way a teacher can encourage representation is to model the use of various methods of representation. In doing so, children see the way representations can be helpful in conveying different mathematical ideas, in explaining thinking and reasoning, and in solving problems. Modeling is an effective teaching tool because children are likely to want to copy the teacher and try each new type of representation.

Use questions, comments, and suggestions to encourage representation.
Teachers also encourage a variety of representations with their questions, comments, and suggestions during interactions with children (e.g., "Show me what you mean… Can you make a drawing…use blocks…write numbers…? Tell me more about how…") Through these exchanges, children learn that representations can help them to remember what they have done and to communicate their reasoning. Teachers can provide opportunities for children to create representations for different audiences. Writing a counting or number book for another class, constructing a playground using blocks and craft sticks for the director of the preschool, or explaining the steps in making a favorite recipe to a parent volunteer are just a few examples of representations for different audiences.

A Routine Example of Making Representations: Children's Work

In a mathematics-rich classroom, children's representations are displayed.

Photo of a block pattern by Sara.

"Down, up, down, up, umm, up, umm, up, umm, up." When Sara was asked why she said, "Umm," when the block was down rather than up, she explained that Patrick had taken all of the square blocks and she couldn't make the pattern the way it was supposed to be made.

Drawing of block tower by Erin.

When asked why her tower picture had a circular shape on top of a rectangular object, Erin said, "It didn't work like that! But it's okay. You can do whatever you want when it's on paper. It doesn't need to really work!"

Each of these pictures shows a different measuring process and unit of measure. The first three show how children used various objects to measure the length of their outlined hands.

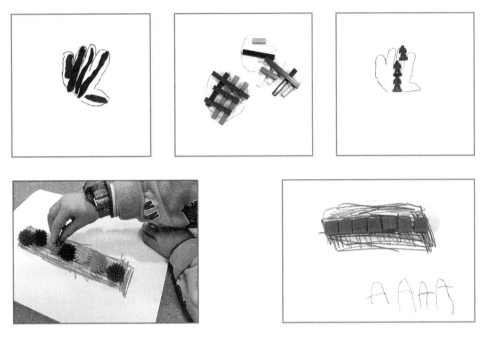

Three-year-old Jeremy's picture showing that he is taller than Mrs. Copley.

As you can see, a mathematically powerful environment is filled with children and teachers who make use of the mathematical process skills throughout the day, during routine experiences and planned activities, and in a variety of contexts. Problem solving, reasoning, communicating, connecting, and representing are all critical to the understanding of mathematical content. Children's unique ways of using the process skills make mathematics exciting for children and teachers alike.

inside this chapter

3

Planning Your Mathematics Program

Chapter 1 explains the components of mathematics. Chapter 2 explains the process skills children need and use as they develop and refine their mathematical thinking. In this chapter, you will see how the goals and objectives of *The Creative Curriculum* align with the content and processes discussed and how mathematics instruction takes place in *The Creative Curriculum* classroom. You will see how teachers purposefully and intentionally plan for children's mathematics learning and how they use the environment, daily routine experiences, and group activities.

Goals and Objectives of Mathematics Learning

The goals and objectives for children's mathematics learning are identified under the cognitive area of development in the *The Creative Curriculum for Preschool* goals and objectives. As shown in the chart, there are three cognitive goals: Learning and Problem Solving, Logical Thinking, and Representation and Symbolic Thinking. Objectives 22–26 relate to the mathematical process skills; Objectives 27–34 are related to mathematics content; and Objectives 35–37 provide a foundation for the symbols and abstractions of mathematics.

Because learning is integrated, children develop an understanding of mathematical concepts as they work all day long. For example, Objective 13, "Uses thinking skills to resolve conflicts," is related to reasoning and problem solving. The language objectives build children's understanding of and ability to communicate mathematical concepts. Therefore, teachers should be familiar with all of the social/emotional, physical, cognitive, and language goals and objectives.

The Creative Curriculum® Goals and Objectives at a Glance

SOCIAL/EMOTIONAL DEVELOPMENT	PHYSICAL DEVELOPMENT	COGNITIVE DEVELOPMENT	LANGUAGE DEVELOPMENT
Sense of Self 1. Shows ability to adjust to new situations 2. Demonstrates appropriate trust in adults 3. Recognizes own feelings and manages them appropriately 4. Stands up for rights	**Gross Motor** 14. Demonstrates basic locomotor skills (running, jumping, hopping, galloping) 15. Shows balance while moving 16. Climbs up and down 17. Pedals and steers a tricycle (or other wheeled vehicle) 18. Demonstrates throwing, kicking, and catching skills	**Learning and Problem Solving** 22. Observes objects and events with curiosity 23. Approaches problems flexibly 24. Shows persistence in approaching tasks 25. Explores cause and effect 26. Applies knowledge or experience to a new context	**Listening and Speaking** 38. Hears and discriminates the sounds of language 39. Expresses self using words and expanded sentences 40. Understands and follows oral directions 41. Answers questions 42. Asks questions 43. Actively participates in conversations
Responsibility for Self and Others 5. Demonstrates self-direction and independence 6. Takes responsibility for own well-being 7. Respects and cares for classroom environment and materials 8. Follows classroom routines 9. Follows classroom rules	**Fine Motor** 19. Controls small muscles in hands 20. Coordinates eye-hand movement 21. Uses tools for writing and drawing	**Logical Thinking** 27. Classifies objects 28. Compares/measures 29. Arranges objects in a series 30. Recognizes patterns and can repeat them 31. Shows awareness of time concepts and sequence 32. Shows awareness of position in space 33. Uses one-to-one correspondence 34. Uses numbers and counting	**Reading and Writing** 44. Enjoys and values reading 45. Demonstrates understanding of print concepts 46. Demonstrates knowledge of the alphabet 47. Uses emerging reading skills to make meaning from print 48. Comprehends and interprets meaning from books and other texts 49. Understands the purpose of writing 50. Writes letters and words
Prosocial Behavior 10. Plays well with other children 11. Recognizes the feelings of others and responds appropriately 12. Shares and respects the rights of others 13. Uses thinking skills to resolve conflicts		**Representation and Symbolic Thinking** 35. Takes on pretend roles and situations 36. Makes believe with objects 37. Makes and interprets representations	

The goals and objectives of *The Creative Curriculum* set the stage for guiding children's mathematics learning, but teachers must also have an understanding of the way in which other mathematical skills and concepts develop. The "Scope of Instruction" in the Appendix provides you with a summary of the content skills and concepts as well as strategies and activities for teaching them. When teachers combine their knowledge of mathematics with their knowledge of child development and each child's unique strengths and needs, they can tailor their instruction and scaffold children's learning appropriately.

Guiding Children's Mathematics Learning

Like literacy learning, mathematics learning cannot be left to chance. Planning is essential. It gives purpose and direction to what takes place each day and helps to ensure that learning opportunities are maximized. A comprehensive, well-planned mathematics program addresses the mathematical components and processes, and the environment and materials. It also takes into account the children's abilities, interests, and learning styles.

In planning for children's mathematics learning, teachers must decide what to teach, how to teach it, and when to teach it. They make these decisions on the basis of

- what children ages 3–5 should know and be able to do mathematically

- the goals and objectives of *The Creative Curriculum for Preschool*

- the strengths, needs, and interests of individual children

Good mathematics instruction requires that teachers use a wide range of teaching strategies. Children have unique learning styles, interests, and temperaments, and they progress at different rates. Some children love to make intricate designs with materials while others gravitate toward dramatic play or large motor activities. An approach that is successful with 4-year-old children may not work with young 3-year-olds. Additionally, the wide range of mathematical concepts and skills requires different teaching approaches. For example, movement activities are ideal for teaching spatial relationships; experiences with manipulatives are essential for teaching number concepts; and activities related to data analysis are done best in small-group settings. Since the environment provides the context for young children's learning, consider the ways in which teachers can create and use the environment to promote mathematics learning.

Creating a Mathematics-Rich Physical Environment

Mathematical thinking is supported by a thoughtfully arranged, well-organized classroom environment. Well-defined interest areas with clearly marked places for materials demonstrate the order that is inherent in mathematics, and focused explorations are more likely to occur in a well-organized environment.

A mathematics-rich environment is full of interesting, novel materials. It fosters the exploration of key concepts in each mathematics component: number and operations, geometry and spatial sense, measurement, patterns (algebra), and data analysis. It stimulates children's thinking and entices them to solve problems, reason, communicate, make connections to what they already know, and represent their learning. In an environment such as this, children can discover patterns and relationships and pose new questions. Here are some basic principles to help you create a mathematics-rich physical environment.

Strategies	Examples
Organize space and materials.	Create orderly, well-defined interest areas. Have designated places for materials. Organize the materials by labeling containers and shelves. Place related materials in close proximity to one another on shelves (e.g., collectibles and sorting trays).
Highlight the use of numbers and other mathematical ideas (patterns, shapes, measurement) in displays.	Create meaningful displays, such as • birthday charts • attendance charts • class phone and address books • daily schedule • calendar of events • interest-area choice boards • instructions for completing jobs or routines (e.g., setting the table or brushing teeth) • class-made charts and graphs • counting songs and rhymes • artwork and photos
Maintain routines so that children can begin to see patterns.	Upon arrival, children put belongings away, check in or sign in, and eat breakfast.
Enhance all interest areas with mathematics materials.	Include tools, concrete manipulatives, and pictorial and symbolic materials (e.g., blocks, counters, collectibles, dice, dominos, timers, graphs, balance scale, number chart, felt or magnetic numerals, tape measure, rulers). Incorporate math-related environmental print appropriate to each area (e.g., telephone book, price tags, and calendar in Dramatic Play; signs). Include appropriate mathematics books in each interest area (e.g., *Icky Bug Counting Book* by Jerry Pallotta in the Discovery Area; *Shoes, Shoes, Shoes* by Ann Morris in the Dramatic Play Area). Provide writing, construction, and other materials in each interest area for children to represent their learning and record observations.

Materials and displays alone do not make the environment mathematics-rich. Mathematics must be incorporated thoughtfully into events throughout the day. Children need to see ways in which mathematics is used in meaningful situations. For example, posting and referring to the daily schedule throughout the day teaches children about time and sequence.

Integrating Mathematics Throughout the Day

Most young children enter school having already been involved in a range of mathematical experiences, most of which occur naturally during their day. Mobile infants explore spatial relationships as they navigate the space around them. They crawl and climb over, under, and around objects, and then they position themselves so they can reach a toy. Toddlers learn about shape and size as they explore blocks, stack them, and knock them down. Two- and 3-year-old children help family members sort laundry, cook, and set the table. Such activities involve sorting, matching, counting, and measuring.

Preschool teachers build on these experiences. They can provide children with meaningful opportunities to count; measure; collect data; and explore space, shapes, and patterns. They can nurture reasoning, problem solving, communicating, and representing all day long. Of course, some of these occasions arise unexpectedly, for example, when a child announces that she found an ant hill with "a million ants." However, chance occurrences are not sufficient; teachers must purposefully incorporate mathematical experiences in each event of the day. Here are some ways to do so. The ideas are discussed in greater detail in other chapters.

Arrival

Preparing the Environment

Create an attendance chart (e.g., *Who's at School? Who's at Home?*).

Post written procedures for routines (e.g., washing hands, toileting). Use numbers to indicate what to do first, second, third, etc.

Post instructions for class jobs that show math used in meaningful ways (e.g., Feed Cottontail: 1 handful of hay, ½ cup pellets, 2 carrots, and 1 bowl of water)

Interactions

Have informal conversations that facilitate mathematics learning and thinking (e.g., "You're wearing a new shirt today with an interesting pattern. Can you read it?").

Remind children to place their name cards in the correct place on the attendance chart.

Talk with children about routine procedures and what they do first, second, third.

Interact to facilitate mathematics learning and thinking (e.g., draw attention to numerals, encourage children to think, reason, and problem solve).

> *Remember, each friend gets one napkin and one spoon. Can you tell me how many of each you will need?*
>
> *What do you need to do first? Next? Last?*
>
> *How many carrots does Cottontail get? Let's read the instructions together.*

Large-Group Time

Preparing the Environment

Refer to the attendance chart.

Post a math-related "Question of the Day" or "Problem of the Week."

Post a picture/word daily schedule.

Post a weekly or monthly class calendar to document and call attention to meaningful events or special days.

Prepare materials, including visuals (e.g., manipulatives, books and related props, charts, posters, pictures, tapes/CDs, or flannel board cutouts), for any math concepts you want to introduce.

Use puppets or props with rhymes and songs.

Interactions

Demonstrate and explain how the attendance chart represents each child and the total number of children at school and at home. Explain how you will use the data/numbers (e.g., to complete reports and to plan for snacks and meals).

Read and review the "Question of the Day." Invite children to predict and later interpret the answers.

Refer to the schedule throughout the day. Talk about what the children will do *after* the group meeting, *before* lunch, etc. Use words such as *morning* and *afternoon* as well as *first*, *next*, and *last*. Discuss the plans for *today*. Review some things that the group did *yesterday*. Use a clothespin to indicate the current time of the day and have a child move it appropriately during the day.

Call attention to upcoming events or special days recorded on the class calendar. Have conversations or discussion about things that happened *yesterday* or might happen *today* or *tomorrow*. Record them on the calendar.

Sing songs, recite rhymes and fingerplays, and use movement activities that develop math concepts (e.g., number, shapes, spatial relations, or patterns).

Introduce new math materials and vocabulary.

Read math-related books. Use comments and open-ended questions to introduce, expand upon, or extend the mathematical concepts presented.

Play math games.

Invite children to share their math discoveries and questions.

Have a small group of children act out math word problems. The remaining children can help solve the problem.

Choice Time

Preparing the Environment

Create choice boards for interest areas that indicate the number of children who may be in a given area at a time.

Organize materials in ways that encourage children to sort and classify.

Equip all interest areas with mathematics materials (see chapter 4), particularly Dramatic Play.

Add math-related books appropriate to each interest area.

Add writing, drawing, and construction materials so children can represent their discoveries and learning.

Post step-by-step instructions for using equipment (e.g., computers) or handling routine tasks (e.g., cleaning up an area).

Add timers so children can learn about and manage their time at a favorite interest area or with a new or favorite toy or game.

Interactions

Talk about the number of children an area can accommodate. Discuss how to figure out whether there is room for others.

Discuss ways to figure out where items belong.

Note similarities and differences among materials and ways in which they are grouped.

Interact with children on a variety of levels. Listen, have informal conversations, pose questions and challenges, model or demonstrate a process, give feedback, or offer clues.

Model and "think aloud" about how you are using a new material, your approach to solving a problem, or ways to collect and report data.

Read math-related books with individuals or small groups of children. Interact with children in ways that intentionally draw their attention to the mathematical concepts presented in the books (e.g., pose questions and problems, and help children make connections to what they already know).

Invite an individual child or a small group of children to work with you or play a game related to a specific skill or concept.

Encourage children to document, or represent, their mathematics learning.

Give children a 5-minute warning before clean-up time.

Observe children and take anecdotal notes regarding children's actions, abilities, and use of materials.

Small-Group Time

Preparing the Environment

Prepare print or visual materials (e.g., recipes, song charts, and rhymes).

Add props, flannel materials, and storyboards for storytelling or retelling.

Prepare materials and supplies such as manipulatives, tapes/CDs, games, or writing materials to conduct a focused activity.

Interactions

Sing songs, recite rhymes and fingerplays, and use movement activities that help children develop mathematical concepts (e.g., number, shapes, spatial relations, or patterns).

Read math-related books. Interact with the children in ways that intentionally draw their attention to the mathematical concept presented in the book (e.g., pose questions and problems, help children make connections to what they already know).

Have children dramatize counting rhymes and fingerplays (e.g., *Five Little Monkeys Jumping on the Bed* by Eileen Christelow).

Tell stories that focus on particular mathematical concepts (e.g., *My Little Sister Ate One Hare* by Bill Grossman focuses on number and patterns).

Have children create mathematics books (e.g., number, pattern, or shape).

Tell oral mathematical problems that give children experience with number (quantity, joining sets, and separating sets), measurement, or geometry.

Play mathematical games indoors and outdoors.

Offer sorting and graphing experiences.

Informally assess children to determine learning strengths and needs.

Snack and Mealtime

Preparing the Environment

Post step-by-step instructions for routines (e.g., washing hands). Use numerals to indicate what to do first, second, third, etc.

Include snack and/or lunch helpers on the job chart (e.g. to set the table, pass out supplies).

Post self-serve snack charts and picture/word recipes.

Include cups, spoons, and other containers in a variety of sizes for children to learn about measurement and quantity.

Interactions

Point out numerals and talk with children about the hand-washing procedure and what they do first, second, third.

Pose open-ended questions to facilitate mathematics thinking and learning (e.g., "Do you have enough chairs at your table? How many more do you need? Shall we cut the carrots into long sticks or circles?")

Read the self-serve snack charts and recipes. Assist children with counting, measuring, and following the appropriate steps in the preparation process. Use open-ended questions and comments as you interact.

Interact to help children make connections between mathematics and this everyday experience.

> *You have three square crackers and one round cracker. How many crackers do you have altogether?*
>
> *I see you sorted your snack mix. All of the square cereal is in one pile, the pretzels are in another, and the raisins are in another.*
>
> *Can you pour milk into your cup until it is half full?*

Create graphs (e.g., "Which color of apple do you want for snack: red, green, yellow?"). Then have the children analyze the data.

Survey the children after snack (e.g., "Did you enjoy the apple cider? Yes/No."). Then have them analyze the data.

Call attention to shapes, sizes, categories, and patterns of foods (e.g., "An orange is like a ball, Dallas. Another name for its shape is *sphere*... Look at the pattern on the rind of this watermelon. Let's read it... This slice of pizza looks like a large triangle. Can you name the shape of other things on your pizza?")

Transitions

Preparing the Environment

Think in advance about appropriate mathematical songs, rhymes, chants, or games to use.

Prepare materials you need for the activity (e.g., numeral cards, geometric shapes).

Interactions

Number (e.g., "If you have more than two pockets, you may get your coat.")

Measurement (e.g., "Make yourself as short [tall] as you can when you walk to the sink.")

Pattern (e.g., "Watch and do what I do as we go outside. Jump, clap, clap; jump, clap, clap.")

Spatial sense (e.g., "Go *through* [*under*, *around*] this circle [hula hoop] as you walk.")

Sorting (e.g., "If you're wearing something green, go with Mr. Alvarez for story time.")

Sing songs and recite rhymes, chants, and fingerplays that have a mathematics focus (e.g., counting: "One, two, three, four, five; I caught a fish alive.") and verbal, physical, or auditory patterns (e.g., "If you're happy and you know it, clap your hands.").

Outdoor Time

Preparing the Environment

Provide measuring tools (e.g., cups for the sand and water area; string or rulers for plants).

Provide equipment such as tunnels, traffic cones, balls, boxes.

Provide writing materials for children to use to record mathematical information.

Interactions

Use math vocabulary as you talk about ways in which children move and play.

Call attention to patterns and shapes in nature and the outdoor environment (e.g., a pipe is a cylinder; the pattern on a caterpillar; shapes and patterns of a wall).

Talk with children about how they might sort and classify collections of natural materials. Invite them to make a graph when you return to the classroom.

Offer movement activities that help children to explore spatial relationships (e.g., *go over*, *under*, *through*, or *around* objects) and measurement (e.g., fast/slow, heavy/light).

Introduce counting and pattern games (jump rope rhymes, hand jive, hopscotch).

Encourage children to look at and draw objects from a variety of perspectives.

Integrate math into projects or other experiences (e.g., measure plants to see how they grow from day to day or week to week; encourage children to make shadow shapes).

(See "Outdoor Interest Area," in chapter 4, *Mathematics Learning in Interest Areas*, for more outdoor activities.)

Rest Time

Preparing the Environment

Establish a rest-time routine.

Play music that has a slow melodic pattern.

Display clock.

Interactions

Remind children of the routines and patterns of rest time (e.g., prepare mat, get blanket, use restroom).

Use open-ended questions during preparation for rest time (e.g., "Where's your cot? Near the aquarium? Between Leo's and Crystal's cot?").

Talk about what happened before rest time and what will happen after rest time.

Use the language of time (*one hour, half an hour*, etc.) to describe the rest period. Let children see you referring to the clock to know when rest time is over.

Offer quiet activities with a mathematical focus to children who do not nap (e.g., stringing attribute beads, working with pattern blocks).

Departure

Preparing the Environment

Review the daily schedule and the calendar of events.

Prepare mathematical materials for children to take home and share with their families.

Interactions

Talk about the events of the day, calling attention to the time they occurred (e.g., in the *morning, before* lunch, *after* lunch). Ask the children to decide on one event of the day that they want to record on the calendar. Review what they chose to record *yesterday*.

Review important events children wish to share with family members.

Call attention to what the clock looks like when it is time to go home.

Planning Learning Experiences

Teaching in the preschool classroom requires a range of approaches. Effective ways of introducing a particular topic or extending learning vary widely. This section begins with a discussion of child-initiated learning experiences and then offers suggestions for teacher-guided instruction. Examples of how to work with children during large- and small-group times and during studies are included.

Child-Initiated Learning

Young children are curious and eager to investigate their environment. As they play and interact with objects and others, they express and represent what they know and they make new discoveries. To fully grasp mathematical concepts, children must have repeated opportunities to participate in a wide range of activities using a variety of materials. They also need opportunities to discuss their observations and discoveries.

In *The Creative Curriculum* classroom, choice time is the segment of the day set aside for child-initiated learning experiences. Children choose where, with what, and with whom they work. Chapter 4, "Mathematics Learning in Interest Areas," helps teachers create mathematics-rich interest areas where children can manipulate and explore with materials, discover interesting mathematical relationships, discuss their observations with peers and adults, and pose new questions.

During child-initiated learning times, teachers observe first and then decide whether, how, and when to engage with children to facilitate learning. They determine the type and level of their involvement with children on the basis of their knowledge of the mathematical skills and concepts to be developed and each child's developmental level. You can read examples of the ways in which teachers respond to and interact with children during choice time in chapter 4.

Teacher-Guided Instruction

In *The Creative Curriculum* classroom, teachers do not rely exclusively on child-initiated experiences to promote mathematical understanding. Opportunities to explore some mathematical topics may not occur during choice time. There are also concepts and terminology that children cannot discover on their own. A child may gain the concept of one-to-one correspondence through repeated experiences with materials in interest areas. However, the same child may not learn what a circle is or that the numeral *4* represents her age without being told. For this reason, *Mathematics: The Creative Curriculum Approach* utilizes a balanced approach to teaching mathematics, one that includes adult-supported, child-initiated experiences and planned, teacher-initiated instruction.

Teacher-initiated instruction occurs most often during large- and small-group times and is used to teach new mathematics concepts or skills explicitly. Previously presented concepts are also revisited during group times to help children see connections among mathematical ideas and connections with other elements of the curriculum. For example, children can combine their knowledge of patterns and shapes as they make patterns with shapes (e.g., square, circle; square, circle; and so forth). Math and literacy are combined as children count and clap the number of syllables in each child's name.

Mathematics activities or lessons are planned in advance by the teacher, usually with a particular concept or skill in mind. Because mathematics is integrated, children will probably learn more than the targeted concept or skill. For example, a lesson on measurement will also include counting, vocabulary, and fine motor skills. Flexibility is key in planning and in teaching. Teachers must continually monitor children's level of interest and understanding, be prepared to respond on a variety of levels, and be willing to incorporate the children's ideas into the experience. Well-constructed plans provide structure and direction, but they also allow for on-the-spot revisions.

When planning experiences in mathematics, teachers must consider the developmental and individual needs of the children. Children are active learners; they should be physically and mentally involved, talking and reasoning, manipulating materials, singing, chanting, or moving about. All children, especially English language learners and children with language delays, need manipulatives and visual materials such as drawings, models, and photographs. Consider various steps in your planning.

Before teaching, think about these questions:

> *What do I want children to know and be able to do?*

> *What do children already know about this topic?*

> *What essential dispositions am I fostering?*

> *How will I evaluate and assess the children's learning?*

During teaching, think about these questions:

> *Is every child learning what I expected?*

> *Is unanticipated learning occurring?*

> *Are things going as planned?*

After teaching, ask:

What worked? What is the evidence?

What needs to be changed?

What do I do next...

> *for the group as a whole?*

> *for individual children?*

The following sections show how two preschool teachers, Ms. Tory and Mr. Alvarez, use large-group and small-group times to teach children about sorting.

Large Groups

The teachers bring children together as a whole group at multiple times of the day and for various reasons. The first group meeting usually occurs in the morning for the purposes of creating a sense of community, sharing news, and discussing plans for the day. Mathematics is not usually the teacher's primary goal for this meeting, but it can be integrated easily and naturally, as described in the earlier section, "Integrating Mathematics Throughout the Day."

Large-group meetings are also ideal times briefly to introduce a new concept or share new mathematical material. In the example that follows, Ms. Tory uses large-group time to introduce the concept of sorting by two categories. The children have had numerous experiences talking about groups that have a particular attribute, such as a particular color, and materials that do *not* have the attribute (e.g., red and *not* red). The notes on the right indicate Ms. Tory's intentions and reflections about this new activity.

Ms. Tory brings a bag with red and blue objects in it to the meeting area.

Plans in advance to have the necessary props ready.

Ms. Tory:	*I would like to talk about something that we'll be doing today and for the next several days. Does anyone know what* sorting *means?* (Children are silent.)

Do you ever help your Mom or another family member put things into groups at home?

Leads children to connect new concept with prior experiences.

Crystal:	*I do! I help Mommy put my socks and things in one pile and Daddy's clothes in another pile.*
Dallas:	*My Dad had a big bucket of screws and nails. I found all the screws and put them into one can, and he put all the nails in another can. I had to be real careful because nails can hurt you.*
Ms. Tory:	*Hmmm. Crystal and her Mommy sort the clean clothes, and Dallas and his Dad sort the nails and screws.*

Recognizes Crystal's and Dallas's responses and invites additional examples.

What else do you sort? Do you sort anything at school? What about at clean-up time?

Tasheen:	*We put all the blocks on the right shelves.*
Zack:	*And we put cars and trucks in one basket and the animals in another.*
Alexa:	*And we put the dishes in the cupboard.*
Ms. Tory:	*Yes, you do all of those things. You sort lots of things at home and at school. When we put clothes in the right piles, separate the screws from the nails, or put all the same kind of blocks or toys together, we're sorting them.*

Reinforces connection between what children already know and the new term.

I brought a bag of things for us to sort. (Ms. Tory opens the bag and spills its contents—various red and blue items—on the rug in front of her.) *What can you tell me about these things?*

Uses concrete objects and a simple example—two colors—to introduce the concept.

Encourages children to observe and talk about what they see.

Zack:	*I see a fire truck and a car and some markers and some Legos®.*
Sonya:	*I see a dish and an apple.*

Crystal:	*Some of the things are red, and some are blue.*	
Ms. Tory:	*You mentioned a lot of different things, and, as Crystal said, they're all red or blue. Let's sort these things by color.*	
	(Ms. Tory makes a circle on the rug with a piece of red yarn and another circle with a piece of blue yarn. She places the red apple in the red circle and a blue car in the blue circle.)	
	What else belongs in the red circle?	Encourages children to think and participate.
Children:	*The fire truck. The dish. The red marker.*	
Ms. Tory:	*What's the same about all the things in this circle?*	Acknowledges children's responses. Leads them to generalize.
Children:	*They're all red!*	
Ms. Tory:	*So we could say they're all the same…*	
Children:	*Color.*	
Ms. Tory:	*Yes. They're all the same color: red. What belongs in the blue circle?*	
Children:	*The blue crayon. The blue Lego®. The cup.*	
Ms. Tory:	*Yes. All the blue things belong in the blue circle. They're all the same color, blue. They're different from the red things.*	Reinforces the terms *same* and *different*.
	We just sorted all these things. We sorted them by color when we put the red things together and the blue things together. (She puts the items and the yarn pieces back in the bag.)	Again uses the term *sort* and explains what they did.
	Some of you may want to sort these during choice time. Ben, will you please put these in the Toys and Games Area?	Provides opportunities for children individually and in small groups to practice the activity introduced during the group meeting.
	Let's look at our schedule to see what we are going to do next. (She points to the daily schedule posted on wall).	Demonstrates the use of the schedule to promote an understanding of sequencing and time.
Children:	*It's choice time!*	
Ms. Tory:	*Listen carefully. If you are wearing red, you may choose an interest area. If you are a wearing blue, choose an interest area.*	Reinforces sorting during transitions.

In this large-group meeting, the class participated in a brief, teacher-led sorting activity. Opportunities were then provided for the children to sort the materials independently or with friends during choice time. Through careful observation of children using these and other materials, Ms. Tory will be able to determine who can sort by color or another attribute and which children need further assistance.

Music and movement experiences are useful in developing many mathematical skills and concepts related to number, shapes, patterns, and spatial relationships. In the scenario that follows, Mr. Alvarez brings the children together after choice time to discuss what they did in interest areas and to provide an enjoyable music and movement activity. He also uses this time to reinforce the sorting concept that was introduced by Ms. Tory, his co-teacher, during the morning meeting.

Mr. Alvarez:	*Everybody was certainly busy this morning. Thank you for telling us about the things you did at choice time.*	
	Today we're going to use streamers as we move to music. I have one for each of you. Sonya, will you please pass out the streamers? (Sonya gives each child a red or blue streamer.)	Chooses materials that will remind children of the morning's sorting activities.
	What can you tell me about your streamers?	
Children:	*They have a stick on the end. They are long. Some are red, and some are blue.*	
Mr. Alvarez:	*The stick on the end is called a* dowel. *Yes, the streamers are long.*	Introduces new vocabulary and validates children's responses.
	Who remembers what we did with the red and blue things that were in the bag Ms. Tory shared at morning meeting?	
Dallas:	*We put them into two groups.*	
Sonya:	*Yeah. All the red things went in the red circle, and all the blue things in the blue circle.*	
Mr. Alvarez:	*Who remembers the word Ms. Tory used to describe what we did?*	Reinforces the word *sort*.
Setsuko:	*Sort! I bet we're going to sort these streamers.*	

Mr. Alvarez:	*That's right, Setsuko! If we wanted to sort the streamers and the people holding them, how would we do it?*	Revisits a concept previously presented. Uses open-ended question to solicit children's ideas.
Leo:	*Have the people with red streamers stand over here* (points to where he is standing with his red streamer) *and the people with blue streamers stand over there* (points to the other side of the rug).	
Mr. Alvarez:	*What do the rest of you think about that idea?*	
Children:	*Yeah! That's a good idea!*	
Mr. Alvarez:	*Okay, everyone who has a red streamer stand by Leo, and those with a blue streamer stand on the other side of the rug.*	Integrates measurement concepts.
	If you have a red streamer, let me see you wave it fast.	
	If you have a blue streamer, wave it slowly.	
	Now, everyone with a red streamer, wave it high. Everyone with a blue streamer, wave it down low.	Integrates spatial concepts.
	When I play the music, I want those of you in the red group to wave your red streamers high and those in the blue group to wave your blue streamers low.	
	You can move any way you want to with the music, but remember that red streamers should stay high and blue streamers low.	
	Okay. Here we go (plays music for a few minutes).	
	Let's change. Blue streamers high; red streamers low.	

◀ Small Groups

While the types of experiences offered at large-group time can also be done with small groups of children, small-group time is usually reserved for activities that allow children to explore concepts more thoroughly. In small groups, teachers are better able to engage each child, to differentiate instruction, and to make accommodations for individual needs and interests. Small groups also are an ideal time to observe children in order to assess their understanding of a concept or skill. When planning small-group mathematics instruction, remember that it should be

- brief (about 10–15 minutes)

- focus on a particular math concept or skill

- offered in groups that are flexible in size and makeup

- active

- hands-on, that is, materials of some kind should be used

- include informal assessment

Knowing each child as an individual is important for effective planning. To know children, you must carefully observe them as they work with materials, listen to them as they explain their thinking or talk about what they are doing, interact with them, and study their representations. Small-group settings enable teachers better to know children and then to scaffold their learning. The sections that follow show how teachers plan for and use small-group times. Other activities appropriate for use with small groups can be found in chapter 5, "Mathematics Activities."

In the two previous scenarios, Ms. Tory introduced sorting to the whole class of children, and Mr. Alvarez reinforced the concept by using music and movement. The teachers do not yet know about individual children's abilities to sort, so together they plan a small-group activity that will help them determine what children know and are able to do. Mr. Alvarez leads the first small-group activity. His reflections are in the right-hand column.

The teachers have prepared four bags, each containing five green and five yellow teddy bear counters and five green and five yellow 1" cubes from the Toys and Games Area.

Plans in advance to have the necessary props ready.

Provides object props to use as visual prompts.

| Mr. Alvarez: | *Do you remember how we sorted things into two groups the other day at morning meeting?* |

| Dallas: | *All the blue things and the red things.* |

| Mr. Alvarez: | *Yes, we sorted things into a group of blue things and another group of red things.* |

I have another set of materials for each of you. (He gives each child a bag.) *Take the materials out and think about how you could you sort them.*

(He watches to see what children do.)

(Ben puts one teddy bear counter on top of each cube.)

(Crystal puts all the yellow bears and cubes in one pile and all the green bears and cubes in another pile.)

(Dallas makes four groups: yellow bears, green bears, yellow cubes, green cubes)

(Alexa watches Dallas and then also makes four groups.)

| Mr. Alvarez: | *You've sorted in different ways. Tell me what you did, Crystal.* |

| Crystal: | *Well, some of the yellow things were bears and some were blocks, but I put all the things that were the same color together, like Ms. Tory did.* |

| Mr. Alvarez: | *You sorted the things by color, making two groups: a group of yellow things and a group of green things. Tell me what you did, Dallas.* |

| Dallas: | *I put all the yellow bears here. Then I put all the green bears here. I put the green blocks over here and the yellow blocks over here.* (She points.) |

Paraphrases child's response. Uses the word *sort*.

Chooses familiar toys. (If the materials were novel, children would be given time to play with them first.)

Ben uses one-to-one correspondence, but he does not sort.

Crystal sorts by color.

Dallas and Alexa sort by more than one attribute, putting items that are exactly alike together.

Acknowledges children's work. Asks children to explain what they did.

Acknowledges each child's explanation by paraphrasing what he or she said.

Mr. Alvarez: *You made four groups of things that are exactly alike. Tell me what you did, Alexa.*

Alexa: *I put the yellow bears here and the green bears here and the green blocks here and the yellow ones here.* (She points.)

Alexa copied Dallas. I'll see if Alexa can sort independently on another day.

Mr. Alvarez: *You also made four groups of things that are exactly alike: green bears, green blocks, yellow bears, and yellow blocks.*

Tell me what you did, Ben.

Ben: *My bears are on chairs.*

Mr. Alvarez: *And you made a rhyme,* bears *and* chairs. (Laughs.)

Uses the opportunity to reinforce rhyming, although the focus was not literacy.

Reinforces the use of the term *cubes*.

You all did different things with your bears and cubes. Crystal sorted into two groups by color. Dallas and Alexa put things that are exactly the same together. Ben didn't sort his things, but he lined them up.

Now, can everyone sort the bears and cubes into two groups: same color and different color?

Wants children to sort by the criterion of *color*, not just *identity*, which is an easier skill.

Crystal: *I already did that.*

Mr. Alvarez: *Yes, I know. See if Ben would like some help.*

Gives Crystal a leadership role and Ben assistance.

(Dallas, Alexa, and Ben [with Crystal's help] put their yellow bears and cubes in one pile and their green bears and cubes in another pile.)

Mr. Alvarez: *Can you tell me why you put all these together?* (He points to yellow bears and yellow cubes.)

Provides children with another opportunity to explain their thinking.

Alexa and Dallas: *They're the same color.*

Crystal: *We sorted by color.*

Mr. Alvarez: *Now, please put all of the yellow objects, both the bears and the cubes, back in the bag.*

Provides an opportunity to demonstrate sorting according to an attribute other than color.

Mr. Alvarez:	*How might you sort the green objects you now have in front of you?*	
	(Crystal and Dallas put all of the green bears in one pile and all of their green cubes in another pile. Alexa watches and then follows their example. Ben makes a new design with his bears and cubes.)	
Mr. Alvarez:	*Crystal, tell us what you did.*	Gives Crystal an opportunity to think through and communicate what she has done.
Crystal:	*I put the bears together and the blocks together.*	
Mr. Alvarez:	*Are the things in this pile the same?*	Acknowledges Crystal's thinking and clarifies the process for other children.
Crystal:	*Well, they're all bears.*	
Mr. Alvarez:	*They're the same because they're all bears. And the things in this pile?*	Reinforces the concept of *same*.
Crystal:	*They're all blocks.*	
Mr. Alvarez:	*Yes, they're the same because they're all blocks.*	
	You all were really thinking today. Please put your green bears and cubes back in the bags.	Encourages thinking rather than answering correctly.
	It's time to go outside. Listen carefully so you will know what to do. If you have something green on today, get your coat and wait for me by the door. (Pauses until children get coats.) *If you have something yellow on, get your coat and stand by Ms. Tory on the rug.*	

This small-group activity gave children an opportunity to participate in another sorting activity. In addition, Mr. Alvarez learned more about the children's skills. Now Mr. Alvarez knows:

- Crystal can sort by color and then re-sort by item.

- Alexa and Dallas are beginning to sort by color, although Alexa followed Dallas' lead.

- Ben needs to be observed more to find out whether he needs practice in simple sorting, does not understand the term *sort,* or simply prefers making designs with the manipulatives.

Assessing children's mathematical skills related to the goals and objectives of *The Creative Curriculum* enables teachers to plan successfully. In the next activity, Ms. Tory uses the book *Five Creatures,* by Emily Jenkins, with a small group of children. During weekly planning for small groups she and Mr. Alvarez determined that the book would be a good way to expand the children's understanding of sorting.

This is the second time the children have heard the story. The first reading was for enjoyment and occurred during large-group time. Much of the discussion revolved around families, cats, and other pets. This time Ms. Tory will use the book intentionally to focus children's attention on the various ways the creatures are sorted. The story also provides a context for counting and exploring quantity. To make the experience active and concrete for the children, Ms. Tory uses people and animal figures from the Toys and Games Area to represent the characters in the story. Join Ms. Tory and six children for a focused small-group time.

Ms. Tory:	*I have a book that I would like to share with you today. It's a book that I've read to you before.* (She holds the book so the children can see its cover.) *Who remembers the name, or the title, of this book?*	Reminds children of a previous reading.
Children:	Five Creatures (Ms. Tory runs her fingers under the title as the children read.)	
Ms. Tory:	*Do you remember who the five creatures are?*	Checks to determine whether children recall the previous reading and discussion.
Children:	*The mother, father, little girl, and the cats.*	
Alexa:	*Two cats.*	
Setsuko:	*The people and the cats are all called creatures.*	
Ms. Tory:	*That's right. Now I'm going to read the book again, and we're going to look at all the different ways the creatures can be sorted and counted. It's like the sorting you did with the yellow and green bears and cubes. Do you remember how you put all the yellow bears and cubes together and all the green bears and cubes together? Then you mixed them up and sorted them again by putting all the bears in one group and all the cubes in another group.* (Children nod yes.)	Gives children a focus for participating in the story reading. Makes connection to a prior activity.

Ms. Tory	*I have some pretend creatures here.* (She opens a bag and takes out a man, a woman, and a girl figure from the dollhouse set and two small cat counters.)	
Juwan:	*Those are like the creatures in the book.*	
Derek:	*But not really.*	
Ms. Tory:	*How are they different, Derek?*	Responds to Derek. Invites him to explain his thinking.
Derek:	*The girl in the book has orange hair, and the cats don't look the same.*	
Ms. Tory:	*You really studied the pictures didn't you, Derek?* (Derek smiles.)	
	The figures I have here don't look exactly like the ones in the story, but they will do just fine.	Ms. Tory could have asked the children to point to the pictures in the book, but she decided to use figures to make the sorting and counting activity more concrete.
	(Ms. Tory reads.) *"Five creatures live in our house. Three humans and two cats."*	
	Setsuko, can you take these figures and show us three humans and two cats?	
	(Setsuko takes the figures and lines them up: man, woman, girl, cat, cat.)	
Ms. Tory:	*Tell us what you did.*	Asks a child to explain her actions.
Setsuko:	*The mommy, daddy, and sister are the people. These are the cats.*	
Ms. Tory:	*So you sorted the creatures by putting the three humans, or people, together and the two cats together. How many creatures is that all together?*	Supports the child by paraphrasing her response.
Setsuko:	*One, two, three, four, five.*	
Ms. Tory:	*So how many creatures do you have?*	Wants to be sure that the child knows that the last counting word tells how *many*.
Setsuko:	*Five.*	
Ms. Tory:	*I wonder how the creatures will be sorted next.* (Ms. Tory continues to read.) *"Three short and two tall."*	
Juwan:	*I know! Some are big, and some are little.*	

Ms. Tory:	*Yes, Juwan, we say the big ones are tall, and the little ones are short.* (Demonstrates differences in height using hands.) *Will you show us three short creatures and two tall creatures with these figures?* (Juwan takes the figures and puts the man and woman together and the girl and two cats together.)	Introduces measurement vocabulary related to height.
Ms. Tory:	*Who's tall?*	Checks to see if the child knows the terms *short* and *tall*.
Juwan:	*The mommy and daddy.*	
Ms. Tory:	*Who's short or **not** tall?*	Revisits a concept previously discussed: *not*.
Juwan:	*The girl and the cats.*	
Ms. Tory:	(Continues to read.) *"Four who like to eat fish."*	
	Alexa, will you show us? Which ones do you think like to eat fish?	Gives each child in this small group a chance to participate actively.
Alexa:	*I like fish sticks.*	
Ms. Tory:	*So do I. Look at the picture. Who's eating fish?*	Acknowledges response but refocuses discussion on topic.
Alexa:	*The mommy and daddy and this cat and this cat.*	
Ms. Tory:	*Can you sort the figures to show us which ones like to eat fish and which ones do not like to eat fish?*	Suggests that the child use concrete figures because they are easier to count.
Alexa:	*Alexa puts the man, woman, and cats together.*	
Ms. Tory:	*How many is that?*	
Alexa:	*One, two, three, four.*	
Ms. Tory:	*So **how many** creatures like to eat fish?*	Again, does not accept counting as an answer to the question, "How many?" Checks to see if child knows that the last counting word tells how many.
Alexa:	*Four.*	
Ms. Tory:	(Ms. Tory turns to the next page where two cats are shown sleeping on the bed with the girl.) *Leo, with the figures, can you show us how many are sleeping on the bed?*	
Leo:	(Leo takes the two cats and the girl figure.)	

Ms. Tory:	*How many, Leo?*
Leo:	*Three.*
Ms. Tory:	*Now, who can figure this out? If there are three creatures sleeping in the girl's bed, how many creatures are sleeping somewhere else?*
	(When no one responds, Ms. Tory offers a prompt.) *Look at the other figures on the rug next to Alexa.*
Carlos:	*The mommy and daddy are sleeping in their own bed.*
Ms. Tory:	*I think so, too.*
	(Ms. Tory turns the page.) *How many of the creatures can button buttons?*
Carlos:	*Three. The people.*
Ms. Tory:	*And who can't?*
Carlos:	*Cats can't do buttons.*
Ms. Tory:	(Ms. Tory continues to read and discuss the pictures with the children.) *"Five who love birds." Show me five creatures, Derek.*
	(Ms. Tory continues.) *"…two who lick each other."*
Children:	*Eeauu!*
Juwan:	*Cats lick to wash themselves.*
Ms. Tory:	*"And five who sit together in the evening by the fire."* (She turns the last page.)
Children:	*The end.*
Ms. Tory:	*The creatures in this story were grouped, or sorted, in many different ways. Can you name some?*
Leo:	*Those that like to lick each other and those that don't.* (The children giggle.)
Setsuko:	*By how tall they were and who could do buttons.*

She suggests that children use the figures to discover the answer.

Alexa: *Those who liked fish and those that didn't like fish.*

Ms. Tory: *You remembered quite a few ways the creatures were sorted. I'll put the book and the figures in the Library Area so you can tell the story, yourselves, or make up a new story about creatures that live in your house. I can't wait to hear about the new and different ways you sort the creatures.*

Responds to children's ideas and follows through.

Derek: *Can we get a boy and a dog?*

Setsuko: *And a baby?*

Ms. Tory: *Derek, why don't you take all of the dollhouse people over to the Library Area? Juwan, can you find a dog in the set of animals and take that over, too?*

Provides materials so children can sort, count, and tell math stories independently.

When used intentionally, books and stories are useful tools for teaching mathematics and helping children make connections between mathematics and everyday life. Small-group settings are ideal for these experiences, because they encourage children to make comments, ask questions, and stay engaged with materials and peers.

Studies

In *The Creative Curriculum* classroom, teachers use studies to help children build content knowledge and develop and use process skills. A study is an in-depth investigation of a topic children are interested in learning more about. Children find answers to their questions through firsthand explorations, and they have opportunities to practice and apply mathematics skills in meaningful ways.

Beginning the Study

To illustrate how children use mathematics to learn, consider the study that evolved in Ms. Tory's and Mr. Alvarez's 4-year-old class.

There was an air of excitement in the classroom as children pressed their faces to the windows to see new construction taking place right on their school grounds!

I wonder what they are going to build?

I bet it's going to be a gigantic room that everyone in the whole world can fit into!

I think it's going to be another classroom for more kids to come to our school.

My dad is a carpenter, and he builds stuff like this all the time.

Ms. Tory noticed the children's curiosity and interest in the new construction and saw the possibility of a study on buildings and construction. While children worked in their interest areas, she noticed children representing their thinking. In the Block Area, Carlos attempted to build a gigantic classroom. Sonya used art materials to draw what she thought the new building would look like. At the group meeting, the conversation continued. Ms. Tory wrote children's predictions about the new construction and discussed their representations. She then asked the children how they thought they could find out about the new building. Children offered various suggestions and decided they would find out.

At planning time, Ms. Tory and Mr. Alvarez discussed their observations of the children and concluded that buildings and construction would be a good topic of study. Their next step was to create a web of big ideas to identify the content children could learn. They started by brainstorming words related to buildings and construction and recording each on a separate Post-it®. Then they grouped the words into categories on a piece of chart paper, drew a circle around each group, and labeled it. The labels identified the big ideas.

In addition to helping Mr. Alvarez and Ms. Tory identify important science and social studies content, the webbing process enabled them to identify important vocabulary that could be taught and to think about the many ways literacy, mathematics, the arts, and technology could be addressed. They also reflected on how their early learning standards would be addressed through the study.

A good study begins with what children know and then leads them beyond their everyday experiences. Ms. Tory brought in a collection of photos and magazine pictures of different types of buildings: schools, office buildings, skyscrapers, garages, warehouses, apartment buildings, homes, thatched-roof huts, and stadiums. Then she led a discussion about them. The children wondered if the new construction project on their school grounds would look like any of the buildings pictured. Ms. Tory listened carefully as they talked about the buildings and began a list of the things they wanted to find out.

She continued to add to the list each day as the children wondered aloud. The list of questions became the heart of their study. The experiences that Ms. Tory and Mr. Alvarez offered were designed to help the children find answers to these questions. Ms. Tory wrote a note to families to let them know about the buildings and construction study and to suggest ways they might participate. She was delighted to find out that many family members were involved in construction work and were eager to come to the class to share their skills with the children.

What We Want to Find Out About Our New Building

What is it going to be?

How long will it take to build it?

Who is going to build it?

What will I be able to do in the building?

Where do you get the stuff to build it?

How big will it be?

Do you have to be strong to build a building?

What kinds of machines will they use?

Investigating the Topic

Ms. Tory and Mr. Alvarez first thought of all the possible experiences that could help the children find answers to their questions and gain a deeper understanding about buildings and the construction process. The following were some of their ideas for incorporating mathematical skills.

Building and Construction Experiences	Ways to Use Mathematical Skills
Visit to construction site	Take photos at various stages of construction. Create a timeline of the project.
	Create observational drawings, calling children's attention to the geometric shapes of the lumber, pilings, bricks, roof, shingles, windows, etc.
	Create a graph of the various kinds of workers at the site.
Create blueprints and build structures from them	Examine blueprints and learn how symbols are used for representing something else.
	Create a blueprint of a dream house.
	Use blocks or boxes to make a model.
Exploration of construction materials and tools	Weigh and measure (using non-standard units) various construction materials such as bricks, lumber, and screws.
	Estimate how many strikes it takes to hammer a sheetrock nail into a piece of wood. Count and record results.
	Place measuring tapes of various lengths, carpenter's ruler, t-square, metal rulers, squares, etc. in the Block or Discovery Area or with woodworking materials.
	Use small ceramic tiles to create patterns.
Classroom visits from construction workers and other experts	Ask a parent to lead a simple woodworking project. Emphasize math skills, e.g., counting, comparing, measuring, spatial relations.
	Use ordinal numbers to repeat a sequence of steps in a project, e.g., "First, you nail the sheetrock to the studs. Second, you tape over the seams. Third, you spread sheetrock mud on it. Fourth, you sand it. Fifth, you paint it."
Walk in community to examine various buildings	Count the features of various buildings, e.g., the number of doors, windows, floors, etc.
	Make comparisons of the buildings in terms of size.
	Notice the patterns in the bricks, tile, shingles.
	Tally and then graph the different kinds of buildings seen on the walk.
Set up a building supply store in Dramatic Play Area	Sort and classify the materials.
	Create price lists for various materials.
	Use a scale for weighing nuts and bolts; use measuring tapes to measure wood.

There were far too many experiences to be completed in a week. Learning takes time. Mr. Alvarez and Ms. Tory used the "Weekly Planning Form" (see *The Creative Curriculum for Preschool*, pages 526–527) to record the materials they needed and to identify what they hoped to accomplish each week. They adjusted their plans on the basis of their observations of children as they engaged in the study.

Over the next few weeks, the teachers guided children through various investigations and activities to help them find the answers to their questions. They used comments and open-ended questions to help children clarify their plans, reason, solve problems, communicate, represent their learning, and make connections between mathematics and the real world. Here are examples of the questions and prompts they used:

> *How can you make a square when you only have these triangular tiles?*
>
> *I see you're building a wall and you've run out of long blocks. How many smaller blocks would you need to be the same length as a long one?*
>
> *This floor reminds me of the floor in our classroom. How are they alike?*
>
> *Can you tell me about the house you built with blocks? I want to draw a blueprint of it without looking. Tell me what it looks like, and I'll draw it.*
>
> *How many tiles do you think it will take to make a floor in this room of your block house?*

Ms. Tory and Mr. Alvarez displayed documentation of the children's work during the study. The documentation included descriptions of mathematical concepts the children were exploring and demonstrating.

Concluding the Study

To conclude the study, the children created a neighborhood of houses that were constructed using blueprints they had drawn. They invited family members and other visitors to an open house similar to one hosted by a real estate firm. The children served refreshments they had made using favorite recipes. They created ads describing their homes and the price of each. When the guests arrived, the children took them on a "home tour," explaining the features of their homes and how they were constructed.

As you can see, this study of buildings and construction enabled children to use mathematics in meaningful and relevant ways. It helped children to understand and apply skills related to number and operations, geometry and spatial sense, measurement, patterns (algebra), and data analysis, and to use mathematical process skills to gain a deeper understanding of the topic.

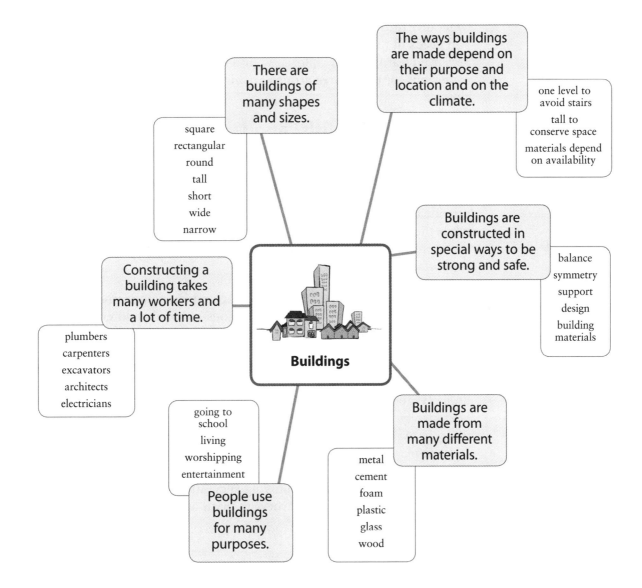

Meeting the Needs of All Children

Young children are similar but different in many ways. They are all eager learners, but some are outgoing, boisterous risk-takers while others are shy, quiet observers. All children learn through active involvement with materials and others, but not all children learn in the same way or at the same pace. Some children need additional support; others need different types of activities or challenges. The sections that follow address ways to modify the environment and your interactions to meet the strengths and needs of three diverse groups of children: English language learners, advanced learners, and children with disabilities. Modifications and extensions for these three groups are also included for each activity in chapter 5.

Supporting English Language Learners

Children who are English language learners come to school with the promise of being fluent in two languages, but in the beginning they may find school an unfamiliar and bewildering place. The teacher's role is to provide an environment where all children feel comfortable and accepted while they grow and learn. Teachers do this when they provide cultural, social/emotional, and family partnership supports, as well as instructional supports.

Language plays a central role in teaching and learning mathematics. Words can help to anchor concepts, and questions can lead children to explore mathematical ideas.

Mathematical concepts can, of course, be learned in any language. Ideally, teachers support children's mathematical explorations in the child's home language, but this is not possible unless you speak that language. Fortunately, *The Creative Curriculum* classroom environment provides many nonverbal mathematical experiences. Children are not expected to learn mathematical concepts from the materials alone, however. Your interactions with English language learners can also support their mathematics learning. The following suggestions can be helpful in engaging English language learners in math activities.

Language Supports

- Keep your language simple. Use short sentences. Pronounce words carefully.

- Determine in advance a few mathematical terms that you want children to learn. Repeat these terms often.

- Use gestures and physical actions along with speech. You can show *big*, *small*, *fast*, and *slow* with hand and body gestures. Modify your speech to facilitate understanding (e.g., a loud voice for *big* and a soft voice for *small*).

- Show and talk. Use manipulatives, pictures, and objects (e.g., show a circle when talking about a circle; hold up four fingers when you say *four*).

- Sing, chant, and recite simple rhymes with the class. Repeat counting songs, finger plays, and chants.

- Let children respond in nonverbal ways (e.g., pointing, drawing, gesturing, acting out).

- Encourage children who speak the same language to work together, communicating their thoughts and ideas in their home language.

- Open-ended questions may be difficult for English language learners. Ask questions that can be answered with one word. Also ask questions that include the word needed for the answer (e.g., "Is this large or small?").

- Include English language learners in conversations regardless of whether or not they respond.

- Talk while doing. Describe what you are doing and what you see the child doing (e.g., "You're putting the red pegs in the red bowl and the blue ones in the blue bowl.").

- Listen closely. Make every effort to understand what the English language learner is telling you and check for understanding (e.g., "Do you want to put all of the cans on the top shelf and all of the boxes on the bottom shelf?").

- Story time may be challenging for English language learners. If possible, have someone who speaks the child's language read the book to the child before the activity or learn a few key mathematical terms or phrases in the child's language. Short books with lots of repetition and hand and body gestures also help understanding.

Cultural Supports

- Provide books, charts, and materials that are related to the family's experiences and cultural and linguistic backgrounds.

- Learn and speak a few terms in the child's home language.

- Encourage the child to talk with other children who speak the same language.

- Post the daily schedule, signs, and labels in the children's home languages as well as in English.

- Sing or listen to tapes or CDs in the children's home languages.

- Teach or use the child's home language in whole-group activities. English-only speakers will benefit from these experiences as well.

Social/Emotional Supports

- Establish and follow regular routines so children can gain confidence, knowing what comes next and what to do.

- Smile and speak often to the English language learner, but do not demand participation or a response until he or she is ready to respond.

- Recognize that the amount of time it takes to feel at home in a new situation varies from child to child. Allow English language learners to watch from a distance that is comfortable for them.

- Become familiar with the stages of learning a second language. (See *The Creative Curriculum for Preschool*, chapter 1, "How Children Develop and Learn," "English Language Learners.")

- Provide many nonverbal ways for children to participate, such as art, music, dance, dramatic play, outside play, and construction.

Family Partnership Supports

- Foster partnerships with families, respecting their culture, inviting them to spend time in the classroom, asking for their advice about how to make a smooth transition for their child, and keeping them informed about their child's activities (through an interpreter if necessary).

- Help parents understand how valuable it is for their children to speak two languages. Encourage them to support their children's home language by speaking and reading to them in their language.

- When possible, send home books and learning materials in the child's home language, so that families can read to children and do learning activities in their own language.

Supporting Advanced Mathematics Learners

Some preschool children are advanced in one or more areas of mathematics. These children do not simply use mathematical terminology or recite facts their older siblings have taught them. The advanced mathematics learner is one who may create complex patterns; build intricate, delicately balanced block structures; or love to analyze problems. It is important to celebrate and challenge children's advanced abilities, but keep in mind that these children are not always advanced in all areas of mathematics simultaneously.

All children need challenges tailored to their abilities and learning styles. Teachers plan for advanced learners just as they do for the children who need more time and assistance to master skills and concepts. Here are some suggestions for working with mathematically advanced learners.

Introduce data collection and analysis activities.

- Pose a question.

- Design a survey.

- Create charts or graphs.

- Interpret and then report results.

Introduce symbolic or more abstract math materials.

- Use dice and dominos.

- Introduce symbolic graphs and graphs with numerals along with graphs with concrete materials.

Introduce advanced computer programs.

- Look at the suggestions in *The Creative Curriculum for Preschool*, chapter 15.

Integrate math with other content areas.

- Pose mathematical problems that enable children to use mathematical skills as they study other areas (e.g., "If the construction workers you see outside work four hours before lunch and four hours after lunch, how many hours do they work in one day?").

- Look for patterns in songs, talk about the refrains in books.

Focus on the mathematics process skills.

- Pose more complex and meaningful problems (e.g., "How can you use the blocks to design a play yard for the guinea pig so that he gets exercise but can't run away? How many more chairs do we need so that everyone can sit for the puppet show? How can we divide the pizza so that everyone will have an equal amount?").

- Challenge children to think of new or multiple solutions to a problem (e.g., "Can you find another way to do it? How else could the man in the story solve his problem?").

- Encourage children to describe and explain their reasoning, probing and prompting if necessary (e.g., "How do you know these are all triangles? Did you count the sides? Did you look at the points?").

- Encourage children to represent their thinking and learning through drawing, writing, or construction. (e.g., "Here are four bears, and here are six cats. If I put them all together, I'll have ten animals.").

- Pose mathematical problems that enable children to make connections among the components of math (e.g., "Can you find a pattern in the numerals between 10 and 30? If our work packets go home every Friday, how many times will your parents see your work this month? What about next month? Where might you look to figure that out?").

As you interact with children who have advanced mathematical abilities, you will discover their interests, find ways to share their enthusiasm, and develop strategies to address their strengths and needs. Continue to challenge children with advanced mathematical skills by introducing more complex materials and posing more difficult problems.

Supporting Children With Disabilities

All children should have opportunities to be actively engaged in mathematical experiences that are challenging yet achievable. For a child with a disability, this may mean that the environment or materials need to be adapted, routines need to be adjusted, or an activity modified. In *The Creative Curriculum* classroom, the teacher's role is to determine what special supports a child needs to participate fully. Some suggestions for general adaptations follow. For additional or more specific recommendations for a child, teachers should request assistance from special educators, the child's parents, and—with the parents' permission—the child's therapist or pediatrician. It is important to observe children with disabilities carefully and continually, to see if the current accommodations and supports are effective and to make changes as needed.

Environmental Supports

- Offer alternative seating options, such as sitting on an adult's lap or next to an adult, for a child who is easily distracted.

- Use tape on the carpet or carpet squares to help children identify the boundaries of their personal space.

- Provide appropriate assistive devices for the computer so all children can use the software. For children with visual impairments, make sure the software has auditory feedback.

- Equip electronic devices, such as tape recorders and CD players, with switches that all children can use independently.

- Make sure that displayed books and other texts are accessible to all children.

- Make sure that manipulatives, puzzles, and other math materials are accessible to all children.

Schedule and Routine Supports

- Preview activities with children who need help with transitions or new experiences.

- Break tasks and activities into smaller parts and provide verbal cues as necessary.

- Encourage children to participate to the degree that they are able.

- Use consistent, predictable routines to help children feel comfortable and secure. Introduce changes gradually to encourage adaptability and flexibility.

- Create a picture board with simple directions or reminders about how to attend during group activities.

Visual Supports

- Provide manipulatives that relate to the topic being discussed. For example, provide a set of shapes for a child to hold while the class is talking about the shapes on the flannel board; provide a large and a small block to hold while the class is discussing size.

- Attach a piece of textured material to the name card of a child, so that he can identify it by touch. Alternatively, let the child choose a special shape for his card, e.g., a circle, if other children's cards are rectangles.

- Include books with large print.

- Introduce and reinforce math vocabulary while the child handles related manipulatives.

- Modify numeral cards or game pieces by adding raised dots to represent numbers. Raised dots can be made with glue.

Language Supports

- Articulate clearly and monitor the speed of your speech so that children are better able to understand.

- Repeat key directions for children.

- Use pictures. Create or purchase picture/symbol cards for basic mathematical concepts such as number (cards with numeral and/or dots), shape, and size.

- Use pictures or objects to represent key concepts. Check for understanding often.

- Encourage children to talk about what they are doing as they manipulate objects.

Many of the suggestions for supporting English language learners may also assist children with language delays.

Sensory and Physical Supports

- Select books and make or purchase charts with clear, simple pictures and familiar concepts.

- Observe to see what manipulatives a child finds easiest to handle. Some children may find it easier to manipulate magnetic numbers, shapes, and objects on a magnetic board.

- Determine what body position makes it easiest for a child to handle manipulatives and writing tools.

- Place large dots made with glue in the upper right-hand corner of book pages. This will separate the pages, making them easier to turn.

- Use Velcro™ or magnetic strips on charts and graphs for children who lack hand strength.

- When possible, have children use their bodies to experience mathematical concepts (e.g., have children hold hands around a tree trunk to form a circle).

- Adapt writing tools for children with limited fine motor skills. Either purchase commercial devices or place a piece of rubber tubing over the pencil or marker to make it easier to grasp.

inside this chapter

4 Mathematics Learning in Interest Areas

The Creative Curriculum classroom has space divided into interest areas where children spend significant time each day in child-initiated play. This design enables children to make choices, explore and experiment on their own, imagine and create, and interact with others. Interest areas are the ideal setting for children to actively and independently explore mathematical ideas and use mathematics to help them make sense of their world.

When each interest area is organized with mathematics in mind, children's time is well spent and mathematics learning is maximized. By integrating mathematics into children's play, children have opportunities to reason; solve problems; communicate; represent their thinking and learning in a variety of ways; and make connections between components, with other content areas, and with the real world. Teachers carefully design and equip each area so that children's strengths, needs, interests, and learning styles are met and important mathematical content is addressed. Then teachers observe children and thoughtfully consider ways in which to interact to guide children's learning and development.

The Toys and Games Area as the Hub of Mathematics Learning

There are opportunities for children to explore mathematics in all interest areas, but the Toys and Games Area is the hub for mathematical activities and learning. As children manipulate puzzle pieces, they learn about shape and spatial relationships. They use collections of objects, such as colored cubes, links, and other collectibles, to count and play number games, sort, make patterns, and measure. Teachers can support and encourage mathematics learning in this area by showing interest and enthusiasm in children's work and interacting in ways that prompt them to share their reasoning, solve problems, communicate their ideas, make connections, and represent their thinking and learning.

Examples of What a Child Might Do	Examples of Related Curriculum Objectives	Examples of How This Relates to Mathematics
Turn a puzzle piece several different ways to get it to fit	23. Approaches problems flexibly	Demonstrates beginning problem solving
Try repeatedly to stack all of the LEGO® to make the tallest tower	24. Shows persistence in approaching tasks	Focuses attention; perseveres
Put all of the red, blue, and yellow circles together	27. Classifies objects	Sorts by shape
Make a chain and then hold it next to a friend's chain to determine whose is longer	28. Compares/measures	Compares length
Line up plastic bears: small, medium, large	29. Arranges objects in a series	Orders objects by size
Make a bead necklace with a red, blue; red, blue pattern	30. Recognizes patterns and can repeat them	Makes a pattern
Say that the bean bag landed outside the circle	32. Shows awareness of position in space	Uses the positional word outside
Put one bear on each cube	33. Uses one-to-one correspondence	Matches a set of bears with a set of cubes
Put five counters on the card labeled 5	34. Uses numbers and counting	Recognizes numeral and counts
Make Xs and Os on paper as a way to show which bug counters have wings and which do not	37. Makes and interprets representations	Uses representation, which is a mathematical process skill

Mathematics Materials for the Toys and Games Area

The Toys and Games Area should have materials that allow children to explore multiple concepts within each component of mathematics and use the mathematical process skills. As described in chapter 8 of *The Creative Curriculum for Preschool*, open-ended materials and collectibles such as buttons, shells, and keys are ideal for such explorations. Symbolic mathematical materials such as dice, dominoes, spinners, graphs, and numeral manipulatives are also important, because they prepare children for later abstract thinking. Books belong in this interest area, too. Many fictional and nonfictional books present mathematical concepts in appealing ways and enable children to see mathematics used in real situations.

To highlight connections among materials, consider their placement. Place a book such as *The Button Box* next to a collection of buttons and a muffin tin to encourage children to sort. Display a shape poster and book about shapes close to the geoboards to encourage exploration of shapes. Remember, too many materials can overwhelm children. When selecting materials for the Toys and Games Area, consider the abilities and interests of the children, as well as key mathematical concepts. Rotate materials as appropriate. For guidance about how to introduce new materials to children, see *The Creative Curriculum for Preschool*, pages 183–5.

materials

- ☐ a variety of counters
- ☐ interlocking cubes
- ☐ connecting links
- ☐ 1" cubes or tiles
- ☐ matching games and materials (e.g., number, shape)
- ☐ collectibles (e.g., buttons, keys, natural materials)
- ☐ containers for sorting (e.g., trays, bowls, hoops, muffin tins, or clean egg cartons)
- ☐ pegs and peg boards
- ☐ stringing beads and pattern cards
- ☐ dominos

book suggestions

All About Where (Tana Hoban) – spatial sense, location

Barn Cat: A Counting Book (Carol P. Saul) – number concepts, numeral recognition

Beep, Beep, Vroom, Vroom! (Stuart J. Murphy) – patterns

The Button Box (Margarette Reid) – sorting, similarities and differences

Cubes, Cones, Cylinders, and Spheres (Tana Hoban) – 3-D shapes

The Handmade Counting Book (Laura Rankin) – number concepts

Let's Count (Tana Hoban) – number concepts

The Line Up Book (Marisabina Russo) – measurement, sorting

More, Fewer, Less (Tana Hoban) – number concepts

Mouse Count (Ellen Stoll Walsh) – number concepts, simple addition and subtraction

materials

- ☐ attribute blocks
- ☐ pattern blocks, parquetry blocks,
- ☐ tangrams, pattern cards
- ☐ geometric solids (cube, sphere, cone, etc.)
- ☐ shape templates for tracing
- ☐ geoboards and rubber bands
- ☐ dice (e.g., with dots, numbers, shapes, or colors) and spinners
- ☐ numeral cards; cards representing quantities 1–10; number strips
- ☐ magnetic and/or felt numbers and shapes
- ☐ writing materials
- ☐ lotto and other games (e.g., number, shape, size, classification)
- ☐ balance scale
- ☐ graphing mat
- ☐ sequencing or seriation materials
- ☐ coins
- ☐ storyboards

book suggestions, continued

One Duck Stuck (Phyllis Root) – number concepts

One Monkey Too Many (Jackie French Koller) – number concepts, location

One of Each (Mary Ann Huberman) – number concepts

Only One (Marc Harshman) – number concepts

Quack and Count (Keith Baker) – number concepts, simple addition

Spirals, Curves, Fanshapes and Lines (Tana Hoban) – shape

Ten Dogs in the Window: A Countdown Book (Clair Masurel) – number concepts, sorting, similarities and differences

Ten Flashing Fireflies (Philemon Sturges) – number concepts

Ten Little Mice (Joyce Dunbar) – number concepts

The Very Hungry Caterpillar (Eric Carle) – number concepts

Where is that Cat? (Carol Green) – spatial sense, location

Where's that Cat? (Eve Meriam and Pam Pollack) – spatial sense, location

Using Toys and Games to Teach Mathematics

Children need time to freely explore the materials in the Toys and Games Area. Through their playful manipulation of objects, they discover many mathematical relationships on their own. Teachers who carefully observe the ways in which children use materials and listen to them as they talk are able to determine the best way to respond and support their mathematics learning. At times teachers will ask a question, pose a problem, introduce a new term, or model the steps in solving a problem. At other times, they simply observe.

Talking helps children clarify and organize their thinking. However, young children are not proficient at expressing their thoughts, particularly if they are English language learners. Your questions and comments can stimulate children's thinking, but be careful not to overwhelm them.

Number and Operations

How many ducks are there? Are you sure? How do you know?

Can you make a chain with more links than mine? Can you make a chain with fewer links?

Which bear is first in line? Which bear is second?

How many shells do you need to put on this card? (Point to the numeral 4.)

If you put two more buttons in the box, how many buttons will there be? How many would you have if you took out one?

Geometry and Spatial Sense

Tell me about these shapes. How would you describe them?

How many different shapes can you make using these straws?

If you put these two triangles together, what shape would you make?

Can you find something in the classroom that looks like a can? How about a ball?

Can you toss the beanbag near the basket? Which beanbag is farthest from the basket?

Measurement

Which one is biggest (smallest, tallest, shortest, and so forth)? How do you know?

What else could you use to measure your tower?

Which shape can you cover with the most tiles?

How do you know which table block is the heaviest? Show me.

Is this a picture of something happening during the day or at night? How can you tell?

Patterns (Algebra)

Tell me about this row of pegs. How do you know it's a pattern?

Can you finish this pattern? It starts out: circle, triangle; circle, triangle; circle,... What shape should come next?

I'd like to make a pattern like yours. Tell me or show me how.

Do you think you could make a pattern like the pattern on your shirt?

How could you read this pattern? Can you read it another way?

Data Analysis (Collecting Data, Sorting and Classifying, and Organizing Data)

Which things do you think go together? Why? What name could you give this group?

How could we sort these buttons? Is there another way to sort the buttons?

Can you find all the cubes that are not green?

Tell me about those marks (tallies). What do they mean?

What other pictures go in the animal column on our graph?

Mathematical Process Skills (Reasoning, Problem Solving, Communicating, Connecting, and Representing)

Why do you think...?

That's an interesting idea. What will you do next?

Are you sure? How do you know?

Can you explain that so that Keri can understand how you did it?

Can you make a picture of that?

Observing Children's Progress

As you observe children playing with toys and games, look for these indications of mathematics learning:

- using one-to-one correspondence

- counting

- using terms such as *some, all, more, less, more than, less than, fewer than, the same as*

- recognizing and/or writing numerals

- recognizing patterns of dots without counting (i.e., subitizing)

- answering the question, *How many?* without recounting

- recognizing, describing, copying, extending, or creating a pattern

- using positional words (e.g., *over, under, in front of, next to, behind, outside, inside*)

- talking about how things are the same and/or different

- describing shapes (e.g., three sides, four sides, straight sides, curved, round, corners)

- naming shapes (e.g., *circle, triangle, square, rectangle, cube, cone, cylinder*)

- using comparative terms such as *big, bigger, biggest; faster, slower; longer, longest, same length; taller, shorter; heavier, lighter; holds more, holds less;* etc.

- using words related to time, such as *morning, afternoon, evening, night, day, noon, soon, tomorrow, yesterday, early, late, a long time ago,* etc.

- sorting

- using the term *not*

- keeping a tally during a game

- constructing a graph with assistance

- interpreting a graph

- explaining reasoning

Mathematics in the Block Area

The Block Area is a favorite among children and one that presents children with numerous opportunities to explore mathematical concepts such as shape, size, space, pattern, and number. Children also acquire and refine mathematical process skills as they address problems such as how to steady a tower so that it does not topple, how to construct a bridge over a raging river, or how to make the roof stay up. Children can persist in solving problems when they are fully engaged in their block-building activity.

Examples of What a Child Might Do	Examples of Related Curriculum Objectives	Examples of How This Relates to Mathematics
Switch to short blocks to finish a road when the supply of long blocks runs out	23. Approaches problems flexibly	Solves a problem through substitution; begins to see the equivalence of two short rectangular blocks to one long rectangular block
Try several ways to get the cylinder to balance on top of a tower	24. Shows persistence in approaching tasks	Uses a variety of strategies to solve a problem
Put blocks away on shelves labeled with outlines of their shapes	27. Classifies objects	Notices similarities and differences; begins to classify objects by shape and size
Try to make a door tall enough for the giraffe to get through	28. Compares/measures	Compares objects according to height; attempts to solve a problem
Line up farm animals according to size: horse, cow, pig, chicken	29. Arranges objects in a series	Orders objects according to height
Decorate the top of castle with a block pattern: triangle, cylinder; triangle cylinder	30. Recognizes patterns and can repeat them	Makes a pattern
Make an enclosure with hollow blocks and sit inside; say, "I'm in my house"	32. Shows awareness of position in space	Beginning to understand geometric concept of enclosure; specifies location
Put a triangular block on top of each square block in a row	33. Uses one-to-one correspondence	Matches sets of objects (triangular blocks and square blocks)
Say, "I made a tower with eight blocks"	34. Uses numbers and counting	Uses counting to measure object
Build a structure, call it a barn, select farm animals, and put them inside	37. Makes and interprets representations	Represents ideas concretely; sorts animals by type (separating farm animals from other animals)

Mathematics Materials for the Block Area

Many of the materials suggested for the Block Area in chapter 6 of *The Creative Curriculum for Preschool* stimulate mathematical thinking. That chapter also suggests ways to organize the area. The materials and books listed in this chart also support children's mathematical explorations.

materials

- ☐ geometric solids
- ☐ everyday materials (e.g., cans, pipes, boxes, traffic cones)
- ☐ maps
- ☐ photographs of buildings and other structures illustrating shapes and patterns
- ☐ photos of children's block constructions, their neighborhoods, and places the class has visited
- ☐ floor tiles, carpet pieces
- ☐ large pieces of cardboard
- ☐ measuring tools
- ☐ writing and drawing materials

book suggestions

The Block Book (Susan Couture)

Building (Elisha Cooper)

Building a House (Byron Barton)

The Busy Building Book (Sue Tarsky)

A Carpenter (Florian Douglas)

Construction Zone (Tana Hoban)

The House in the Meadow (Shutta Crum)

How a House Is Built (Gail Gibbons)

The Lot at the End of My Block (Kevin Lewis)

Louise Builds a House (Louise Pfanner)

One Big Building: A Counting Book About Construction (Michael Dahl)

Unit Blocks

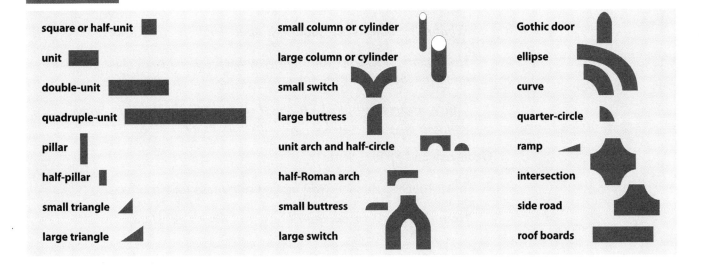

square or half-unit	small column or cylinder	Gothic door
unit	large column or cylinder	ellipse
double-unit	small switch	curve
quadruple-unit	large buttress	quarter-circle
pillar	unit arch and half-circle	ramp
half-pillar	half-Roman arch	intersection
small triangle	small buttress	side road
large triangle	large switch	roof boards

Using Blocks to Teach Mathematics

Understanding the developmental stages of block play helps teachers interact with children in appropriate ways (see *The Creative Curriculum for Preschool*, pages 256–9). For example, a teacher who observes a child pulling blocks off the shelf and piling them into trucks will recognize that the child is at Stage 1: Carrying Blocks. He is learning about the properties of blocks and gaining an understanding of what he can and cannot do with them. Knowing this and considering math content, the teacher may talk with the child about his choice of blocks and call his attention to their physical characteristics. She may try to interest the child in counting the blocks in his truck or matching them to the labels on the shelves when choice time is over.

Teachers first observe children in the Block Area and listen as they talk about what they are doing. Then, using carefully chosen questions and comments, they introduce mathematical vocabulary, nurture children's understanding of mathematical concepts, and support their development as serious builders, problem-solvers, and players in the Block Area. Here are examples of what teachers might say as they interact with children in the Block Area.

Number and Operations

There are many people in your house. How many live there? How many are visiting?

This is the bedroom. Do these children share a room? How many beds will you need?

An upstairs and a downstairs! Your house has two floors.

That's a tall tower! How many blocks did you use to build it? How many would there be if you added two more blocks to the top?

What other objects are about the same height as your tower?

How many blocks do you think you used for the road? Did you use more for the road or the tower?

Can you carry five blocks to the shelf and put them away? Wow, that was easy for you! Can you carry six blocks?

Geometry and Spatial Sense

What other shapes can you make using these four triangles?

How will you get from your house to Derek's gas station?

It doesn't look like there are any more of the longest rectangles. What other blocks could you use to finish your building?

That block is called a cylinder. *It looks like a column in front of your house.*

I'm looking for blocks that have three sides. Next, I'm going to look for blocks that are curved.

Measurement

Yes, your road is longer; it goes straight across the rug. Aisha used more blocks for her shorter, curved road.

I think this tower is even taller than the one you built yesterday. What do you think?

I wonder if it would take more tiles or more carpet pieces to cover the floor of your house. What do you think?

Will you car fit under the bridge? What about the truck? Will it fit?

You made a bed of hollow blocks that is long enough for you to sleep on. I wonder how many blocks you'd need to make a bed long enough for me.

Patterns (Algebra)

I see you've placed one block up, one block flat, one block up, and another block flat. That's a pattern! What will go next?

I want to make a fence with a pattern just like yours. Will you tell me how to do it?

I'm making a pattern with square blocks and triangular blocks. Can you help me finish it?

You created a patterned floor for your house with the tiles. Tell me about it.

Data Analysis

You've put all the long rectangular blocks in one pile and all the short rectangular blocks in another pile.

Can you make a road that is the same length by using blocks of a different size?

Mathematical Process Skills (Reasoning, Problem Solving, Communicating, Connecting, and Representing)

Sometimes one road goes over another road, like on the freeway. How could you make an overpass for your highway?

What do you suppose would happen if...? Why do you think that?

How did you figure that out?

How is your shopping mall similar to the one in your neighborhood?

You worked so hard on your building. Would you like me to take a picture of it so we can remember what it looked like?

Observing Children's Progress

While children are engaged in block play, look for these indications of mathematics learning:

- talking with peers and adults to describe what they have built

- placing blocks or other objects in one-to-one correspondence

- using mathematical words such as *longer, shorter, inside, outside, square, triangle, round, more, less*

- describing size and position

- counting blocks

- making a pattern with blocks

- solving problems, for example, balancing a block or constructing a bridge

- matching shapes when returning blocks to the shelves

- comparing length or height

- describing or naming the shape of some blocks (e.g., three sides, triangle, sphere, like a can, etc.)

- using two or more shorter blocks to equal a longer block

- constructing a structure that represents something (e.g., a house, car, or farm)

- arranging objects in a series (e.g., small to large)

Mathematics in the Dramatic Play Area

In the Dramatic Play Area, children experience mathematics in ways similar to their mathematical experiences at home and in their communities. Enacting real-life situations such as setting the table, sorting laundry, or shopping for shoes allows them to experience mathematics in meaningful ways and to deepen their understanding of everyday experiences. They also have opportunities to solve real problems like determining how to divide a pizza equally among friends. Children's ability to engage in dramatic play, to imagine and recreate past situations, or to substitute one toy for another provides practice with abstract thinking and using the symbols of mathematics.

Examples of What a Child Might Do	Examples of Related Curriculum Objectives	Examples of How This Relates to Mathematics
Use a plastic banana as a bottle to feed the baby if no bottle is available	23. Approaches problems flexibly	Solves a problem through substitution
Try to get a friend to be the patient. Finally say, "OK, you can be the other doctor," and get a doll for the patient	24. Shows persistence in approaching tasks	Tries various means to solve problem; perseveres until solution is found
Put the cereal boxes on one shelf and the soup cans on another	27. Classifies objects	Begins to classify objects by shape and type
Look for clothes of the right size to fit a doll	28. Compares/measures	Compares length and width of doll to length and width of dress
Stack the measuring cups	29. Arranges objects in a series	Orders objects according to size
Tell a friend, "First she gets her bottle, and then I put her to bed. When she wakes up, I change her diaper"	30. Recognizes patterns and can repeat them	Talks about patterns in everyday life
Ask a teacher to babysit; say, "I'll be there in 10 minutes"	31. Shows awareness of time concepts and sequence	Begins to understand time concepts and to use time vocabulary
Say to a friend, "The store is too far away; we need a car"	32. Shows awareness of position in space	Uses the positional words near and far
Set the table with a plate and spoon at each place	33. Uses one-to-one correspondence	Demonstrates one-to-one correspondence, a critical requirement of counting
Put 4 candles on a pretend cake and say, "I'm 4"	34. Uses numbers and counting	Counts in meaningful situations
Create a menu by using pictures and symbols	37. Makes and interprets representations	Uses a symbol to represent something

Mathematics Materials for the Dramatic Play Area

In most preschool classrooms, the Dramatic Play Area is initially set up like a home so children can enact the familiar roles of family life. As time passes, children's play extends beyond family life to include situations such as going to the doctor, a restaurant, or the post office. Mathematics can be integrated into any play topic by including materials that encourage children to count, sort, classify, and measure, as well as solve problems, reason, and communicate. Children who are experienced with dramatic play will enjoy using symbolic or abstract mathematical materials such as play money, a timer, a check book, price tags, recipes, or a telephone book.

An organized Dramatic Play Area, with props arranged in labeled containers or displayed on hooks, promotes order and organization—important aspects of mathematics. The following chart lists mathematics-related props, accessories, and books for this interest area.

materials

- ☐ calendar
- ☐ clock
- ☐ timer
- ☐ writing materials
- ☐ recipes
- ☐ cookbook
- ☐ list of emergency telephone numbers
- ☐ phone book
- ☐ coupons
- ☐ measuring cups and spoons
- ☐ bowls, pots and pans, and wooden spoons of varying sizes
- ☐ muffin tins and egg cartons
- ☐ clothes and accessories of varying sizes (e.g., socks, shoes, hats)
- ☐ wallets and purses
- ☐ newspapers (advertisements)

book suggestions

Alfie's 1, 2, 3 (Shirley Hughes)

Anno's Counting House (Mitsumasa Anno)

The Big Brown Box (Marisabina Russo)

The Cake That Mack Ate (Rose Robart)

Car Wash (Sandra Steen and Susan Steen)

Come Back, Hannah! (Marisabina Russo)

The Doorbell Rang (Pat Hutchins)

The Glorious Day (Amy Schwartz)

Jesse Bear, What Will You Wear? (Nancy White Carlstrom)

One Monday Morning (Uri Shulevitz)

Rise and Shine, Mariko-Chan! (Chiyoko Tomioka)

The Secret Birthday Message (Eric Carle)

The Teeny-Tiny Woman (Paul Galdone)

Ten, Nine, Eight (Molly Bang)

We Were Tired of Living in a House (Liesel Moak Skorpen)

As children demonstrate interest in other aspects of community life, the Dramatic Play Area should change or be modified to address the changing roles, language, and mathematical experiences associated with each new topic. The charts that follow offer suggestions for integrating mathematical materials and books into four settings: a grocery store, a doctors' office, a shoe store, and a restaurant. There are many other possibilities, of course.

materials

Grocery Store

☐ flyers, signs, coupons, and advertisements from local supermarkets

☐ paper, cardboard, markers, and tape for making signs for different sections (e.g., meat, dairy) and labels for shelves

☐ empty food containers

☐ stick-on labels or price tags

☐ number stamps and stamp pads

☐ cash register

☐ play money, checkbooks, credit cards

☐ shopping list pads and/or receipt pads

☐ balance scale

☐ materials for a cake-decorating center if your local supermarket has one

book suggestions

At the Supermarket (David Hautzig)

Each Orange Had 8 Slices (Paul Giganti, Jr.)

I Shop with My Daddy (Grace Maccarone)

Jelly Beans for Sale (Bruce McMillan)

Just Shopping With Mom (Mercer Mayer)

Lemonade for Sale (Bettina Ling)

The M&M Counting Book (Barbara McGrath)

More M&Ms Math (Barbara B. McGrath)

Pigs Go to Market (Amy Axelrod)

Pigs Will Be Pigs: Fun with Math and Money (Amy Axelrod)

The Supermarket (Anne F. Rockwell)

Tommy at the Grocery Store (Bill Grossman)

materials

Doctor's office

☐ sign-in sheet on clipboard

☐ patient charts

☐ telephone

☐ appointment book

☐ clock and calendar

☐ scale

☐ measuring tape

☐ prescription pad and pencils

☐ blood pressure cuff

☐ thermometer

☐ play syringe

☐ X-rays

☐ play money, checkbooks, credit cards

☐ paper, cardboard, markers, and tape for making signs

book suggestions

Doctor Tools (Inez Snyder)

Going to the Doctor (Fred Rogers)

Going to the Doctor (Melinda Beth Radabaugh)

The Hospital (Debbie Bailey)

How Do Dinosaurs Get Well Soon? (Jane Yolen)

Kevin Goes to the Hospital (Lisbet Slegers)

My Doctor (Harlow Rockwell)

What to Expect When You Go to the Doctor (Heidi Murkoff)

materials

Restaurant

- ☐ cash register
- ☐ plates, cups, silverware, napkins
- ☐ order pads
- ☐ menus or materials for children to make menus
- ☐ play money, checkbooks, credit cards
- ☐ wallets and purses
- ☐ paper, cardboard, markers, and tape for making
- ☐ signs, e.g., "Daily Specials" or "Pay here"

book suggestions

A Chef (Douglas Florian)

Dim Sum for Everyone! (Grace Lin)

Dinner at the Panda Palace (Stephanie Calmenson)

Hi, Pizza Man (Virginia Walter)

In the Diner (Christine Loomis)

Marge's Diner (Gail Gibbons)

Miss Mabel's Table (Deborah Chandra)

One Pizza, One Penny (K. G. Hao)

Spaghetti and Meatballs for All (Marilyn Burns)

materials

Shoe store

- ☐ shoes of various sizes and styles
- ☐ shoeboxes of various sizes
- ☐ ruler or shoe-size measure
- ☐ order forms and receipt pads
- ☐ sticky labels or price tags
- ☐ cash register
- ☐ play money, checkbooks, credit cards
- ☐ wallets and purses
- ☐ paper, cardboard, markers, and tape for making signs (e.g., men, women, children)

book suggestions

Hello, Shoes! (Joan Blos)

My Best Shoes (Marilee Robin Burton)

New Shoes for Silvia (Johanna Hurwitz)

New Shoes, Red Shoes (Susan Rollings)

Shoes, Shoes, Shoes (Ann Morris)

Whose Shoe? (Margaret Miller)

Whose Shoes Are These? (Ron Roy)

Using Dramatic Play to Teach Mathematics

A teacher observes children engaged in dramatic play and then thoughtfully considers ways in which to promote their mathematics learning. Sometimes a teacher may let a child wrestle with a problem; at other times she may pose a question, model the use of a material or the way in which a problem is solved, or become a full-fledged player. Here are some examples of what teachers might say or do as they interact with children in the Dramatic Play Area to promote mathematical skills and thinking.

Number and Operations

Lunch is ready for you, Marla, Andre, and Keisha. How many places do you need at the table?

Let's see. I'm buying an apple for 3 cents and a pear for 2 cents. One, two, three (puts down 3 cents); one, two (puts down 2 cents). That's one, two, three, four, five. I owe you 5 cents.

Your shoe store has a wonderful selection of shoes. Are there more shoes for children or for adults?

Yes, I may come to the birthday party. I'll need you to give me directions to your house and your address.

You have four bracelets on your arm. If you shared two with a friend, how many would you still have?

Geometry and Spatial Sense

What shapes of cookies have you made? May I have a round one, please?

Where do you think we should put the baby's bed?

Apples, oranges, grapes, and pears are all fruits. Tell me another way that they are alike. What about their shapes?

How are the coffee can, the oatmeal box, and the roll of paper towels similar in shape?

How is the shape of an egg different from the shape of a ball?

Measurement

How do you know that this tablecloth is big enough to cover the table?

I'm not sure what size shoe I wear. Will you help me find out?

I see you set the timer for 5 minutes. Is that how much longer the cake needs to bake?

Your baby's growing so fast. How much does she weigh now?

What time do you begin serving lunch? Hmmm, what size pizza should I get: large, medium, or small?

Patterns (Algebra)

Your baby's dress is like the flag: red, white; red, white; red....

I wonder why the rind on this watermelon has a pattern (dark green, light green, dark green, light green) and the other does not. What do you think?

You've chosen just the right beads to match your dress. Do you see a pattern? Tell me about it.

There is a pattern on the sole of this shoe. How would you describe it?

Data Analysis

I see you're doing laundry. I usually sort the light-colored clothes from the dark-colored clothes. Does your mother do that?

Where does the Cheerios® box go? Where does the dog food belong?

She wants a shoe that does not have laces. Can you help her?

You've been busy measuring everyone. Would you like to make a chart showing how tall your friends are?

Mathematical Process Skills (Reasoning, Problem Solving, Communicating, Connecting, and Representing)

What will you do first? What will you do next?

I wonder...

Tell me more about that.

How did you figure that out?

Show me how you...

How is this like...?

 ## Observing Children's Progress

As you observe children engaged in dramatic play, look for these indications of mathematics learning:

- placing objects in one-to-one correspondence (e.g., putting one sock and one shoe on each foot of the doll; setting the table)

- counting

- using ordinal numbers (e.g., to describe what to do first, second, third, and so on when cooking)

- reading or writing numbers (e.g., on recipes, addresses, or price tags)

- measuring (e.g., children height and weight in the doctor's office; feet in the shoe store)

- comparing sizes (e.g., shoes or cereal boxes)

- sorting (e.g., groceries or clothing)

- using math terms such as *same-different, more-less, bigger-smaller, some-all, not*

- using positional or directional terms (e.g., *near-far, in front of-in back of, on-off, on top of, under, behind*)

- using time and relational words (e.g., *morning, afternoon, evening, tomorrow, yesterday, early, late, fast, slow*)

- solving problems

- using pictures or symbols to represent something else (e.g., using checkers for pepperoni)

- talking about plans and ideas

Mathematics in the Art Area

The Art Area is rich in opportunities for mathematics learning. Children explore size, shape, and spatial relationships as they use three-dimensional materials for sculpting and collage. They describe patterns in wallpaper samples and create their own patterns with stencils or paint and sponges. Representation, which is basic to art, is also fundamental to mathematics, which relies on symbols to represent concepts.

Examples of What a Child Might Do	Examples of Related Curriculum Objectives	Examples of How This Relates to Mathematics
Try many ways to get an acorn to stick on a collage	23. Approaches problems flexibly	Tries alternative ways to solve problem
Choose only red objects for a collage	27. Classifies objects	Sorts (classifies) objects by color
Say that the roller makes wide lines and the marker makes narrow lines	28. Compares/measures	Uses comparative terms, *wide* and *thin*
Roll play dough into large, medium, and small balls to make a snowman	29. Arranges objects in a series	Seriates according to size
Make a pattern of round, square; round, square sponge prints	30. Recognizes patterns and can repeat them	Makes a pattern
Observe that the fingerpaint takes longer to dry in the places where it is thicker	31. Shows awareness of time concepts and sequence	Notices time intervals
Say that the sky is above the house and the tree is beside the house in the drawing	32. Shows awareness of position in space	Uses the positional terms *above* and *beside*
Glue one seed on each leaf in a collage	33. Uses one-to-one correspondence	Matches sets of objects (seeds and leaves)
Count out five buttons for the playdough snowman	34. Uses numbers and counting	Counts in a meaningful situation
Draw and name family members	37. Makes and interprets representations	Uses representation, which is a mathematical process skill

Mathematics Materials for the Art Area

All of the items in a well-stocked Art Area have possibilities for mathematical discoveries. The following materials and books may inspire additional mathematical explorations.

materials

- ☐ templates or stencils of geometric shapes
- ☐ shape sponges
- ☐ wallpaper and fabric samples
- ☐ easel paper cut into a variety of shapes
- ☐ rulers
- ☐ pipe cleaners
- ☐ brushes and/or rollers in two or more widths
- ☐ thick and thin crayons
- ☐ shape and numeral cookie cutters
- ☐ printmaking materials (e.g., corks, spools, sponges, stamp pads)
- ☐ modeling materials and tools
- ☐ collage and construction materials (e.g., Styrofoam® packing sheets in assorted sizes)
- ☐ geometric solids
- ☐ everyday materials in the shape of geometric solids (e.g., spools, boxes, cardboard tubes, cone-shaped cups)

book suggestions

Harold and the Purple Crayon (Crockett Johnson)

I Spy Shapes in Art (Lucy Micklethwait)

I Spy Two Eyes: Numbers in Art (Lucy Micklethwait)

It Looked Like Spilt Milk (Charles G. Shaw)

Mouse Paint (Ellen Stoll Walsh)

Ten Black Dots (Donald Crews)

Using Art to Teach Mathematics

Your primary role in the Art Area is to facilitate children's art explorations and creations. By observing children and listening to them describe and tell about their work, teachers can decide if and when to call children's attention to mathematical concepts. Here are examples of what you might say.

Number and Operations

You've punched many holes in your clay. Shall we count them?

Please put one paint brush in each of the paint pots.

Can you make a picture using only three colors of paint?

You drew a picture of your family. Who are these two large persons? Who are the three smaller persons? How many are there altogether?

Geometry and Spatial Sense

I see triangles, circles, and rectangles in your picture.

Can you make your playdough into the shape of a ball? What will happen if you flatten it into a pancake? Is the same amount of playdough in the ball and the pancake?

Tell me about your sculpture. How did you decide which shapes to use? How did you get the sphere to balance on top of the tower?

Tell me where you plan to place that piece on your collage.

Measurement

You made long lines and short lines, big circles and little circles.

Will you use the thick paintbrush or the thin one for your picture?

Your snake is long. Mine is shorter and fatter. What can I do to make mine as long as yours? How will we know when they are the same?

You drew the moon and stars in the sky above the house. It must be nighttime. Tell me what's happening.

Patterns (Algebra)

Red dot, blue dot; red dot, blue dot. You made a pattern!

Look at the pattern the truck tires made in the paint.

I see you drew a pattern on your snake just like the one we saw in the photo. Can you read it?

Data Analysis

Do you have something on your collage that's the same as this? What do you have that's different from this?

You and Shakira both used the same yarn and cotton balls, but your pictures are quite different.

Tell me why you drew this line down the middle of your paper and glued these things here. Are they alike in some way?

Mathematical Process Skills (Reasoning, Problem Solving, Communicating, Connecting, and Representing)

Can you draw some of the animals that we saw yesterday?

How did you get your playdough snake so long?

Tell me how you made that color of paint.

Tell me about your picture.

How did you decide...

I wonder what would happen if you...

Observing Children's Progress

As children create and explore in the Art Area, look for these indications of mathematical development:

- counting, recognizing, or writing numerals (e.g., printing numerals and then naming them, forming cookies with clay and counting them, drawing and labeling a picture of three friends)

- naming, drawing, or sculpting two- and three-dimensional shapes

- making patterns (e.g., color, shape, object)

- using measurement terms (e.g., *long, short, thin, thick, wide, narrow, taller, shorter*)

- sorting materials (e.g., making a collage of things that are red and things that are not red)

- using the terms *same* and *different*

- telling what they will be making and then painting or constructing it

Mathematics in the Library Area

In the Library Area, children explore books and listen to or retell stories that highlight mathematical concepts. *My Little Sister Ate One Hare* (Bill Grossman) has a growing number pattern and repetitive, patterned text. Children enjoy hearing the story repeatedly, and, with picture props, teachers can intentionally call children's attention to the growing number pattern. When the book and props are left in the Library Area, children can continue to use them to build language, literacy, and mathematical skills.

Books such as *Titch* (Pat Hutchins) help children learn about size differences. The Spot books (Eric Hill) invite children to use positional terms to answer *where* questions. *Mr. Gumpy's Outing* and many other books are filled with characters to be counted. Adding concept books such as Tana Hoban's *Let's Count* or *Shapes, Shapes, Shapes* to the Library Area increases opportunities for children to learn about number and geometry. The Library Area can nurture children's literacy and mathematical development as well as broaden their understanding of the world.

Examples of What a Child Might Do	Examples of Related Curriculum Objectives	Examples of How This Relates to Mathematics
Stack caps, putting like colors together, while acting out *Caps for Sale*	27. Classifies objects	Sorts objects by color
Say that the hungry caterpillar is growing bigger and bigger	28. Compares/measures	Compares sizes
Arrange the three billy goats, from smallest to largest, on the flannel board	29. Arranges objects in a series	Seriates according to size
Describe the patterns pictured in *Pattern Fish* (Trudy Harris)	30. Recognizes patterns and can repeat them	Recognizes and describes patterns
Repeat the order of clothes the boy puts on in *The Jacket I Wear in the Snow*	31. Shows awareness of time concepts and sequence	Repeats sequence of actions
Say that Spot is under the chair	32. Shows awareness of position in space	Uses the positional term *under*
Put one cap on each flannel board monkey	33. Uses one-to-one correspondence	Matches set of caps with set of monkeys
Hold up fingers while reciting "Five Little Monkeys"	34. Uses numbers and counting	Counts and uses fingers to represent numbers
Tell the story of the three little pigs, using a brick, wood, and some straw to represent the houses	37. Makes and interprets representations	Uses representation, which is a mathematical process skill

Mathematics Materials for the Library Area

The Library Area in your classroom probably already contains books that can be used to talk about mathematical concepts with children. In fact, many picture books address several mathematical ideas. For example, in the book *Five Creatures* (Emily Jenkins), the child narrator counts the creatures that live in her house: three humans and two cats. She then groups and counts them in different ways: "three short and two tall," "three who can button buttons," "four who like to eat fish, and two who like to eat mice."

The Library Area should include nonfiction that reflects mathematical ideas as well as fiction that tells a good story and invites children to explore mathematical concepts. The following chart lists materials and a few of the many books that entice children to explore mathematics through literature.

materials

- ☐ felt props for recalling counting or number stories or rhymes

- ☐ props for dramatizing or retelling stories that also address mathematical concepts (e.g., three sizes of bowls and chairs for acting out *The Three Bears;* hats for *Caps for Sale;* small plastic animals and a mitten for *The Mitten*)

- ☐ paper and writing/drawing tools so that children can make their own representations of a story or make number/counting books

- ☐ story tapes or CDs that reinforce the development of mathematical concepts

- ☐ charts of counting/number rhymes or chants (e.g., *Two Little Blackbirds Sitting on a Hill*)

- ☐ class-made books (e.g., counting books, books of patterns children have created)

book suggestions

Biggest, Strongest, Fastest (Steve Jenkins)

Caps for Sale (Esphyr Slobodkina)

Chicka Chicka 1 2 3 (Bill Martin, Jr., Michael Sampson, Lois Ehlert

Come Back, Hannah! (Marisabina Russo)

Cook-a-Doodle-Doo (Janet Stevens and Susan Stevens Crummel)

Counting Crocodiles (Judy Sierra)

Cubes, Cones, Cylinders, and Spheres (Tana Hoban)

Do You See a Mouse? (Bernard Waber)

A Dozen Ducklings Lost and Found (Harriet Ziefert)

Five Creatures (Emily Jenkins)

Five Little Monkeys Wash the Car (Eileen Christelow)

Freight Train (Donald Crews)

book suggestions, continued

Inside Mouse, Outside Mouse (Lindsay Barrett George)

Is It Larger? Is It Smaller? (Tana Hoban)

The Jacket I Wear in the Snow (Shirley Neitzel)

Lemons Are Not Red (Laura Seegar)

Lots and Lots of Zebra Stripes (Stephen R. Swinburne)

The Mitten (Jan Brett)

Mrs. McTats and Her Houseful of Cats (Alyssa Satin Capucilli)

One for Me, One for You (C. C. Cameron)

One Lighthouse, One Moon (Anita Lobel)

One More Bunny; Adding from One to Ten (Rick Walton)

A Pair of Socks (Stuart J. Murphy)

Pattern Fish (Trudy Harris)

Rosie's Walk (Pat Hutchins)

Shrinking Mouse (Pat Hutchins)

Ten Go Tango (Arthur Dorros)

Ten Mice for Tet! (Pegi Deitz Shea and Cynthia Weill)

Ten Puppies (Lynn Reiser)

The Relatives Came (Cynthia Rylant)

The Teeny-Tiny Woman (Paul Galdone)

Uno, Dos, Tres = One, Two, Three (Pat Mora)

We're Going on a Picnic (Pat Hutchins)

When I Was Little: A Four-Year-Old's Memoir of Her Youth (Jamie Lee Curtis)

Where Is the Green Sheep? (Mem Fox and Judy Horacek)

Using the Library Area to Teach Mathematics

The primary goal of the Library Area is to motivate and encourage children to enjoy and explore books. Books also offer teachers numerous opportunities for presenting mathematical ideas to children. In the same way that you teach children about letters, rhyme, and print, you can call their attention to concepts of number, size, shape, space, pattern, and sequence. Here are some examples of questions and comments you might use as you share books with children.

Number and Operations

Look at all the mice. I've never seen so many! How many do you think there are?

Do you remember which billy goat crossed the bridge first (second, third)?

Are there more red sheep or more blue sheep? How do you know?

Geometry and Spatial Sense

What shapes do you see? How do you know they are triangles?

Do you remember where Rosie the hen walked after she went across the yard, around the pond, and over the haystack?

Can you find the mouse? Where is he?

Measurement

Do you think all of the animals can fit into the mitten? Why? How large do think the mitten will get?

That pig is so funny! Cook-a-Doodle-Doo told him to measure the flour, so he measured it with a ruler. What should pig have used to measure the flour for the cake?

Can you tell me some of the things Jesse wore in the morning? How about at noon and at night?

Patterns (Algebra)

If the little girl in the story ate one hare, two snakes, and three ants, how many of the next animal do you think she will eat?

Do you remember what the dog, cat, and goose told the Little Red Hen each time she asked for help? Read it with me.

Now that you know the pattern, read with me. "Polar Bear, Polar Bear, what do you hear? I hear a…"

Data Analysis

You chose books about animals. Do you want to find all the books about animals and put them on this shelf?

Some of you like this version of The Three Bears, *and some of you like the version that Mr. Alvarez is holding. If you like this one, sit by me. If you prefer the other version, sit by Mr. Alvarez. Which book do most of you like best?*

What's different about these two versions of The Three Bears?

Mathematical Process Skills (Reasoning, Problem Solving, Communicating, Connecting, and Representing)

I wonder why... What do you think?

Have you ever been told to share your cookies? How can the children in the story share their cookies so everyone has the same number?

Can you think of another way for the peddler to get his caps back?

Would you like to draw a picture of that?

◀ Observing Children's Progress

As you observe and share books with children in the Library Area, look for these indications of mathematical development:

- counting, using one-to-one correspondence, or identifying numerals

- telling who's first, second, or last; recalling the sequence of events in a story

- identifying quantity or using terms such as *some, all, more, less*

- recognizing patterns in a story or the language of the text

- naming or describing shapes

- using positional words such as *over, under, in front of, next to, behind*

- using comparative terms such as *big, bigger, biggest; faster, slower; longer, longest*

- talking about how things are the same or different

- suggesting solutions to problems presented in stories

Mathematics in the Discovery Area

The Discovery Area has materials that spark children's curiosity and wonder. Children handle and examine objects, experiment, and make discoveries. As they explore, children can use mathematical thinking to help them focus their observations, organize their thoughts, and record their investigations.

Mathematics and science are closely related. In both content areas, children observe, count, sort and classify, compare objects, measure, discover patterns, and collect data. The mathematical process skills—reasoning, problem-solving, communicating, connecting, and representing—are also needed by scientists. In the Discovery Area, teachers help children develop their observation and reasoning skills as they use their senses to explore.

Examples of What a Child Might Do	Examples of Related Curriculum Objectives	Examples of How This Relates to Mathematics
Turn the prism, holding it in many different ways while looking for rainbows	23. Approaches problems flexibly	Demonstrates beginning problem solving
Observe the planted seed daily, looking for signs of growth	24. Shows persistence in approaching tasks	Focuses attention; perseveres
Put objects attracted to a magnet on one tray and those not attracted to a magnet on another tray	27. Classifies objects	Classifies objects by property
Pick up a pumpkin and say, "This pumpkin is bigger and heavier than that one."	28. Compares/measures	Uses comparative measurement terms
Notice that a shell has stripes	30. Recognizes patterns and can repeat them	Recognizes a pattern in nature
Follow picture/word instructions for planting seeds	31. Shows awareness of time concepts and sequence	Begins to use system to measure time
Say that the gerbil is hiding inside the tube	32. Shows awareness of position in space	Uses the positional term *inside*
Put each rock from a collection in a separate section of an egg carton	33. Uses one-to-one correspondence	Matches one rock with each section of the egg carton
Count three carrots to feed the pet rabbit	34. Uses numbers and counting	Counts in a meaningful situation
Draw a picture of the sprouting zinnia plant	37. Makes and interprets representations	Uses representation, which is a mathematical process skill

Mathematics Materials for the Discovery Area

Standard Discovery Area equipment such as magnifying glasses, magnets, prisms, balance scales, eyedroppers, thermometers, tweezers, and clear plastic cups are also useful for mathematics explorations as children observe, measure, count, and sort. Writing and graphing materials enable children to represent and record information. For example, they might draw a picture each day of the changes that occur in a bean seed resting on a wet paper towel, or they might put a tally mark next to the picture of the food the gerbil eats first every day.

The following chart lists books and materials that support mathematical experiences. You can add other items related to your current topic of study to help children see the connections between mathematics and science.

materials

- [ ] collections of natural materials for sorting (e.g., shells, leaves, seeds, soil, rocks)
- [ ] saorting trays, bowls, or other containers (e.g., muffin tins, ice cube trays, clean egg cartons)
- [ ] standard measuring tools (e.g., rulers, tape measure, liquid and dry measuring cups, balance scale, timers, calendar)
- [ ] nonstandard measuring tools (e.g., string, paper clips, popsicle sticks)
- [ ] writing materials to record
- [ ] observations and data
- [ ] graphs and charts
- [ ] sequencing charts (e.g., step-by-step instructions for planting seeds)

book suggestions

Apples and Pumpkins (Anne Rockwell)

Fish Eyes: A Book You Can Count On (Lois Ehlert)

The Icky Bug Counting Book (Jerry Pallotta)

It's Fall, It's Summer, It's Spring, It's Winter (four books by Linda Glaser)

Lots and Lots of Zebra Stripes: Patterns in Nature (Stephen R. Swinburne)

One Bean (Anne Rockwell)

One Child, One Seed: A South African Counting Book (Kathryn Cave)

One Guinea Pig Is Not Enough (Kate Duke)

Pumpkin, Pumpkin (Anne Titherington)

Red Leaf, Yellow Leaf (Lois Ehlert)

Seeds! Seeds! Seeds! (Nancy Elizabeth Wallace and Marshal Cavendish)

Sense Suspense: A Guessing Game for the Senses (Bruce McMillan)

The Surprise Garden (Zoe Hall)

Ten Flashing Fireflies (Philemon Sturges)

Ten Seeds (Ruth Brown)

Two Bad Ants (Chris Van Allsburg)

Using the Discovery Area to Teach Mathematics

The Discovery Area invites children to observe, explore, and investigate natural materials. In the Discovery Area, they sort classify, compare, and measure. By supporting children's investigations in the Discovery Area, you also promote their mathematical development, especially their mathematical process skills: reasoning, problem solving, communicating, connecting, and representing. Your most effective interactions may begin with "I wonder why…" or "What would happen if…?" The following questions and comments may be useful in drawing children's attention to the mathematics involved in their explorations. Encouraging children to ask questions is even more important than asking questions, yourself.

Number and Operations

These X-rays are so interesting. How many ribs did you count?

Yes, you may add the leaves you found on the playground to our collection. How many do you have in your hand?

How many more small rocks are there than large rocks? How do you know? Show me.

Geometry and Spatial Sense

I wonder why the balls roll down the ramp but the boxes don't. What do you think?

Where is the gerbil hiding today?

Hmm, what happens…?

Measurement

Do you want to keep track of how tall your plant grows? Now it's short. We could put one of these connecting cubes next to it, because it's just that tall. When it gets as tall as two cubes, you can add another one.

This side of the balance scale went down when you put the rock on it. I wonder how many acorns you'd have to add to the other side to make it level. Would you like to find out?

If you put another block under the ramp, do you think the ball will roll faster or at the same speed?

Wow! The gak is getting longer and longer and thinner and thinner!

Patterns (Algebra)

How are these shells alike? How are they different?

You chose lots of different kinds of rocks. Tell me about them.

Did you notice the pattern on this leaf? How would you describe it? Would you like to make a rubbing of it?

Data Analysis

How could you sort all the things you found in the soil? Are there more rocks or more twigs? How can you tell without counting?

Why do these belong together?

Can you find another feather that would go in this group? What name could you give to this group?

What does your graph tell you?

Mathematical Process Skills (Reasoning, Problem Solving, Communicating, Connecting, and Representing)

Tell me why you think that.

Can you think of a way to…?

Tell me what you're working on.

Can you think of another time when…?

Would you like to draw a picture or make a sign about that?

Observing Children's Progress

As children explore in the Discovery Area, look for these indications of mathematical development:

- counting

- using terms such as *some, all, more, less*

- identifying, describing, copying, or creating patterns

- describing shapes and their properties

- using positional words such as *over, under, in front of, next to, behind*

- measuring with standard and nonstandard tools

- using terms related to weight such as *heavy, heavier, light, lighter*

- using terms related to time (e.g., *days, minutes, faster, slower*)

- describing how things are the same and/or different

- contributing to or creating a chart or graph

- talking about their investigations

- representing their thinking and learning (e.g., creating a model, drawing a picture, dictating, or writing)

Mathematics in the Sand and Water Area

The soothing properties of sand and water make this area one of the children's favorite. Here, children have many opportunities to informally explore mathematical concepts, particularly measurement. As they experiment with various sizes and shapes of containers, filling them up and emptying them, children estimate, count, and learn about weight, volume, and capacity. Adding water to sand along with molds and other tools and props allows children to explore shapes, patterns, and other dimensions of mathematics.

Examples of What a Child Might Do	Examples of Related Curriculum Objectives	Examples of How This Relates to Mathematics
Try different strategies to prevent tunnel from collapsing (e.g., add more water; use hands; then use a scoop)	23. Approaches problems flexibly	Tries alternative ways to solve problem
Try repeatedly to get water into the turkey baster; carefully watch to see how another child does it	24. Shows persistence in approaching tasks	Focuses attention and perseveres until solution is found
Put things that float in one tub and things that sink in another	27. Classifies objects	Classifies objects by a property: floating/non-floating
Say, "This is the tallest mountain of all."	28. Compares/measures	Estimates size; uses simple measurement terms
Sift sand to find shells and then line them up from largest to smallest	29. Arranges objects in a series	Orders objects according to size
Create a pattern in the sand by using a rake	30. Recognizes patterns and can repeat them	Identifies one type of pattern
Say, "My truck is at the top of the hill, and yours is at the bottom"	32. Shows awareness of position in space	Uses positional words.
Put one bear in each boat	33. Uses one-to-one correspondence	Matches one bear with each boat
Count *one, two, three, four…* as each scoop of sand is poured into a pail	34. Uses numbers and counting	Counts in a meaningful situation
Say, "This is a farm. The tractor made this road in the sand"	37. Makes and interprets representations	Makes a simple map of sand and talks about the process

◖ Mathematics Materials for the Sand and Water Area

The addition of well-chosen materials and books can enhance mathematics learning experiences. The materials listed in the chart below are not meant to be added all at once. Choose props on the basis of your current mathematical focus or topic of study.

materials

Sand

☐ rakes and large combs for creating patterns

☐ collections for sorting, counting, weighing (e.g., shells, rocks, other natural materials)

☐ sorting and counting trays (e.g., muffin tins, ice cube trays, or clean egg cartons)

☐ standard and nonstandard measuring tools (e.g., popsicle sticks, links)

☐ molds of various shapes and sizes (e.g., cube, cone, cylinder)

☐ cookie cutters (e.g., numeral and shape)

☐ balance scale

☐ props related to a current topic of study

Water

☐ magnetic fishing pole and fish (for counting and sorting or labeled with numerals)

☐ containers of various dimensions (e.g., tall, short, narrow, wide).

☐ containers with holes punched in sides and/or bottom

☐ clear plastic liquid measuring cups

book suggestions

Drip Drop (Sarah Weeks)

Five Little Ducks (Ian Beck)

Is This a House for Hermit Crab? (Megan McDonald)

Math in the Bath (Sara Atherlay)

One Less Fish (Kim Michelle Toft)

Sea Shapes (Suse MacDonald)

Sea Sums (Joy Hulme)

Splash (Ann Jonas)

Underwater Counting (Jerry Pallota)

Water (Frank Asch)

Water, Water (Eloise Greenfield)

What Lives in a Shell? (Kathleen Weidner Zoehfeld)

Who Sank the Boat? (Pamela Allen)

materials, continued

☐ boats or small trays that will serve as boats

☐ collections of objects (e.g., plastic animals or people; materials for exploring the concepts of *sink* and *float*, such as corks)

☐ tubing and funnels, cooking baster

☐ strainers of various sizes

☐ vinyl graph

☐ plastic sorting bowls or trays

Using Sand and Water to Teach Mathematics

Teachers can take advantage of children's natural in and enjoyment of sand and water to introduce the language of mathematics and to teach many concepts and skills. Encourage children to talk about and explain what they are doing, e.g., "Tell me how you made this tunnel." Supply words, e.g., "It's full. Now it's half-full. Now it's empty." Describe what children are doing, e.g., "You are splashing water over the side of the water table." Wonder aloud, e.g., "Hmmm, I wonder if there is a way to make the water wheel turn faster. What do you think?" Ask questions, e.g., "Which one is heavier? Why do you think that is?"

Some children enjoy using sand and water for pretend purposes, e.g., "I added sugar; now it's lemonade." You can support their creative play through your responses and expression of interest. Because you recognize that free exploration is valuable for children, you will want to observe for a while before stepping in to promote their understanding of mathematical concepts and vocabulary.

Questions and comments can help focus children's attention on the mathematics involved in sand and water play, but be mindful that questioning can also interrupt children's thinking and distract from their learning. Always begin by observing. Then thoughtfully determine whether, when, and how you should step in.

Number and Operations

How many bears did you put in your boat before it sank?

You found lots of rocks in the sand. I see you've put two in each section of the muffin tin. How many do you have altogether?

How many scoops of sand do you think you'll need to fill this bowl? How can you check your estimate?

How many fish did you catch?

Geometry and Spatial Sense

How did you get your hill so smooth and round on the top? Could you make a hill that's pointed on the top?

What container do you think Derek used to make his castle? How could you find out?

*Which container did **not** make this shape? How do you know?*

Measurement

I wonder how much sand you would need to make a hill big enough to hide this truck.

Do you think this bottle holds more water than the bowl? Why? How could you check to be sure?

If you try to pour the sand back into the bowl, do you think it will fit? How could you find out?

Which bowl is heavier, the one with wet sand or dry sand? How could you find out? Why do you think one is heavier than the other?

Patterns (Algebra)

Look at the tire tracks! Which vehicle made these? How do you know?

I see that you used tiles to make a path around your hill. Tell me about the pattern you created.

You discovered lots of shells in the sand. Can you read the pattern on this one?

Data Analysis

*Tell me how you decided to put the stick, boat, and Styrofoam®
peanut in this basket and the key, rock, and screw in this basket?*

How are these shells alike? How are they different?

*Can you think of a way to organize our water props so everyone
can find what they need easily?*

Mathematical Process Skills (Reasoning, Problem Solving, Communicating, Connecting, and Representing)

Tell me why you think...

*The funnel is missing. What else could you use to get the sand
through the narrow neck of the bottle?*

Tell the class what you discovered!

*When you pour water on the sand, the sand washes away. That
reminds me of what happened to the hill on our playground.*

*Would you like to record your recipe for mudpies in the notebook?
That way, you can remember exactly how you made it.*

◀ Observing Children's Progress

As children explore sand and water, look for these indications of
mathematics learning:

- estimating and counting (e.g., the number of scoops to fill a pail)

- comparing capacity (e.g., using terms like *some, all, more, the
  same amount, less, too much, not enough, left over*)

- recognizing and/or creating patterns (e.g., using sand combs or
  making impressions in the sand)

- comparing sizes (e.g., *tall, taller, tallest; wide, wider, widest;
  highest, lowest; thin, narrow; shallow, deep*)

- comparing mass (e.g., *heavier, lighter*) and speed (*fast, faster,
  fastest; slow, slower, slowest*)

- using nonstandard measurements (e.g., tubful, bowlful)

- sorting and classifying collections of objects

- describing shapes (e.g., *round, curved, straight*)

- using positional words (e.g., *around, on top of, over, under, through*)

Mathematics in the Music and Movement Area

Music and movement activities can enhance children's understanding of mathematical concepts. As children clap and dance to the beat of the music, they experience patterns physically. Moving to the tempo, or speed, of the music enables them to experience time, a measurement concept, firsthand. Children explore geometrical and spatial concepts as they transform their bodies into a ball and move forward and backward, around and through, back and forth, or up and down. Counting is reinforced by singing songs such as "Five Little Ducks" or "The Ants Go Marching."

Examples of What a Child Might Do	Examples of Related Curriculum Objectives	Examples of How This Relates to Mathematics
Try several different ways of holding a triangle in order to get the desired sound	23. Approaches problems flexibly	Demonstrates beginning problem solving, an important mathematical process skill
Put all the drums on a shelf, the rhythm sticks in a tub, and the bells in another tub	27. Classifies objects	Classifies objects by type even though they differ in size and shape
Respond to directions using comparative words such as *higher-lower* and *louder-softer* in music and movement activities	28. Compares/measures	Demonstrates understanding of some comparative terms
Play xylophone loudly, softly, and very softly	29. Arranges objects in a series	Seriates according to loudness of sound
Follow the teacher's lead: stamp, clap, clap; stamp, clap, clap	30. Recognizes patterns and can repeat them	Copies a pattern of sounds
Sway with arms overhead, first slowly like a gentle breeze and then fast like an approaching storm	31. Shows awareness of time concepts and sequence	Demonstrates understanding of *fast* and *slow*
Respond to motion words, such as *forward, backward, up,* and *down*	32. Shows awareness of position in space	Demonstrates understanding of some positional terms
Tap stick in time to a steady beat: *1, 2, 3, 4*	33. Uses one-to-one correspondence	Matches one beat with one movement (tapping)
Sing counting songs, such as "One, two, three, four, five, I caught a fish alive"	34. Uses numbers and counting	Counts by rote
Pretend to fly like a bird	37. Makes and interprets representations	Uses one action (flapping arms) to symbolize another (flying)

Mathematics Materials for the Music and Movement Area

You can support children's mathematical development in the Music and Movement Area by offering a variety of musical instruments for them to explore and experiment with and by providing enough space for movement activities. The following chart lists suggestions for mathematics-related materials and books.

materials

- ☐ tapes or CDs of counting and shape songs
- ☐ picture/word charts of counting songs
- ☐ props related to favorite counting songs and chants (e.g., felt ducks for *Five Little Ducks*)
- ☐ shakers that will make distinctive sounds (e.g., cans or boxes filled with materials such as bottle caps, pebbles, or sand)
- ☐ materials that encourage children to explore, copy, or create patterns (e.g., cards illustrating actions such clapping, stamping, tapping)

book suggestions

The Ants Go Marching One by One (Richard Bernal)

The Aunts Go Marching (Maurie Jo Manning)

Five Little Ducks: An Old Rhyme (Pamela Paparone)

Five Little Monkeys Jumping on the Bed (Eileen Christelow)

Max Found Two Sticks (Brian Pinkney)

Over in the Meadow (versions by Ezra Jack Keats and Olive A. Wadsworth)

Roll Over! A Counting Song (Merle Peek)

Shape Space (Cathryn Falwell)

She'll be Comin' 'Round the Mountain (Philemon Sturges)

Ten Go Tango (Arthur Dorros)

Ten in the Bed: A Counting Book (David Ellwand)

This Old Man (Carol Jones)

Using Music and Movement to Teach Mathematics

In many preschool classrooms, music and movement experiences typically occur during large-group times. Children need additional time to explore musical instruments independently and to experiment with ways to move their bodies and navigate space. This helps them gain a deeper understanding of mathematical concepts. As you observe children in action, you will be able to determine when and how to interact, whether it is to introduce new vocabulary, reinforce an idea, or ask a question to encourage or clarify a child's thinking.

Number and Operations

One, two, three, four, five. You hopped five times.

Last time, the ants went marching three by three. How many will march together this time? Show me.

If there were three monkeys jumping on the bed and one fell off, how many would be left?

Geometry and Spatial Sense

You're waving the streamer above your head? Can you make it go behind you? Now wave it beside you.

You're marching around in a circle. Do you think you could march in a triangle?

Can you dance forward?...backwards?...sideways?

Measurement

You played some very fast beats. How will it sound if you play the drum slowly?

Can you march low? How about high on your toes?

Some streamers are long; some are short. Which would you like?

Patterns (Algebra)

I hear your drum pattern. It sounds like DA, da, da; loud, soft, soft. Can you do that again?

Let's see if I can make the same pattern that you did. I think it was one, two, three; one, two, three.

Follow Leo! Clap front, clap back, then shake, shake, shake; clap front, clap back, then shake, shake, shake...

Data Analysis

Sonya wants to know what everyone's favorite song is. How could we find out?

Why did you put the cymbals, triangle, and bells together in a group?

Some of you have red streamers, and some of you have streamers that are not red. How could we figure out which group has more without counting?

Mathematical Process Skills (Reasoning, Problem Solving, Communicating, Connecting, and Representing)

Why do you think the smallest bar on the xylophone makes the highest sound?

Since you can't find the finger cymbals, can you think of another instrument that would be good to represent the sound of a mouse scurrying across the floor?

You're playing that drum slowly and loudly. It reminds me of how an elephant walks, heavily, like this.

You made up new words to that song. Would you like to record it on tape?

Observing Children's Progress

As children explore music and movement, look for these indications of mathematical development:

- counting while singing

- making predictions or estimating (e.g., how many baby steps it would take to walk from one point to another)

- making rhythmic sounds or movement patterns

- responding to or using directional or positional language (e.g., *forward-backward, high-low, up-down, around, through*) to describe their motions

- describing rates of movement (e.g., *fast* or *slow*)

- using the terms *same* and *different* to compare sounds

Mathematics in the Cooking Area

Cooking provides children with opportunities to develop and use mathematical skills in meaningful ways. Through cooking, children are able to see the connection between mathematics and everyday life experiences. Recipes involve measuring, counting, and following a sequence of steps. Working with fruits and vegetables, for example in preparing vegetable soup or fruit kabobs, provides opportunities to explore shape, size, and pattern. Children use mathematical process skills as they attempt to explain why a recipe did not turn out as planned or as they try to determine how to divide a snack equally among a group. Of course, eating makes mathematics learning even more fun!

Examples of What a Child Might Do	Examples of Related Curriculum Objectives	Examples of How This Relates to Mathematics
Try different ways to divide dough so that everyone at the table will have a piece of about the same size	23. Approaches problems flexibly	Demonstrates beginning problem solving, an important mathematical process skill
Shake a bottle of cream until it turns into butter	24. Shows persistence in approaching tasks	Perseveres with a task
Put the red apples in a red bowl, yellow apples in a yellow bowl, and green apples in a green bowl	27. Classifies objects	Classifies objects by color
Measure 2 tablespoons of sunflower seeds when following a recipe	28. Compares/measures	Uses standard unit of measurement
Return the measuring cups to their sequentially arranged outlines on the pegboard	29. Arranges objects in a series	Sequences objects by size (following model)
Follow a recipe to create a patterned fruit kabob: slice of apple, strawberry, banana; slice of apple, etc.	30. Recognizes patterns and can repeat them	Copies a pattern
Set the timer for 10 minutes	31. Shows awareness of time concepts and sequence	Begins to use standard time intervals
Say that the seeds of the strawberry are on the outside, not the inside	32. Shows awareness of position in space	Uses the positional terms *inside* and *outside*
Put one piece of cheese on each cracker	33. Uses one-to-one correspondence	Matches one piece of cheese with each cracker
Point to 5 on the Trail Mix recipe chart then count out five raisins	34. Uses numbers and counting	Recognizes numeral on recipe; counts in a meaningful situation

◀ Mathematics Materials for the Cooking Area

Many standard cooking utensils such as measuring spoons and cups are also mathematical tools. Much of the mathematics-related equipment listed in the chart below may already be in your Cooking Area. Recipe charts, recipe cards, and class-made cookbooks are useful for promoting mathematical skills. You will find some sample recipes in *The Creative Curriculum for Preschool*, pages 461–6.

materials

- ☐ picture/word recipes and charts
- ☐ graduated measuring cups and spoons
- ☐ clear, liquid measuring cup, marked ¼, ½, 4 oz., etc.
- ☐ cookie cutters in geometric shapes
- ☐ timer
- ☐ candy thermometer
- ☐ ruler
- ☐ Food guide pyramid (U. S. Dept. of Agriculture Center for Nutrition Policy and Promotion)
- ☐ Class-made graphs showing, for example, children's favorite kind of apples or what they like on their pizza

book suggestions

10 for Dinner (Jo Ellen Bogart)

Bread, Bread, Bread (Ann Morris)

Cook-a-Doodle-Doo (Janet Stevens and Susan Stevens Crummel)

The Doorbell Rang (Pat Hutchins)

Eating Fractions (Bruce McMillan)

Feast for 10 (Cathryn Falwell)

Growing Vegetable Soup (Lois Ehlert)

Let's Eat! (Ana Zamorano)

The Little Red Hen Makes a Pizza (Philemon Sturges)

Magda's Tortillas (Becky Chavarria-Chairez)

Pancakes for Breakfast (Tomi DePaola)

Pretend Soup and Other Real Recipes: A Cookbook for Preschoolers and Up (Molly Katzen and Ann Henderson)

Round Is a Pancake (Joan Sullivan Baranski)

Seaweed Soup (Stuart J. Murphy)

Today is Monday (Eric Carle)

Too Many Tamales (Gary Soto)

Two Eggs, Please (Sarah Weeks)

Using Cooking to Teach Mathematics

Mathematics, especially number and measurement concepts, can be taught through cooking experiences. Children will learn more if they do more. Therefore, plan experiences that include the use of picture/word recipes so children can do their own measuring, counting, pouring, and mixing.

As you interact with children in the Cooking Area, talk with them about similarities and differences in food. For example, have them compare the size and taste of oranges, tangerines, satsumas, and clementines. Call attention to the shapes of fruits and vegetables and the patterns that occur naturally in foods. Invite children to predict how many apples it will take to make a cup of applesauce or half a cup of apple juice. Then let them test their predictions.

Number and Operations

How many seeds did you find in your apple?

How many tablespoons of flour does the recipe call for? Count aloud as you add each one.

Each person will need a cup for juice and a bowl for snack mix. How many cups will we need altogether?

How many strawberries do you think are in this basket?

Geometry and Spatial Sense

If we slice the carrot crosswise, what shape do you think the slices will be?

How will you cut your cheese so that it fits the cracker?

I'm thinking of a fruit that is smooth and round like a ball. Can you guess which one it is?

A slice of pizza has three sides and three points. What shape is the pizza slice?

Measurement

We need a bowl that will hold the batter for everyone's muffins. Can you find a bowl that will be big enough?

Fill each cup so that it is half full.

We need to set the timer for 15 minutes. Can you do that?

Which pitcher do you think will hold more juice?

Patterns (Algebra)

Tell me about the pattern you see on the watermelon rind.

You made a pattern with your raisins and pumpkin seeds.

Even the mixing bowl has a pattern on the outside. Let's read it!

I see you have arranged the crackers in a pattern on the tray. I see a row of round crackers and then a row of square crackers, a row of round cracker and then a row of squares. If there were still some space, what shape would you put next?

Data Analysis

Some of you made blueberry muffins, and some of you made banana muffins. How could we tell which kind of muffins we made the most of without counting?

Let's look at our snack chart for today. Did more people have apple juice or orange juice?

Why did you put these two fruits in the same group? How are they the same?

What food group do you think these tortillas belong to? What about the cheese?

Mathematical Process Skills (Reasoning, Problem Solving, Communicating, Connecting, and Representing)

Now that the juice is frozen, it is taller than the cup. Why do you think that is?

The Jell-O® is really hot. I don't know if it will be ready for lunch. What should we do?

Crystal, why are you adding more flour to your dough?

This popcorn smells so good! Do you remember what happened in the story we read when the children popped popcorn?

You're enjoying your trail mix. Would you like to write the recipe so you can remember all of the ingredients you used?

◀ Observing Children's Progress

As children participate in cooking experiences or prepare snack, look for these indications of mathematical development:

- using numbers (e.g., counting, reading and writing numerals, showing quantity)

- using one-to-one correspondence (e.g., putting one liner in each section of a muffin tin)

- recognizing, copying, or creating patterns

- naming, describing or making shapes

- using measurement terms or tools (e.g., setting the timer for 10 minutes; saying, "This is the coldest thing I've ever tasted!")

- telling how items are the same and/or different

- contributing to or creating a graph

- making a sign or recipe with pictures

- explaining and/or demonstrating how to prepare a recipe

- making connections among home, school, and community experiences

- solving a problem (e.g., dough is too sticky or too dry; dividing a snack equally among children)

- explaining reasoning (e.g., why cream turns to butter)

Mathematics in the Computer Area

By using computers, children can experience mathematics in new or different ways. They can create a character having a specific number of body parts; they can change the size, position, or location of an image on screen; and they can create three-dimensional shapes. Children also can use the computer to practice skills, represent their ideas, or investigate topics such as the mole that has created long mounds on the play yard.

Discovery-based computer programs are ideal for promoting mathematical thinking while kindling children's imaginations and fostering creativity. Children solve problems such as figuring out how to transform an object; create patterns; and experiment with size, shape, color, number, and space.

Examples of What a Child Might Do	Examples of Related Curriculum Objectives	Examples of How This Relates to Mathematics
Try many drawing tools in KidPix® to achieve a particular effect	23. Approaches problems flexibly	Explores alternatives before choosing
Try many different paths to get "home"	24. Shows persistence in approaching tasks	Focuses attention; perseveres
Select all of the four-sided figures from a group of shapes	27. Classifies objects	Classifies geometric shapes according to one attribute (number of sides)
Select the right-sized shoes to fit a character in Millie's Math House	28. Compares/measures	Compares sizes and matches size of shoe with size of foot.
Line up the animals, shortest to tallest	29. Arranges objects in a series	Seriates according to size
Make a snowflake pattern with KidPix®	30. Recognizes patterns and can repeat them	Uses technological tools to design a pattern
Follow the steps for turning on the computer, selecting a program, and getting started	31. Shows awareness of time concepts and sequence	Follows sequence
Uses the ↑ key to move up and the ↓ key to move down	32. Shows awareness of position in space	Uses arrow symbols for up and down
Give every dog one bone	33. Uses one-to-one correspondence	Matches sets of objects (dogs with bones)
Count images and select the correct numeral	34. Uses numbers and counting	Recognizes numeral and counts objects
Use icons and tell what they mean	37. Makes and interprets representations	Recognizes and uses symbols (icons)

Mathematics Materials for the Computer Area

The arrangement of the Computer Area affects how children use it. If you cluster computers together and place two chairs at each computer, children are likely to share their discoveries and assist one another. Learning is enhanced when children interact and communicate.

Choosing appropriate software to enhance mathematics learning can be challenging. Software that is open-ended and engages children in thinking, problem solving, and creating supports the development of mathematical process skills and promotes children's overall cognitive development. The computer programs listed in the following chart are interactive and allow children to explore a variety of mathematical concepts and skills.

software suggestions

Clifford Thinking Adventures (Scholastic)

Curious George Downtown Adventure (Knowledge Adventure)

Does it Belong? (Navarre)

Fredi Fish 5: The Case of the Creature of Coral Cove (Humongous Entertainment)

How Many Bugs in a Box? (Simon & Schuster Interactive)

KidPix (The Learning Company)

Millie's Math House (Edmark/Riverdeep)

Nick Jr. Little Bill Thinks Big (Scholastic)

Ollo and the Sunny Valley Fair (Plaid Banana Entertainment)

Putt-Putt: Pep's Birthday Surprise (Atari)

Putt-Putt Joins the Circus (Atari)

Stuart Little: His Adventures in Numberland (The Learning Company)

Thinkin' Things (Edmark/Riverdeep)

Thomas and Friends: Trouble on the Tracks (Hasbro Interactive)

The interactive opportunities that software programs offer can be increased when controls are used that are designed for young children. The standard mouse and keyboard (with over 100 keys) are not child friendly. Other options are available at computer supply stores and through catalogs that provide better ways to control what happens on the screen.

Mouse Alternatives

- **touch screen:** This clear screen fits over the monitor. Children touch the screen instead of clicking the mouse.

- **trackball:** A large "upside-down" mouse. Children move the ball to move the pointer on the screen. A separate button is clicked to make a choice.

- **squeezable mice:** instead of using one finger to click, smaller mice are available that children squeeze rather than tap.

Keyboard Alternatives

Keyboards designed for children often include the following features:

- fewer keys that are larger and colorful

- keys that are rearranged for easier use (e.g. the arrow keys are in the correct direction)

- keys in ABC order that make letters easier to find

Using the Keyboard

Software for young children often requires the use of just a few keys. Consider highlighting the important ones with stickers, Velcro®, or raised dots.

Using Computers to Teach Mathematics

Your guidance, enthusiasm, and responsiveness foster children's computer learning. As in the other areas, you can give encouragement, ask open-ended questions, provide assistance, pose problems. Share your wonder, "Wow! Look what you made using these simple shapes!" You help children focus by asking them to communicate their intentions and describe their actions. You can also make suggestions as needed, e.g., "What if you tried...?"

Help children see the connections between what they are doing on the computer and what they draw, build, or create in other classroom areas. When appropriate, call attention to mathematical concepts in the computer programs and use mathematics vocabulary. Taking time to explore the computer program, yourself, will increase your awareness of its mathematical possibilities.

Number and Operations

How many bugs will you put in that box?

Do you want more or less?

If you added one more piece here, how many would there be altogether? What if you took one piece away?

Can you find another way to show five?

Geometry and Spatial Sense

All of your shapes have curved sides.

Are there any other ways that you could put those shapes together?

Your creature can go backwards, forwards, up, and down, just like you do.

Hmm, how do you think you can get there?

Measurement

Wow! They're getting bigger and bigger and bigger!

How many of those little boxes do you think will fit in this box?

Which shape can you cover with the most squares?

Don't forget to set the timer so you know when your turn at the computer is over.

Patterns (Algebra)

What an interesting pattern!

Tell me your plan.

I see you created a snake with shapes. You made a pattern! Will you read it for me?

Do you see any patterns in this photo?

Data Analysis

Which things do you think go together?

Are you looking for shapes that are the same or different?

What if you wanted a different color?

Mathematical Process Skills (Reasoning, Problem Solving, Communicating, Connecting, and Representing)

Hmmm, I wonder why that happened. What do you think?

You figured out your problem. Will you show me how you did it?

How did you make that color?

Would you like to see if we can find some information about that on the Internet?

If you print a copy of that, do you think you could make one like it out of blocks?

Observing Children's Progress

As children explore the computer and use various software programs, look for these indications of mathematics learning:

- counting

- recognizing numerals

- copying or creating patterns

- recognizing, matching, naming, describing, and/or drawing shapes

- comparing or matching size (e.g., putting the right-sized shoes on characters in Millie's Math House)

- sorting figures by color, shape, or size

- problem solving (e.g., figuring out what icons mean, how to use the mouse)

- showing a friend how to get a desired result

- explaining a process

- creating representations

- making home/school connections

Mathematics in the Outdoor Area

Mathematics can be an integral and important part of most outdoor play experiences: counting each rung while climbing the slide's ladder, considering which tree is tallest, noting the striped pattern on a caterpillar, or crawling through a tunnel. Mathematics vocabulary easily becomes a part of outdoor conversations. For example, children talk about who will ride the tricycle *first*, *second*, or *third*; announce who pedals *faster*; explain how they wove *around* traffic *cones*, or tell the teacher about the *length* of a friend's turn with a new toy.

Organized games such as Hopscotch require children to use numbers, while "Mother, May I?" requires that they have an understanding of both measurement and directional concepts (e.g., "May I take two giant steps?" "No, you may take four baby steps backwards.")

Examples of What a Child Might Do	Examples of Related Curriculum Objectives	Examples of How This Relates to Mathematics
Try different bubble wands and blowing strategies to get bigger bubbles	23. Approaches problems flexibly	Tries alternative ways to solve problem
Find all the red leaves and put them in a pile	27. Classifies objects	Sorts or classifies objects by color
Say, "I'm bigger than my shadow."	28. Compares/measures	Observes differences in size; uses comparative term (e.g., taller, shorter)
Line up the balls, biggest, middle-sized, smallest	29. Arranges objects in a series	Seriates according to size
Notice the pattern made on the sidewalk by wet boots	30. Recognizes patterns and can repeat them	Recognizes a pattern
Ask a friend, "Remember how we pretended to feed the bears yesterday?"	31. Shows awareness of time concepts and sequence	Uses relational term (e.g., yesterday, today, tomorrow)
Say that she is on top of the world, even above the clouds, when she is on the climber	32. Shows awareness of position in space	Uses positional terms (e.g., on top of, above)
Plant one pea in each small hole in the garden	33. Uses one-to-one correspondence	Matches set of peas to set of holes
Attempt to write numerals with chalk on hopscotch board	34. Uses numbers and counting	Begins to write numerals
Pretend to be a seed sprouting and growing	37. Makes and interprets representations	Uses representation, which is a mathematical process skill

Mathematics Materials for the Outdoor Area

A well-planned Outdoor Area provides opportunities for children to make many mathematical connections. *The Creative Curriculum for Preschool* provides information about setting up and equipping the Outdoor Area to maximize learning. The chart has suggestions for books and materials to stimulate problem solving and encourage children to find their own answers to mathematical questions related to nature.

materials

- [ ] equipment of varying sizes (e.g., small, medium, large balls; streamers or ribbons of various lengths)

- [ ] magnifying glasses and binoculars for observing things near and far

- [ ] materials to create an obstacle course or equipment that invites children to go over, under, around, and through

- [ ] standard and nonstandard measuring tools (e.g., rulers, yardstick/meter stick, measuring tapes, popsicle sticks, connecting cubes, and plastic links)

- [ ] nature guides (plant and animal)

- [ ] identification books

- [ ] rain gauge

- [ ] wind sock or weather vane

book suggestions

At the Edge of the Woods (Cynthia Cotton)

Bugs Are Insects (Anne Rockwell)

Countdown to Spring: An Animal Counting Book (Janet Schulman)

Counting on the Woods: A Poem (George Ella Lyon)

Counting Wildflowers (Bruce McMillan)

Deep Down Underground (Olivier Dunrea)

Dots, Spots, Speckles, and Stripes (Tana Hoban)

Icky Bug Counting Book (Jerry Pallotta)

Inch by Inch (Leo Lionni)

Millions of Snowflakes (Mary McKenna Siddals)

materials, continued

□ sundial

□ materials for outdoor sand and water mathematical explorations (see "Mathematics in the Sand and Water Area")

□ muffin tins, egg cartons, or ice cube trays for sorting collections

□ traffic signs related to direction or speed (e.g., one way, u-turn, speed limit, yield)

□ clipboards, paper, and writing materials (for creating representations and drawing items from a variety of perspectives)

book suggestions, continued

Over, Under, Through (Tana Hoban)

Shapes, Shapes, Shapes (Tana Hoban)

Turtle Splash!: Countdown at the Pond (Cathryn Falwell)

What's Up? What's Down? (Lola M. Schaefer)

Ten Flashing Fireflies (Philemon Sturges)

The Wildlife 1 2 3: A Nature Counting Book (Jan Thornhill)

Wonderful Worms (Linda Glaser)

Using the Outdoors to Teach Mathematics

Respond to children's calls to "Look how high I am!" or "Look at the line the plane made in the sky!" with simple comments or questions. You might say, "Wow, you're on the highest rung! You're even taller than I am," or "I wonder what made that line. What do you think?" By using mathematical language in your casual conversations with children, you help them develop important mathematical process skills, concepts, and vocabulary. More importantly, you demonstrate an enthusiasm for learning that is sure to be contagious. Here are examples of what you might say.

Number and Operations

You're on the first rung of the climber. How high do you think you'll climb? Up to there, the fourth rung?

Will you collect all of the balls and put them in this cart?

How many bugs do you have in your bug box?

Do you have more red leaves or more yellow leaves?

Yes, Setsuko, our tricycle track does look like the numeral 8.

Geometry and Spatial Sense

Are you ready? When I say, "Go," run around the tree, through the tunnel, and then straight back here.

Remember to keep the tricycles inside the area marked by the orange cones.

Do you get dizzy, going around and around on the merry-go-round?

Can you find something on our playground that is shaped like a can?

How does that jump rope rhyme go? Teddy bear, teddy bear, turn around. Teddy bear, teddy bear, touch the ground...

Measurement

How many footsteps will it take to go from the climber to the slide? Will you take big steps or small steps?

Can you find a bush that's just as tall as you are? ...that's taller? ...that's shorter?

How wide is this tree? Can you reach around it? What if we hold hands with each other? Can we reach around it now?

Let's check the rain gauge to see how much it rained last night.

How can we find out how deep the snow is? Do you think some places have more snow than other places?

Patterns (Algebra)

Do you see the pattern that the tricycle tire made when it came out of the puddle?

Look at this footprint. Do you know who made it? How can you find out?

That's an interesting pattern on the caterpillar. How would you describe it?

Would you like to take photos of patterns we see on the playground? Let me know when you see one.

Follow me back to the classroom. Hop, hop, jump; hop, hop, jump; hop, hop, jump.

Data Analysis

You found two kinds of yellow flowers: dandelions and buttercups. What's different about them? How are they the same?

You found a stone that writes like chalk. Do you think there are other stones that will make marks on the pavement?

Can you put the leaves shaped like this one on this tray, and the leaves shaped like that one on that tray?

Can you put a mark on your clipboard for every step it takes to get from the door to the slide? Then we can do the same thing from the door to the climber and see which is farther away.

Mathematical Process Skills (Reasoning, Problem Solving, Communicating, Connecting, and Representing)

How can you tell it's windy?

There are not enough tricycles for everyone to have one. What can we do so that everyone who wants a turn on that tricycle will get a turn?

You learned to swing all by yourself. Tell what you did to learn.

You've drawn lots of pictures of clouds. They remind me the pictures in the book, It Looked Like Spilt Milk. *Would you like to make yours into a book?*

The seeds we planted are starting to sprout. How can we keep track of how much they grow each week?

Observing Children's Progress

As children play and explore in the Outdoor Area, look for these indications of mathematical development:

- counting (e.g., collections of objects; during games and activities)

- using ordinal numbers (e.g., first, second, third)

- using terms such as *some, all, more, less*

- recognizing, describing, copying, or creating patterns

- using positional words such as *over, under, in front of, next to, behind*

- measuring with standard units (ruler or tape measure) or non-standard units (arm's-length, footsteps, or connecting cubes)

- using comparative terms (e.g., *taller, shorter; higher, lower; smaller, larger*)

- recognizing or describing two- and three-dimensional shapes

- discussing similarities and differences

- collecting, organizing, and representing data (e.g., sorting and classifying collections of natural objects)

inside this chapter

5 Mathematics Activities

Mathematics instruction includes planning learning experiences and interacting with children in intentional ways to teach specific concepts and skills explicitly. This chapter includes 39 activities to be used during large- and small-group times or with individual children during choice time. Each activity shows how to teach concepts and skills in each of the five components of mathematics and the five mathematical process skills.

The activities are organized by component and identify the concepts or skills that are the instructional focus. The Appendix includes an "Activity Matrix" that guides choices by showing which core activities address the various components of mathematics. The activity extensions address additional concepts and skills, and they often relate to multiple components. The extensions are not shown on the matrix.

Keep in mind that the child is always the focus of instruction. Because children are at various stages in their development and learning, you will need to combine your knowledge of children and your knowledge of mathematics to make instructional decisions for each child and the group. Each activity includes guidance on how teachers might adapt it to meet a range of abilities and skill levels.

Each activity is organized in the same way.

Goals and Objectives are from *The Creative Curriculum for Preschool* and *The Creative Curriculum for Preschool Developmental Continuum for Ages 3–5*. These help teachers plan for and assess children's mathematics learning.

Other Concepts identify additional mathematical skills and concepts that are addressed through the core activity. These concepts are often related to multiple components of mathematics.

Materials and Preparation includes the materials and books you will need to conduct the activity and explains what you need to do to get ready for the activity. Some of the activities require the use of the blackline masters found in the Appendix.

Guiding Children's Learning describes how to lead the activity and interact with children to promote thinking and learning.

Closing offers suggestions for ending the activity. In most cases, we recommend placing materials in interest areas so children can have extended experiences after participating in the teacher-led activity.

Developmental Progression describes the activity as a sequence of experiences, from simple to complex. With this guidance, teachers can help every child participate in the activity, and they can scaffold each child's learning.

Meeting the Needs of Diverse Learners includes ways to adapt the activity for children who are English language learners, for children with disabilities, or for children who are advanced mathematics learners.

Going Beyond includes suggestions for extending the core activity. These activities encourage integration among components of mathematics and with other subject areas.

At the end of each activity, a table indicates the recommended setting for the core activity, the interest areas where the activity might occur, and the length of time the activity might take. Please note that an activity identified as a single-day activity may be repeated on multiple occasions.

Compare It

<table>
<tr><td>**Goal(s) & Objectives**</td><td>

Objectives

28. Compares and measures; 33. Uses one-to-one correspondence; 34. Uses numbers and counting

Other Concepts

- Understands the concepts of *more*, *less*, *same*, and *equal*
- Interprets data

</td></tr>
</table>

Materials and Preparation

☐ Ice cube trays, muffin tins, or sanitized egg cartons

☐ Sandwich bags that zip

☐ Collections of objects (e.g., counters, coins, colored chips)

Prepare five bags. Each bag should have a different type and number of objects (e.g., place one counter in one bag, two coins in a second bag, three colored chips in a third, and so forth). Although the items in the bags are different, the items should be similar in size.

Guiding Children's Learning

Display the bags. Explain that each bag has a different number of objects. Have two children each pick a bag and place it on the table or floor so the other children can see it. Ask these questions:

Which bag has more? How did you decide?

How could you find out which bag has more?

Have the children demonstrate how they can find out which bag has more.

If no one suggests matching or comparing the two sets, explain that you are going to show them a way to compare the items to see which set has more and to check their guesses.

Recite the following rhyme as you bring out the ice cube tray.

More, fewer, the same—

Which will it be?

Line them up;

Then we will see.

Place an ice cube tray in front of the two children. Have one child take the items from his bag and place them in the left column, beginning at the bottom of the tray.

Have the second child place her objects in the right column while the other children recite the rhyme again.

Hold the ice cube tray for all the children to see. Then pose the following questions:

> *Which column has more? How do you know?*
>
> *Is there another way you can find out if there are more objects in one column than another?*
>
> *How many more (fewer) are in this column than that one? How many in this column do not have a match?*

Explain that the column that has objects without matches has *more* objects and the other column has *fewer* objects. Introduce the term *same* or *equal* when there are the same number of objects in the collections. Use other comments, such as these:

> *A set of four rocks is more than a set of two rocks.*
>
> *This group has fewer objects than that group. There are only three teddy bears in this group* (teacher points), *and there are five buttons in this group* (teacher points).

Repeat this process of comparison several times, using different bags of objects.

Closing

Tell the children that the materials will be in the Toys and Games Area, where they may use them during choice time. Encourage the children to work in pairs and take turns asking each other questions or saying *more, fewer, the same.*

Developmental Progression

Simple ↓ **Complex**	Have the children predict which of two groups of objects has more. Then verify their prediction using the ice cube tray. Use collections of 1–5 objects.
	Use two bags with the same number of items but objects of very different sizes. Have children predict which group has more. Then use an egg carton or muffin tin to verify the answer. Talk about the difference between *number* and *size*.
	After determining which of two sets has more objects, have the children determine how many more (fewer) objects are in the set.
	Give children three bags. Then have them tell which has the *most* or *least* number of objects. Muffin tins or ice cube trays with three rows can be used to make the comparison.
	Extend the activity to cover more complex topics in number composition (e.g., *adding on* and *taking away*) by asking: *How many more objects would you need to add to make the groups equal? If you take away two objects from the first group, which group would have more (fewer) then? How do you know?*

Meeting the Needs of Diverse Learners

Larger objects and larger zippered bags will make it easier for some children to participate. A large two-column graph or rows of shoeboxes or crates may be used instead of egg cartons or muffin tins for one-to-one comparison.

Have a set of bags with a limited number of items. Some children may need hand-over-hand assistance to put the items into each section.

For advanced learners, make word cards such as *more*, *less*, *fewer*, *equal*, or *the same* and have children use them to label a specific set.

For advanced learners, adapt an egg carton by cutting off two egg cups from one end of the carton. This will form two rows of five. Use these egg cartons with children to build a conceptual understanding of the numbers five and ten.

Going Beyond

Set up other kinds of matching problems where children have to decide if there are more (fewer) objects in a group than another (e.g., cars and garages, cups and saucers, or boys and girls.) Use the blackline master in the Appendix to make a "more/fewer" spinner. Provide collections of objects (e.g., interlocking cubes, links). Then have children make a set of a given number, for example, four cubes. Choose a child to spin the spinner. If the spinner lands on *more*, have the children make a set having more than four objects; if it lands on *fewer*, have them make a set having fewer than four objects.

Make up stories similar to the one that follows. Then have children tell which set has *more, fewer*, or the *same* number of objects.

> *Once upon a time there was a group of three girls who decided to go for a walk in search of blueberries. On the way to the blueberry patch, they met a group of five boys. Tell me, "Which group has more people, the group of girls or the group of boys?"*

Have the children give their answers and explain their reasoning. Invite them to act out the story if they like.

Individual	Small Groups	Large Group	Interest Area	Single Day	Multi-Day	Time
●	●	●	Toys and Games	●		20 minutes

Counting Calisthenics (Aerobics)

Goal(s) & Objectives	**Objectives** *33. Uses one-to-one correspondence; 34. Uses numbers and counting* **Other Concepts** • Recognizes patterns in number • Estimates • Understands positional words • Understands and uses measurement words

Guiding Children's Learning

Have the children count aloud to a specific number using a variety of movements. Here are five different ideas.

- Have children perform a two-step action (e.g., move up and down, bending at the knees) as they count 1, 2; 1, 2; 1, 2; a three-step action (e.g., jump forward, jump backward, clap) as they count 1, 2, 3; 1, 2, 3; a four-step action (e.g., arms out front, arms opened wide at shoulder level, arms down by side, hands on hips) as they count 1, 2, 3, 4; 1, 2, 3, 4.

- To call attention to number patterns, have children alter the volume of their voices as they count aloud. For example, 1 (whisper), 2 (whisper), 3 (whisper), 4 (whisper), **5 (shout)**, 6 (whisper), 7 (whisper), 8 (whisper), 9 (whisper), **10 (shout)**, 11 (whisper), 12 (whisper), 13 (whisper), 14 (whisper), **15 (shout)**, and so forth. Combine this with movement, such as 1 (hands in air), 2 (touch head), 3 (touch shoulders), 4 (hands on hips), **5 (touch knees)**, 6 (hands in air), 7 (touch head), 8 (touch shoulders), 9 (hands on hips), **10 (touch knees)** and so forth.

- Choose an action for children to perform as they count aloud to a specified number. For example, have the children tap their nose (stamp their foot, clap, or jump) ten times as they count to 10.

- Pose counting problems that also involve movement, such as

  How many hops do you think it will take you to get from the door to the playground? Let's hop and count to check your guess.

  How many times will you jump before the timer runs out?

  How many giant steps do you think it will take you to go from the Block Area to the Library Area? Let's count to find out.

- Play counting games that also require children to follow two- and three-step directions (e.g., jump forward four times, turn to the right, and take seven baby steps). This can be done indoors using smaller numbers and outdoors with larger numbers.

Closing

Comment on the many different ways the children counted. Encourage them to think of other ways to move and count aloud.

Developmental Progression

Simple ↓ **Complex**	Have children count to 5 by rote.
	Have children count to 10 by rote.
	Have children count by rote to 10; then to 20, to 30, and so forth.
	Have children count to 10, performing one action or movement for each number named.
	Provide a set of quantity, numeral/quantity, or numeral cards from 1–10. Have children draw a card and then count aloud as they perform an action or movement the number of times specified by the card.
	Have children count to 20, performing one action or movement for each number counted.

Meeting the Needs of Diverse Learners

Adjust the action to one all children can perform. (e.g., nod your head, clap your hands). Children can also select the number cards or type of movement.

Several options can be programmed into a recording device and used by children to count aloud. Make sure all children participate in the activity in some way.

Post the action cards. Point to them while counting aloud (e.g., nose and chin while counting 1, 2, 1, 2, 1, 2.)

Going Beyond

Duplicate the numeral cards and action cards from the Appendix on card stock. Laminate the cards for durability. Turn both sets of cards face down. Then have a child select one of each from each set. Have the child perform the action shown on the card the number of times shown on the numeral card.

Draw ten adjacent squares on the sidewalk with chalk (similar to hopscotch). Let children take turns counting aloud as they step, hop, jump, or tip-toe from one square to another. Pose problems such as these:

Jump two squares. Now jump one more. How many squares did you jump altogether? Two and one more make three altogether.

Alternatively, write one numeral (*1–10*) in each square. Then pose number problems, such as

Hop to 3. What numeral are you on? What numeral will you be on if you hop backwards one square? You are really thinking. Three take away one is two.

Post a hundreds chart. Have an advanced mathematics learner circle the numerals that are shouted, for example, 5, 10, 15, 20, and so forth. Then have the child read or describe the pattern she sees.

Individual	Small Groups	Large Group	Interest Area	Single Day	Multi-Day	Time
	●	●	Music and Movement, Outdoors	●		10–15 minutes

Dinner Time

Goal(s) & Objectives	Objectives
	33. Uses one-to-one correspondence; 34. Uses numbers and counting
	Other Concepts
	• Understands part-whole relationships
	• Adds and joins sets of objects and tells *how many*
	• Subtracts and separates sets of objects and tells *how many*
	• Understands positional words and relationships

Materials and Preparation

☐ One of the following books or another related to meal- or snack time

  Feast for 10 by Cathryn Falwell (Clarion, 1993)

  10 for Dinner by Jo Ellen Bogart (Scholastic, 1989)

☐ Paper or plastic dishes, cutlery, napkins, and glasses

☐ Placemats

☐ Play food or pictures of foods such as pizza, cookies, strawberries, juice boxes, milk (at least enough of each to solve the story problems described)

Guiding Children's Learning

Read the book. Have the children count aloud as you point to the pictures in the text.

Display the dishes, cutlery, napkins, and glasses. Tell the children to pretend that they are going to have friends for dinner. Invite them to discuss what they might serve or whom they might invite.

Demonstrate and describe how to set a table. Use positional words such as *beside, above,* or *on top of*. Pose story problems and then have the children take turns solving them using the tableware and play food. Use questions and comments that encourage children to describe how they solved a problem and to explain their reasoning. Some examples follow.

Two friends are coming to dinner. Please set the table for them. Don't forget to set a place for you, too. How many plates (forks, glasses, napkins) will you need?

One other friend just called, and he is coming to dinner as well. What do you need to do? Show me.

Everyone wants pizza for dinner, but one child wants cheese pizza and three want pepperoni. How many slices of pizza will you need altogether? How do you know?

Is there enough pizza for everyone to have a second slice? How could you find out?

Two friends want apples for dessert, and two friends want peaches. How many pieces of fruit will you need altogether?

You have four boxes of juice. Two friends want juice with their pizza, and the other two want milk. How many boxes of juice do you have left?

If you wanted to give each friend two cookies, how many do you need? How could you find out?

Closing

Comment on how well the children prepared and served dinner for their friends. Remind them that the dishes and foods will be in the Dramatic Play Area to use at choice time.

Developmental Progression

Simple ↓ **Complex**	Display collections of the objects (e.g., strawberries, cookies, juice boxes). Have children match the objects in one collection with the objects in another collection. Have them tell which has *more* or *fewer*; have them count the number of objects in each collection.
	Pose story problems that help children understand one-to-one correspondence. Use small number quantities (1–5)
	Pose story problems that help children understand quantity and see part-part-whole relationships (e.g., 1 slice of cheese pizza and 3 slices of pepperoni pizza equals 4 slices of pizza; the children ate 4 pieces of fruit: 2 apples and 2 peaches). Use small number quantities (1–5).
	Pose story problems that require children to add and join sets of objects or to subtract and separate sets of objects. Use small number quantities (1–5).
	Repeat the steps above using 6–10 objects. Use higher quantities if children demonstrate understanding.

Meeting the Needs of Diverse Learners

Use laminated placemats with shapes of dishes, cutlery, and glasses to help children match and place objects on each one.

Offer larger play food items such as pizza, cookies, strawberries, juice boxes, and milk that are easy to pick up and hold. A large two-column graph or rows of shoeboxes or crates may be used for one-to-one comparisons.

Going Beyond

Read math-related books with a similar theme, such as *Miss Spider's Tea Party* by David Kirk or *The Doorbell Rang* by Pat Hutchins. With advanced mathematics learners, you can offer props and then have them solve problems presented in the story. For example, after reading *The Doorbell Rang*, give children paper cookies and pose a problem such as this: "How many cookies would each person get if four friends had to share twelve cookies? Show me, using your cookies."

Offer experiences similar to the one presented in the activity. For example, have the children pack a picnic lunch or plan a party for a specific number of children. For children who need an additional challenge, include items that are packed in multiples (e.g., two cookies; a bag of three carrot sticks; a sprig with five grapes). Challenge them to figure out how many of each item they will need for all of the picnic or party participants.

Assign breakfast, lunch, or snack time helpers to pass out napkins, straws, and other items. Pose problems such as this: "Leo, Crystal, and Dallas need spoons for their cereal. Derek, you are our helper today. Will you get the spoons please? How many will you need?"

Draw attention to the three-dimensional shapes of the foods and other items used in the activity. Use the phrases *like a ball*, *like a can*, and *like a box* as well as the names for the geometric shapes in your discussions. Talk about the attributes of each item.

Individual	Small Groups	Large Group	Interest Area	Single Day	Multi-Day	Time
●	●		Dramatic Play, Cooking	●		20 minutes

Learning About Numerals

Goal(s) & Objectives	**Objectives** *33. Uses one-to-one correspondence; 34. Uses numbers and counting* **Other Concepts** • Connects number words and numerals to the quantities they represent • Makes numerals

Materials and Preparation

☐ *Counting with Apollo* by Caroline Grégoire or another counting book

☐ Modeling dough or clay

☐ Numeral/quantity cards master (see Appendix)

☐ Card stock or heavy paper

Make a set of numeral/quantity cards (1–5) out of card stock for each child in your group. Laminate the cards for durability.

Guiding Children's Learning

Introduce the book to the children. As you read, invite the children to count the items referenced in the book (e.g., Apollo's two beautiful ears and two beautiful eyes). Point out the numeral on each page, tracing it with your finger. Explain that a numeral is a way to tell or show *how many*. Help the children make connections to the story by asking questions such as these:

> *Apollo only has one tail. Can you think of a body part that you have only one of?*

> *How many beautiful eyes and ears do you have? Let's count them.*

> *What would it be like if you had four legs like Apollo? What do you think it would be like if Apollo only had two legs like you?*

After finishing the book, continue the discussion with questions such as these:

What kind of dog is Apollo? Do you or anyone you know have a dachshund?

Tell us about Apollo's shape and size. What does he look like?

What was Apollo able to do with his body?

Would you like to try to make a numeral by using your body? You may invite friends to help if you need them.

Next, have a child choose a card from the set of numeral/quantity cards. Show the card to the children. Name the numeral as you trace it with your finger. Call attention to the set of dots at the bottom of the card. Remind the children that the numeral tells *how many* dots are on the card.

Explain that you are going to use modeling dough to make an Apollo-like numeral. Demonstrate how to roll the dough into a long, slender shape like a dachshund and place the dough along the numeral outline. Talk about the features of the numeral (e.g., *curved, straight,* or *diagonal* lines) and the way in which it is formed.

Give each child a set of cards and have them find the same numeral. Give each child some dough to form an Apollo-like shape. Then have them place the dough along the outline of the numeral. Demonstrate again, if necessary.

Continue making dough numerals as long as the children are interested.

Closing

Tell the children that the modeling dough and numeral cards will be in the Art or Toys and Games Area to use at choice time.

Help the children make the transition to the next activity, using instructions such as these:

If you are wearing red, find the card with the numeral 2. Then tiptoe to an interest area.

Show me the numeral 5 and *then get your coat and hat.*

Provide assistance to children as needed (e.g., have them find the set of two dots and then name the numeral).

Developmental Progression

Simple ↓ **Complex**	Have the children use counters or dough to form a set with a specific number of dachshunds, or dogs. Show the numeral card as you comment, e.g., *You made a set of three dogs: one, two, three. Let's label the set with the numeral 3.*
	Have the children make a set of a given number of objects. Let the children find the matching numeral/quantity card and use it to label the set. Begin with sets 1–5 and then expand to include sets 6–10.
	Have the children arrange the numeral/quantity cards in order from the set having the smallest number of objects to the set having the largest number of objects. Have the children point to and name the numeral representing the set. Begin with sets 1–5 and then include sets 6–10.
	Introduce numeral cards. Show children a card. Then ask them to use counters to form a set having the appropriate number of objects. Begin with sets of 1–5 objects. Then expand to include sets of 6–10 objects.
	Have children outline the numeral on the numeral card by using dough. Talk about the numeral as the children form it, e.g., "You placed your dough on the numeral *1*. It looks like a straight line. When we write the numeral *1*, we start at the top and pull straight down. Trace it with me as we say its name: *one*."
	Have children write the numeral to identify the quantity in each set. Offer a variety of media for writing (e.g., shaving cream, sand, chalk, and starch in sealed baggies).
	Add the number word to each of the numeral/quantity cards. Call attention to the number word during activities using the cards so children will make the connection among all three (i.e., the numeral, the number of objects/pictures, and the written number word).
	Introduce numerals greater than 10.

Meeting the Needs of Diverse Learners

For children who cannot see the numbers, use cards with raised or textured numerals and objects. To make raised or textured cards, write numerals on cards and then trace them with white glue. Let the glue dry. If necessary, help children place the clay along the raised outline of the numerals.

Cut out numeral shapes or use large magnetized numerals on an inclined board. Make sure there is space between the numerals so they are easy to distinguish and pick up.

Shape a pipe cleaner into a numeral and glue it on a card. Use a card in a contrasting color so children can see and feel the shape of the numeral. The raised pipe cleaner makes it easier to guide the clay.

If 5 numeral cards overwhelm a child, offer 2–3 numeral cards.

Use the children's home languages when naming numerals and objects and when counting the objects.

Learn and use sign language for numerals.

Going Beyond

Have the children work together to use their bodies to form a numeral.

Place the numeral cards alongside counters in the Toys and Games Area. Have the children identify the numeral and then create a corresponding set. Show them how to check their answers using the numeral/quantity cards.

Give each child a set of numeral cards. Show the children a set of objects. Then have them hold up the numeral card that corresponds to the set. Also hold up a numeral card and have the children form a corresponding set.

Provide a variety of collage and sculpting materials. Have each child roll a die, write the corresponding numeral on a collage tray, and then create a sculpture using that number of collage materials.

Challenge advanced learners to figure out how many eyes or ears there are altogether in a small group of children or in their family. Some children may be able to do this in their heads; others will need drawing materials.

Individual	Small Groups	Large Group	Interest Area	Single Day	Multi-Day	Time
●	●		Toys and Games, Art, Library	●		20–25 minutes

Let's Go Fishing

<table>
<tr>
<td>Goal(s) & Objectives</td>
<td>

Objectives

33. Uses one-to-one correspondence; 34. Uses numbers and counting

Other Concepts

- Understands part-whole relationships
- Understands *same*, *equal*, *more*, or *fewer*

</td>
</tr>
</table>

Materials and Preparation

☐ Wading pool

☐ Child-size fishing pole(s) with a magnet attached to the line or pole(s) made from a stick or dowel, string, and magnet

☐ Set of fish cards

☐ Paper clips

Duplicate the fish cards (see Appendix) on card stock and color the worms. Cut the cards apart and laminate them for durability. Attach a paper clip to each card.

Set up a wading pool or define an area to serve as a pond (e.g., a piece of blue carpet; an area defined with yarn). Place the fish cards in the pond. Spread the cards far enough apart so that children can easily catch one card at a time.

Guiding Children's Learning

Have the children gather around the pond. Ask,

Who would like to tell about a time when you or someone you know went fishing?

What do you need to catch fish? What kinds of tools would you use?

What do you think fish like to eat?

Show the fishing pole to the children and encourage them to pretend they are on a fishing trip. Explain that they will each have an opportunity to fish and then tell how many worms the fish they caught has eaten.

Sing a modified version of the song "Who Wants to Go Fishing?" (tune: "Did You Ever See a Lassie?")

Who wants to go fishing, go fishing, go fishing?

Who wants to go fishing

Down at the pond?

Demonstrate how to fish, using the magnetic fishing pole.

Take the fish card off the line. Show it to the children and then count aloud the number of worms pictured on the card. To show one-to-one correspondence, touch each worm as you count it. Call attention to the fact that the last number said is the number that tells how many worms the fish ate (quantity).

Sing the song again. Then choose a child to go fishing. Afterward, ask the child to tell how many worms are inside his fish, counting them one by one if necessary. Have the child place the card face up on the floor in front of him so that all the children can see it.

Sing the song and have the last child who fished choose someone who has not had a turn. Ask,

> *How many worms are inside the fish you caught?*
>
> *Did your fish eat more (fewer) worms than (child's name)'s fish or the same number? How do you know?*

Draw children's attention to the different patterns and arrangements of the same number of worms. For example:

> *You each caught a fish that ate three worms. Let's count them: one, two, three. The three worms on this card are arranged in a row. Let's count the fish on the second card: one, two, three. These three fish are not in a row. It doesn't matter how the worms are arranged. There are still three worms.*
>
> *These three fish ate the same number of worms: five. In the first fish, two worms are close to the fish's tail and three worms are in the center of its body. A set of two and a set of three make five altogether: one, two, three, four, five. The second fish also ate five worms. They are arranged like the dots on a die or a domino. The five worms in the third fish are in a row: one, two three, four, five.*

Encourage the children to continue singing and fishing until everyone has had a turn.

After all the fish in the pond have been caught, have the children

- take turns finding one (two, three) other friend(s) with a fish with the same number of worms; then talk about the ways the arrangement of worms on the cards are similar and different

- work as a group to sort the cards by the number of worms; then have them compare and discuss the cards within each sorted collection

Closing

Explain that the fishing pole and cards will be in the Toys and Games Area so they may use them to fish and count at choice time.

Developmental Progression

Simple ▼ **Complex**	Cut fish shapes from construction paper. Give children play worms to use as counters. Have them create sets of small quantities (1–3).
	Count small sets of worms (1–3).
	Recognize small sets of worms (1–3) without counting.
	Pair two cards having the same number of worms (1–3), regardless of arrangement.
	Describe the parts of a small set of worms (e.g., *This fish ate four worms. Two are near the tail, and two are near the head*).
	Sort multiple fish cards by the number of worms (quantity), regardless of the arrangement.
	Repeat the steps above with larger sets (4–6 and then 7–10).
	Match or label sets of worms with the appropriate numeral.
	With a given a set of worms, identify how many *more* or *fewer* are needed to make a new set (e.g., a child who has a set of two worms says, "Two more worms are needed to make a set of four.")

Meeting the Needs of Diverse Learners

Provide toy worms or cards with raised or textured figures of worms that are easy to see and to catch in the pond. Have children work together in pairs to catch the fish and count the worms.

Include cards with more than five worms for those who need more of a challenge.

Adjust the size and grip of the fishing pole to make it easier to hold. A stiffer string (use colored yarn, twine or a pipe cleaner) is easier to see and makes it easier to catch the fish.

For English language learners, count aloud in the children's home language as well as English.

When appropriate, use sign language for the hearing impaired.

Going Beyond

Include a blank fish card to represent zero or none.

Place the cards in the pond faceup. Name a number (1–5) and have the children catch a fish card with the specified number of worms.

Provide numeral cards. Have the children match the fish cards with the same number of worms to each numeral card. Add number word cards for children who need an additional challenge.

Have children add (join sets) and subtract (separate sets) by posing questions such as these:

> *If you caught a fish that ate two worms and I caught a fish that had eaten one worm, how many worms were eaten in all?*

> *If you caught three fish and each ate two worms, how many worms would have be eaten altogether? How many worms were eaten if one fish got away before he ate any?*

Have a child with advanced skills draw a number from a set of numeral cards (6–10). This card represents the number of worms he wants to use as a target number. Have the child fish, identify the number of worms on the fish card, and then tell how many more worms he needs to reach the target number. After the child fishes a second time, have him tell whether he reached his target number, has more than his target number, or still needs more worms.

Individual	Small Groups	Large Group	Interest Area	Single Day	Multi-Day	Time
●	●		Toys and Games, Dramatic Play, Outdoors	●		15–20 minutes

Merry Monkeys

Goal(s) & Objectives

Objectives

33. Uses one-to-one correspondence; 34. Uses numbers and counting

Other Concepts

- Understands part-whole relationships
- Adds and joins sets of objects and tells *how many*
- Subtracts and separates sets of objects and tells *how many*
- Recognizes patterns in number

Materials and Preparation

- ☐ *Five Little Monkeys Jumping on the Bed* by Eileen Christelow
- ☐ Monkey cards
- ☐ Card stock or heavy paper
- ☐ Adhesive Velcro® or magnet
- ☐ Flannel, Velcro®, or magnetic storyboard
- ☐ Markers

Use the monkey card master and card stock to create two sets of monkey cards. Each set of cards should have sets of 1–5 monkeys (i.e., two cards with one monkey, two cards with two monkeys, and so forth.) Laminate the cards for durability. Attach Velcro® or a magnet to the back of each card so it will attach to the storyboard.

Position a large storyboard so children can view and reach it easily. Display the label *On the Bed* on the left side of the board and the label *Off the Bed* on the right side. Display the felt monkeys in an area where children can see them.

Before using these materials, teach children the rhyme "Five Little Monkeys Jumping on the Bed." Allow them multiple opportunities to recite and dramatize the rhyme.

Guiding Children's Learning

Have the children sit facing the storyboard. Explain that you have a book and some pictures to go along with a favorite rhyme, "Five Little Monkeys Jumping on the Bed."

Invite the children to tell in their own words what happens in the rhyme. Then introduce the book.

Read the headings, *On the Bed* and *Off of the Bed*, that are displayed on the storyboard. Run your fingers under the text as you read. Ask a child to find a monkey card that shows how many monkeys are on the bed (five) and place it under the appropriate heading. Provide assistance with counting or placing the card on the storyboard.

Restate what is shown on the storyboard after each verse. For example,

Since all the monkeys are on the bed, the card with five monkeys is under the heading On the Bed. *Let's count the monkeys pictured on the card: one, two three, four, five. No monkeys have fallen off the bed yet, so there is no card under the heading* Off the Bed.

Continue reading the rhyme. After each verse, invite a different child to find the pieces that represent the number of monkeys on the bed and off the bed. Have the child place them in the appropriate space on the story board (see illustration below.) Use open-ended questions and comments that encourage children to count and develop concepts related to quantity (part-whole relationships) and separating sets (subtraction). Use words and phrases like *altogether* and *how many are left*.

Closing

Refer to the storyboard and point out all the groupings in the story. Have the children count aloud as you point to the monkeys on the cards.

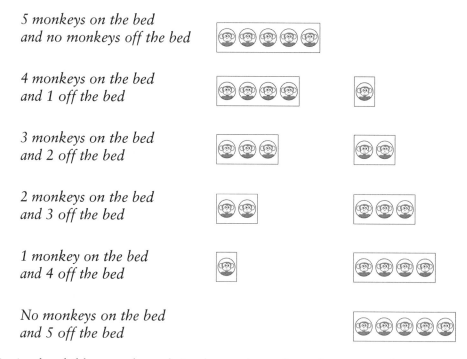

*5 monkeys on the bed
and no monkeys off the bed*

*4 monkeys on the bed
and 1 off the bed*

*3 monkeys on the bed
and 2 off the bed*

*2 monkeys on the bed
and 3 off the bed*

*1 monkey on the bed
and 4 off the bed*

*No monkeys on the bed
and 5 off the bed*

Invite the children to share their observations about the groups, for example, the growing pattern of one. Point out that each group totals five, regardless of the arrangement.

Tell the children that the *Five Little Monkeys* book and materials will be in the Toys and Games or Library Area to use during choice time.

Developmental Progression

Simple ⯆ **Complex**	Have children recite and/or dramatize the story.
	Use concrete objects such as toy monkeys and a toy bed to retell the number rhyme.
	Use the pictures of the monkeys to represent the number of monkeys *on the bed* and *off the bed*.
	Place numeral cards next to the picture sets of monkeys to show the number of monkeys *on the bed* and the number *off the bed*.
	Use numeral cards or write the numerals to show the number of monkeys *on the bed* and the number *off the bed* after each verse. Introduce the minus symbol (-).

Meeting the Needs of Diverse Learners

Teach the verses to English language learners in their home languages first.

For children who can't hear, use sign language gestures for the numbers and the monkeys as you read the books.

Simplify the steps and guide children through the counting process. Give children five chips or colored tiles. Have them drop one into a small container each time a monkey falls off the bed. Then have them count their chips as the other children count pictures of the monkeys.

Use a communication board or recording device so children who do not speak can tell how many monkeys are on the bed.

Going Beyond

Expand the quantity of monkeys from sets of 1–5 monkeys to sets of 6–10 monkeys (see Appendix).

Use this same strategy with other counting rhymes and finger plays, such as "Five Little Speckled Frogs," "Five Little Ducks," or "Ten in the Bed."

Read other stories about playful monkeys, such as *Five Little Monkeys with Nothing to Do, Five Little Monkeys Sitting in a Tree,* and *Five Little Monkeys Wash the Car,* all by Eileen Christelow.

Individual	Small Groups	Large Group	Interest Area	Single Day	Multi-Day	Time
		●	Music and Movement, Library	●		15–20 minutes

More or Fewer Towers

Goal(s) & Objectives

Objectives

33. Uses one-to-one correspondence; 34. Uses numbers and counting

Other Concepts

* Understands concepts of *more, less, same,* and *equal*

Materials and Preparation

☐ Interlocking cubes

☐ More/Fewer spinner

☐ Large paper clip and a brad (paper fastener)

☐ Numeral/quantity cards or die

Make a More/Fewer spinner by duplicating the spinner in the Appendix on card stock. Laminate it for durability. Attach a large paper clip to the center of the circle by using a brad.

Guiding Children's Learning

Give each child a collection of interlocking cubes.

Place the cards in a stack facedown. Have a child draw a card from the top of the stack and identify the numeral. If a child has difficulty recognizing the numeral, use the dots on the cards to help the child make the connection between the numeral and the quantity it represents. Then have all the children make a tower using the specified number of interlocking cubes.

Next, have another child spin the More/Fewer spinner. If the spinner lands on *More,* the children should make another tower having more cubes than their first tower. If the spinner lands on *Fewer,* they should make a new tower having fewer cubes than their first tower. Have the children compare their two towers by height. Ask questions such as these:

How many cubes are in your first tower? How many are in your second tower?

Does your second tower have more *or* fewer *cubes than your first? How do you know?*

How many more (fewer) *cubes do you have in your second tower?*

Does your tower have more than, fewer than, *or the* same (equal) *number of cubes as (child's name)'s tower?*

Whose tower has the fewest *number of cubes? Whose tower has the* most? *How do you know?*

Would you say the tower with the fewest *cubes is* shorter *or* taller *than the other tower?*

Repeat the process, letting children take turns using the spinner.

Closing

Review the activity, emphasizing vocabulary such as *more, less, fewer,* the *same,* and *equal.* Encourage the children to construct towers with more and fewer cubes at choice time in the Toys and Games Area or the Block Area.

Developmental Progression

Simple → Complex	
	Have children build towers using the number of cubes specified by a quantity card or die. Have children work with small quantities (1–3).
	Have children build two towers, the first one with a specified number and the second one with *more* cubes than the first.
	Have children build two towers, the first one with a specified number and the second one with *fewer* cubes than the first.
	Use numeral/quantity cards to indicate the number of cubes to use in building a tower or to tell how many more cubes to add or take away from a tower.
	Have children determine how many *more (fewer)* cubes one tower has than another.
	Have children represent their work through drawing or with other media.

Meeting the Needs of Diverse Learners

Use larger cubes or those that connect with Velcro® or magnets to make a tower easier to build. Working in pairs, one child can select a card and the other can build the tower.

Translate the words *more, fewer, equal* and *the same* into children's home languages.

Going Beyond

Gather a small group of children. Have each child select a different numeral card and construct a tower. Have them compare their towers to determine if they have *more* or *fewer* cubes than another.

Have the children make a tower, using a specific number of cubes and two different colors of cubes. Have them see in how many ways (color combinations) they can represent the number. As children work, ask questions such as these:

How many ways did you find to make a tower of five cubes?

Tell me about this combination. How many of each color did you use?

If you used three yellow cubes, how many blue cubes would you have to use to make a tower of six? How can you find out?

Give children two colors of interlocking cubes. Have them select a numeral card or roll a die. Then use cubes of one color to make a block tower. Have them select a second card or roll the die again. Then use cubes of another color to make a tower. Have the children compare the two towers to determine if one has *more, fewer,* or the *same* number of cubes as the other.

The red tower has five cubes, and the yellow tower has three cubes. A tower with five cubes has more than a tower with three cubes.

Your green tower has four cubes. That is just one more than your blue tower, which has two cubes. If you stand them side by side, you can see that there is only one more green cube than blue cube.

Give each child two colors of interlocking cubes. Have them make a tower, using a specific number of cubes but using any colors. After they are finished constructing the tower, have them tell which color of cubes they have *more of (fewer of)* in their tower. Use comments or questions such as these:

You used four white cubes and two brown cubes to make your tower of six cubes. Which color of cube do you have more of, white or brown? How do you know? How could you find out?

Individual	Small Groups	Large Group	Interest Area	Single Day	Multi-Day	Time
●	●	●	Toys and Games	●		15 minutes

Nursery Rhyme Count

Goal(s) & Objectives	Objectives
	33. *Uses one-to-one correspondence*; 34. *Uses numbers and counting*
	## Other Concepts
	• Understands quantity

Materials and Preparation

☐ Cotton balls or white pompoms

Guiding Children's Learning

Gather a small group of children and sing the familiar song, "Mary Had a Little Lamb."

Give each child a collection of cotton balls. Then explain that they are going to play a counting game in which they pretend to count Mary's lambs. Tell them to listen carefully because the song will tell how many lambs Mary had.

Sing an altered version of the song "Mary Had a Little Lamb," as shown below. Then have the children count the appropriate number of lambs (cotton balls). Observe to see who is counting with one-to-one correspondence, who can form sets of small numbers of objects without counting (*subitizing*), who has difficulty keeping track while counting, and who needs other assistance.

> *Mary had* four *little lambs,*
>
> *Little lambs, little lambs*
>
> *Mary had* four *little lambs,*
>
> *Let's count them as they go.*
>
> *One, two, three, four.*

Continue as long as the children are interested. Invite the children to take turns, substituting a number in the rhyme and singing the song.

Closing

Comment on the children's ability to listen and count. Invite the children to suggest an interest area in which to put the cotton balls or pompoms so they can use them at choice time.

Developmental Progression

Simple → Complex	
Simple	Have children show or count out 1–5 lambs (cotton balls or pompoms).
	Have children show or count out 6–10 lambs.
	Show children a numeral/quantity card or numeral card. Have them form sets with the appropriate number of lambs.
	Have children count out to 20 (lambs).
Complex	Engage children in activities that help them to see part-whole relationships (e.g., give children two differently colored pompons). Have them make a set of lambs and tell how many of each are in the set (e.g., "I have six lambs. Three are white, and three are black.").

Meeting the Needs of Diverse Learners

Teach the song to English language learners in their home languages before conducting the activity.

Use sign language or visual cues as you sing the song and count the different sets, so that all children understand.

A child who is sensitive to touch may prefer a harder object, such as a golf ball, to use in counting.

Going Beyond

Sing the song twice, inserting different numbers in the song each time. After the children have formed two sets of lambs, have them tell which set has *more* or *fewer* lambs.

After singing the song and forming a set of an identified number, pose story problems such as these:

If Mary had six lambs and three ran away, how many would be left?

If Mary had five lambs and she bought two more, how many lambs would she have then?

If you and Mary both had three lambs, how many would you have altogether? If two of your lambs wandered away to Mary's farm, how many lambs would you have left? How many would Mary have?

Engage children in activities that help them see part-whole relationships. For example, provide black and white pompoms to represent lambs. Then pose the following problem:

Show one way to make a set of five lambs by using the black and white pompoms. Can you show me another? And another?

Alter other songs and nursery rhymes for use in counting and number games. Buy counters or make felt counters as suggested below.

- "Little Jack Horner" (plastic or purple felt plum counters)
- "Little Miss Muffet" (spider counters)
- "Little Bo Peep" (cotton ball sheep)
- "Hickory, Dickory, Dock" (plastic or felt mouse counters)
- "Sing A Song of Sixpence" (plastic or felt bird counters)
- "Jack Be Nimble" (have the children jump a specified number of times)

Individual	Small Groups	Large Group	Interest Area	Single Day	Multi-Day	Time
●	●	●	Music and Movement, Toys and Games	●		15 minutes

Secret Numbers

Goal(s) & Objectives

Objectives

33. Uses one-to-one correspondence; 34. Uses numbers and counting

Other Concepts

* Understands quantity

Materials and Preparation

☐ Quantity cards

Use the blackline master in the Appendix to make quantity cards. Make one complete set and then enough additional cards so that each child has a card.

Guiding Children's Learning

Gather the children and have them sit in a circle. Explain that they are going to play a game called "Secret Numbers."

Give the children cards and have them place them facedown on the floor in front of them without looking at the cards.

Explain that you will recite a rhyme and then each child will pass his or her card to the person seated next to them. Model how to pass the cards to the person sitting to their left and explain that this is called passing the cards *clockwise* (i.e., moving in the same direction as the hands of a clock).

Recite the following rhyme. Teach children the second verse of the rhyme so they can join in with you.

I've got a secret number.

What could it be?

I'm ready to show you.

Are you ready to see?

Sing rinky, dinky, dinky,

Sing rinky, dinky do.

Sing rinky, dinky, dinky.

I'll pass my card to you. (Have the children point to the child sitting to their left.)

Have the children pass their cards. Each child then looks at the new card without showing it to others. Reveal the secret number to the children (one of the cards from your set of cards). Ask the children if their card matches the secret number. Some children may be able visually to recognize the quantity without counting (subitize) while others may have to count. Have those with a matching quantity perform a specific action (e.g., if the secret number is four, have the children holding a matching card hop four times).

Closing

Invite the children to tell what they liked about the game. Tell them the cards will be in the Music and Movement Area to use during choice time.

Developmental Progression

Simple / Complex	
Simple	Have children play the game by using the quantity cards having quantities 1–4.
	Have children play the game by using the quantity cards having quantities 5–10.
	Have the children play the game by using the numeral/quantity cards. Use those cards that have numerals that look distinctly different from or like one another (e.g., numerals that have curves/do not have curves; numerals with straight lines). Use descriptive words that help children recognize the numerals.
	Have the children play the game by using numeral/quantity cards that include numerals with less distinct differences.
Complex	Have the children play the game with numeral cards 1–10.

Meeting the Needs of Diverse Learners

Provide raised or textured numbers on the cards for children to feel. Provide an inclined board or light box to make them easier to see.

Whisper the secret number to children who can't see or identify it.

Use number words in the children's home languages as well as in English.

Use sign language for the hearing impaired.

Change the task for advanced mathematics learners by giving them a numeral card with *10* on it. Challenge them to figure out what number would result if 10 more were added to the secret number.

Going Beyond

Create a memory game by duplicating two sets of quantity cards. Turn all the cards facedown on a table or floor, placing them randomly. Have the children take turns turning two cards over to find a pair that match. Have the children identify the quantity each time they turn a card over. The child that finds the matching pair places the pair on the floor in front of him.

To simplify the game, place only one set of quantity cards facedown. Show and name one of the cards from the second card set and have the children try to find its match. When they do, give them the pair of cards. The game is over when all the cards have been matched. When children are ready, introduce the numeral/quantity cards and numeral cards.

Make multiple sets of large quantity cards (e.g., 11" x 14") and laminate them. Decide upon which quantities you wish to focus (e.g., 1–4). Then spread them on the floor faceup in random order. Have the children spread out and invite them to move as you play music. Periodically stop the music, and give instructions such as, "Find a card with four and touch it with your right hand. Put your toe on a two. Tiptoe to a three." For children who need more support, show the quantity card.

Give each child a small box or other container and tell the children to pretend the containers are treasure chests that they are going to fill with treasure. Create a story about going on a treasure hunt. While telling the story, pause periodically to show a quantity or numeral/quantity card. Have the children identify the number and put the same number of items into their chests. Here is a sample story:

> *Once upon a time, a group of children were playing in the sand at the beach. One of them saw something glistening brightly in the sun. Now, the children's parents had told them stories about a treasure that was lost many, many years before. They weren't sure that the story was true—until today. The first child to find something was (insert child's name). He found six shiny silver coins. He gathered the coins and counted them as he placed them in a chest. (Child's name)'s friend, who was digging right next to him, came upon four sparkling jewels. She couldn't believe her eyes! She scooped up the four jewels and put them into the chest. The next friend to find treasure was exploring close to the water's edge when she found three golden nuggets...*

If children are attentive and engaged, encourage them to sort the treasure and create a graph.

Individual	Small Groups	Large Group	Interest Area	Single Day	Multi-Day	Time
	●	●	Music and Movement, Outdoors, Toys and Games	●		15–20 minutes

Shake, Rattle, and Roll

Goal(s) & Objectives	## Objectives *33. Uses one-to-one correspondence; 34. Uses numbers and counting* ## Other Concepts • Understands part-whole relationships • Recognizes and identifies shapes and their attributes • Sorts by shape • Recognizes and identifies numerals

Materials and Preparation

☐ Five cubes (dice) with blank faces

☐ Shape stickers (circle, triangle, square)

☐ Parquetry or pattern blocks (5 of each shape per child)

☐ Container with lid

☐ Paper plates or counting mats

Choose two shape stickers and place three of each on the faces of each cube.

Guiding Children's Learning

Have a small group of children sit in a circle on the floor.

Demonstrate how to play "Shake, Rattle, and Roll" following these steps.

• Place all five cubes in the container and secure it with the lid. Shake the container and then roll the cubes onto the table or floor.

• Sort the cubes into groups by the shape that appears on the top face. For example, there may be two triangles or three circles. Talk about what you are doing as you demonstrate.

• From the collection of shapes, find a match for the shape represented on the top face of each cube and place it on the paper plate or counting mat. Count and think aloud as you demonstrate.

Explain that each child will have a turn to shake, rattle, and roll the cubes and then sort them by shape. After each roll, the children will find the matching shapes from their collections and place them on their paper plate or counting mat.

Play music and have the children pass the container around the circle. Invite the children to move to the beat of the music. When the music stops, the child holding the container rolls the cubes.

After each roll, pose questions like these:

How many triangles (circles, squares) are there?

Which group has the most (least)? How do you know?

For a challenge, ask questions such as these:

How many more circles are there than squares?

If there are two triangles in a group, how many more would you need to make a group of three?

If I counted all of the shapes in each group, how many shapes would I have altogether?

Continue passing the container until every child has had a turn.

Closing

Tell the children the "Shake, Rattle and Roll" materials will be in the Toys and Games Area so they can play at choice time.

Developmental Progression

Simple ↓ **Complex**	Have children roll 3–5 cubes with only two shapes and then sort them by shape. Then count the number in each group. Describe or have the children describe parts of the whole set.
	Have children form the sets represented on the cubes by using pattern blocks.
	Have the children use a quantity card or numeral/quantity card to label *how many* of each shape are in the set they form. Describe their work (e.g., "There is one square, so you labeled it with the numeral *1*. There are two circles, so you used a *2*.")
	Use a permanent marker and write each of the numerals *1, 2,* or *3* on two faces of a blank cube. Put the numeral cube and one shape cube in a container. Choose a child to shake, rattle, and roll the cubes. Have the children identify the numeral and shape on the top face of each cube. Then have them place the appropriate number of shapes on their counting mats.
	Give each of two children one shape cube and one numeral cube. Have them roll the cubes and identify the numeral and shape on the top face of each cube. Next, have the children form a set reflecting the number of each shape. Describe or have the children describe the set (e.g., "This set has five shapes in all: two circles and three triangles.")

Meeting the Needs of Diverse Learners

Larger cubes and containers are easier to hold and count.

Put raised figures on the cubes to use with children who can't see the dots. Make sure that the weight of each side of the cube is about the same so there is an equal chance for rolling each side.

Provide parquetry shapes or three-dimensional shapes for children to place on their plates and pick up to count.

Duplicate the tally graph from the Appendix ("Question of the Day: Form 2"). Write the question, "Which shape was rolled most often?" Draw a circle at the left-hand side of row one, a square on row two, and a triangle on row three. Invite an advanced mathematics learner to act as the Tally Grapher and record a tally mark on the appropriate rows to represent the shapes shown on the dice with each roll. At the end of the game, have the Tally Grapher count the total number of tally marks in each row and record the numeral in the box at the end of the row. Have the Tally Grapher summarize the data and report to the rest of class.

Going Beyond

Increase the number of cubes so children can practice counting and solving problems with larger collections and numbers.

Use counters that are a different color on each side. Place 5–10 counters in a container and have the children pour them out. Have the children use a grid graph to line the counters up by color. Use questions and comment such as these:

> *How many red counters are there? How many yellow?*

> *Are there more or fewer red counters than yellow?*

> *Four red counters and two yellow counters make six altogether. What numeral will you write to tell how many red counters there are? Show me how you can make a 4 with this red crayon. What will you write to show how many yellow counters there are? Show me.*

> *Do you think the counters will look the same or different when you spill them out again? Let's find out.*

Introduce additional or less familiar shapes.

Give children a set of numeral cards. After sorting the cubes by shape, have them match the numeral to the number of shapes in a group.

Place one cube with numerals and another cube with shapes, pictures, or other symbols in the container. Shake, rattle, and roll the cubes. Read the top face of each cube and have the children place the appropriate number of shapes on their counting mats. For example, a triangle on one cube and a three on the other would mean that a child would place three triangles on the counting mat. Roll the number cube again to tell how many the second set will have. Have the children find out how many they have altogether.

Provide construction paper shapes, glue sticks, and paper for children to represent different combinations that total five. For example, a child who rolled three triangles and two circles would glue the respective shapes on paper. After a roll of one circle and four squares, the child would find the matching construction paper shapes and glue them to the paper.

Individual	Small Groups	Large Group	Interest Area	Single Day	Multi-Day	Time
●	●		Toys and Games	●		15–20 minutes

Show Me Five

Goal(s) & Objectives	Objectives *33. Uses one-to-one correspondence; 34. Uses numbers and counting* Other Concepts • Understands part-whole relationships

Materials and Preparation

☐ Collection of materials (e.g., toothpicks, buttons, seeds, two-sided counters)

☐ Crayons and chart paper

Guiding Children's Learning

Use materials from one of the collections to create a set of five (e.g., five buttons arranged in a column). Ask, "How many do you see? How do you know?"

Create a second set of five, using the same materials but arranging them differently from those in the first set (e.g., five buttons arranged in a circle). Ask,

Are these two sets the same or different? How do you know?

How many are here now? Are there more, fewer, or the same number? How do you know?

Ask a child to show a third way to make a set of five. Have the child tell how this set is the same as and different from the other two sets.

Give each child a collection of materials and challenge them to see how many different sets of five they can make. When the children have found all the possible sets, invite them to take turns showing and telling others about one of her arrangements. After each child shares, draw a representation of her set on chart paper. Make comments such as these:

I see you've arranged your five buttons into two rows: three buttons in the first (top) row and two buttons in a second (bottom) row.

You have a column with four buttons and then a column with one button. Four and one make five altogether.

These five buttons are arranged like the pips on a domino or die.

Closing

Refer the children to the chart. Invite them to share what they discovered as they explored the number five. Encourage children to continue to explore five and other numbers, using different materials. Remind them that drawing and writing materials are in the interest areas for them to document their discoveries.

Developmental Progression

Simple → Complex	
Simple	Provide collections of objects (e.g., buttons, keys, beads, cubes). Have children form multiple sets of a given quantity, using each type of material. Begin with quantities of 3–5.
	Create two sets having the same quantity of objects but arranged in different ways. Have children tell how the sets are the same and different. Begin with quantities of 3–5.
	Have children create multiple sets of a given quantity. Have them describe the parts of each set (e.g., "Three buttons are going up and down, and these two are side by side"). Expand quantities beyond five if appropriate.
Complex	Have children represent their discoveries about a specific quantity by drawing, graphing, or other means.

Meeting the Needs of Diverse Learners

Pair children of different abilities. Give each child a role that they can do successfully.

Make sure that at least two sets of objects are large enough to pick up and place easily. Placing the objects on a non-skid material keeps them from being moved accidentally.

For English language learners and children who are hearing impaired, display the respective numeral/quantity card when asking children to make a set.

Learn key words (e.g., body parts and numerals) in the home languages of the children in your class. Use them along with the English words.

Going Beyond

Give the children a collection of objects of two different colors (e.g., blue and yellow chain links). Challenge them to see how many ways they can make a set of five, using various color combinations. Display the combinations in the order below, on a bulletin board, dowel, or hanger. Then invite the children to share their observations. Observe to see if they notice any patterns. In this example, the combinations include the following:

- 0 blue and 5 yellow
- 1 blue and 4 yellow
- 2 blue and 3 yellow
- 3 blue and 2 yellow
- 4 blue and 1 yellow
- 5 blue and 0 yellow
- 5 yellow and 0 blue
- 4 yellow and 1 blue
- 3 yellow and 2 blue
- 2 yellow and 3 blue
- 1 yellow and 4 blue
- 0 yellow and 5 blue

Challenge children to work with one another to make sets having a specific number of body parts. For example, upon signaling, have the children make a set of four feet. Two children might stand touching feet to feet, or four children might connect one foot each. Continue challenging children to make sets of six knees, eight thumbs, and so forth as long as they are interested. Take pictures of children forming sets, mount them on heavy paper, and combine them to make a number book. Put it in the Library or another interest area for children to read and think about.

Have children form groups of a specified quantity, and then give them instructions to form shapes or other objects. For example, have children form a group of three and then create a triangle, or have a group of seven create a circle.

Gather a small group of children. Give each child an ice cube tray or egg carton to use as a counting board and a collection of objects. Roll a die, identify the quantity (e.g., 6), and then tell the children to show a collection of six in their ice cube trays. Invite children to show and tell about their arrangements (e.g., all six in one row, three in one row and three in another, five in a row and one in another row, and so forth). Use numeral cards in place of or in addition to the die.

Let each child select a numeral or numeral/quantity card and identify the numeral. Provide various collections of objects and have each child create a variety of sets having the specified quantity but arranged in different configurations (e.g., three toothpicks laid end to end vertically, horizontally, or in a "T" shape; four double-sided counters—three white and one red, four red, four white, two white and two red.) Use questions and comments such as these:

Tell me what number you are working with.

How many are in this set? And this one?

Does it matter that the objects are arranged differently? Why or why not?

Tell me how this set is different from the other sets.

Tell me about the arrangement of these two sets.

I see you've created a pattern using your seven straws. Can you make another pattern using your seven straws?

Individual	Small Groups	Large Group	Interest Area	Single Day	Multi-Day	Time
●	●		Toys and Games	●		15–20 minutes

The Fishing Trip

Goal(s) & Objectives	**Objectives**
	33. Uses one-to-one correspondence; 34. Uses numbers and counting
	Other Concepts
	• Adds or joins sets of objects and tells how many
	• Subtracts or separates sets of objects and tells how many

Materials and Preparation

☐ Pictures of various kinds of fish

☐ Fishing props (rod and reel or pole, tackle box, lures with hooks removed, waders, net)

☐ Fish-shaped crackers

☐ Two paper cups or containers per child, one to represent water (e.g., pond, stream, ocean) and the other to represent a bucket

For each child, place approximately 10–15 snack crackers in one of the containers.

Guiding Children's Learning

Invite the children to tell what they know about fish or tell about their fishing experiences. Share the pictures and fishing props. Then introduce the activity.

Today we are going on an imaginary fishing trip.

Each of you will get an imaginary pond (stream, ocean) filled with fish. You will also get an empty bucket to put your fish in when you catch them. From time to time, you'll get to eat some of the fish. You'll need to listen carefully as I describe what happens on our imaginary fishing trip.

Teach the song "Let's All Go Fishing" (tune: "Did You Ever See a Lassie?").

Let's all go fishing, go fishing, go fishing.

Let's all go fishing

Down at the pond.

Then distribute the materials.

Create a story in which children bait an imaginary hook; get a nibble or bite; and then catch different kinds of fish, such as bass, trout, flounder, redfish, or tuna. Each time fish are caught, have the children move different quantities of crackers from the water to their bucket. Pose questions such as these:

How many fish are in your bucket? How do you know?

Are there more fish in your bucket now?

If you put one more fish in your bucket, how many will there be?

Occasionally, pretend it is time for a snack and have the children eat a fish. Ask questions such as these:

How many fish are in your bucket now? How did you get your answer?

How many would there be if you ate one fish? How do you know or how could you find out?

Continue the imaginary fishing trip as long as the children are interested or until the fish are gone.

Closing

Comment on how well the children fished and have them share their favorite part of the imaginary trip. Explain that next time they will help tell the imaginary fishing trip story.

Developmental Progression

Simple ↓ **Complex**	Use small quantities (3–5) when telling the story.
	Use larger quantities (6–10) when telling the story.
	Have children add or take away two fish at a time.
	Use quantity/numeral cards to show the children how many fish to catch and eat during the fishing trip.
	Introduce symbols to the children, such as +, -, and =. Demonstrate how to use them to write simple equations for the problems you describe in the story.

Meeting the Needs of Diverse Learners

Use larger crackers or containers to make it easier to move the fish. You can also secure the containers to the table or floor with non-skid material or Velcro®.

Use cups of contrasting colors or sizes to make them easier to see. Highlight the lip of the cup with colored tape to define its boundary.

With children who are advanced mathematics learners, record equations that express the operations in the story. For example,

> *I caught three fish and put them in my bucket. Then I caught one more: 3+1=4. I got hungry and ate two for a snack: 4-2=2.*

Going Beyond

Create other stories that invite children to solve similar counting, addition, or subtraction story problems. For example, go on an imaginary berry-picking trip using blueberries, blackberries, raspberries, or cherries.

Make a set of numeral and/or quantity cards. During the story, hold up a numeral card instead of orally telling the children how many fish to catch or eat.

Individual	Small Groups	Large Group	Interest Area	Single Day	Multi-Day	Time
●	●		Cooking, Toys and Games	●		10–15 minutes

Oh, Where, Oh, Where Has My Little Dog Gone?

Goal(s) & Objectives	Objectives
	33. *Uses one-to-one correspondence;* 34. *Uses numbers and counting*
	Other Concepts
	• Understands quantity

Materials and Preparation

☐ Small plastic dogs, photos, or drawings of dogs

☐ Half-pint milk cartons

☐ Art supplies such as construction paper, markers, glue

Follow these instructions to make doghouses:

Wash the milk cartons and let them dry.

Staple the top of each carton closed and cut out the bottom.

Cover each carton with construction paper and draw a door on one side for the door.

Guiding Children's Learning

Teach the song, "Oh, Where, Oh, Where Has My Little Dog Gone?"

Oh, where, oh, where has my little dog gone?

Oh, where, oh, where can he be?

With his ears cut short and his tail cut long.

Oh, where, oh, where can he be?

Explain to the children that they will act out the song. Two children will pretend to search for lost dogs while the rest of the children pretend to be dogs.

Ask for two volunteers and have them close their eyes while the dogs (children) hide.

Sing the song. At the end, send the volunteers to find the lost dogs and bring them to you. Upon returning, have each child count the number of dogs they found. Repeat the process several times.

Next, display the doghouses and toy dogs. Explain to the children that they are going to play the "Oh, Where, Oh, Where Has My Little Dog Gone?" game by using these props.

Arrange two groups of doghouses in the following manner. Place the dogs next to the houses, counting aloud as you do so. Tell the children to look very carefully at the number of dogs next to each doghouse. Then cover the dogs with a doghouse.

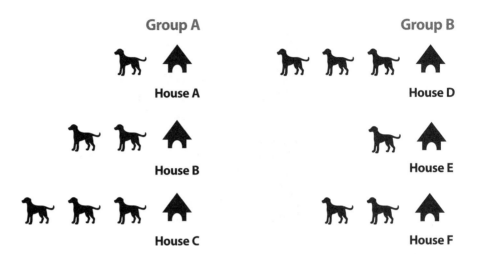

Group A	Group B
House A	House D
House B	House E
House C	House F

Next, have one child lift a house in Group B and tell how many dogs are there. Then have the child choose the house from Group A that he thinks has the same number of dogs. If the child chooses correctly, he removes the house and keeps the dogs in Group B. If the number of dogs in the house differs, the child replaces the house.

Make note of which children visually recognize and name the number of dogs in each set (subitize) and which children count the dogs. Continue playing until each child has had a turn. Rearrange the order of the houses in Group B as needed but maintain the order of the houses in Group A.

As children become more skilled, rearrange the houses in both groups. Remember to maintain a set of one, two, and three dogs in each group. Once children can easily identify, count, and match sets with up to three objects, play the game with sets up to five.

Closing

Tell the children that the "Oh, Where, Oh, Where Has My Little Dog Gone?" game will be placed in the Toys and Games Area for them to use at choice time.

Developmental Progression

Simple ↓ **Complex**	Sing "Oh, Where, Oh, Where Has My Little Dog Gone?" Then have the children act it out, taking turns counting the number of dogs found.
	Play the "Oh, Where, Oh, Where Has My Little Dog Gone?" game with sets of 1–3 dogs and rearrange only one group of doghouses.
	Play the "Oh, Where, Oh, Where Has My Little Dog Gone?" game with sets of 1–3 dogs and rearrange both groups of doghouses.
	Play the "Oh, Where, Oh, Where Has My Little Dog Gone?" game with sets of 1–5 dogs. Repeat the game, rearranging the doghouses as described in the previous two steps.
	Play the "Oh, Where, Oh, Where Has My Little Dog Gone?" game, replacing the dogs in group B with numerals. Have the children uncover a numeral and find the corresponding set of dogs in group A.

Meeting the Needs of Diverse Learners

Have the volunteers work in pairs to find the lost dogs. One can find the dogs, and the other can count them.

Use larger objects and laundry baskets to make it easier to uncover and count the dogs.

Record the song so that children who do not speak can play the recording when the group sings.

Going Beyond

Make a duplicate game for children to borrow to play with family members.

Count aloud as you display a set of five dogs. Use a doghouse to cover a portion of the dogs in the group and then ask,

How many dogs are outside the doghouse?

How many dogs do you think are inside the doghouse?
How do you know?

Lift the doghouse and ask the child to confirm or count to confirm
her answer. Say and/or write a number sentence that describes what is
represented. For example, explain,

> *Sonya said there were three dogs outside of the
> doghouse and two dogs inside the doghouse. Three
> dogs and two dogs make five dogs altogether.*

After a child uncovers a set of dogs, pose problems such as this:

> *If four dogs are here, how many more would you
> need to make five? Can you show me which house
> has the set of five dogs?*

Individual	Small Groups	Large Group	Interest Area	Single Day	Multi-Day	Time
	●	●	Toys and Games, Music and Movement, Outdoors	●	●	15 minutes

Buried Treasure

Goal(s) & Objectives	Objectives
	22. *Observes objects and events with curiosity*; 27. *Classifies objects*

Other Concepts

- Identifies basic geometric shapes and their properties
- Describes, classifies, and sorts basic geometric shapes
- Compares and measures

Materials and Preparation

- ☐ Shape patterns (see Appendix)
- ☐ Card stock or heavy paper
- ☐ Attribute blocks (circles, rectangles, and triangles in various sizes and colors)
- ☐ Three boxes with hinged lids
- ☐ A book about treasure (optional)

    The Secret Birthday Message by Eric Carle
    Spot's Treasure Hunt by Eric Hill
    Treasure Map by Stuart J. Murphy
    Elliot Digs for Treasure by Andrea Beck

- ☐ Sandbox or tub of sand
- ☐ Small brushes

Decorate the boxes to look like treasure chests. Use the shape patterns in the Appendix to cut a circle, rectangle, and triangle from construction paper or card stock and put one on the lid of each box.

Bury the attribute blocks in the sand. If you do not have attribute blocks, use the patterns to make multiples of each shape from construction paper or card stock. Laminate or cover them with clear contact paper for durability.

Learn the "Shape Song." (See the end of this activity.)

Guiding Children's Learning

Read the book to the children. Lead a discussion about treasure and what it means to go on a treasure hunt.

Explain that they are going to pretend that they are on a treasure hunt and search for treasure buried in the sand.

Display the treasure chest with the circle on the lid. Explain that some of the treasure is in the shape of a circle. Point to the circle. Sing the first verse of the "Shape Song." Run your fingers around the outside edge of the circle as you sing. Have the children draw a circle in the air and sing along with you. Repeat the process with the other two treasure chests.

Demonstrate how to use the brush to gently brush away the sand. Then let the children take turns searching for treasure. Each time treasure is discovered, have the child identify the shape and place it in the appropriate treasure chest. Use questions and comments such as these:

How did you decide where to put the treasure?

How is a triangle different from the rectangle? How are they the same?

How many sides does this rectangle have? Let's count as we touch them.

How are these two triangles different? How are they the same?

Closing

After all the treasure is found, open the treasure chests to verify that each one contains the correct shapes. Allow the children to make changes if necessary. Have them explain their reasons for making changes.

Developmental Progression

Simple ⟶ Complex	
	Conduct the activity as described, using only two shapes that are distinctly different from one another.
	Give children the three basic shapes. Have them hold up the shape described in each verse of the "Shape Song."
	Have children sort shapes by putting them into the appropriate treasure chests.
	Have children name each shape and describe its attributes.
	Have children sort shapes that are different sizes or different types within one category (e.g., triangles can vary by both type—right, equilateral, isosceles—and size).

Meeting the Needs of Diverse Learners

Before focusing on shapes, have children search for and sort broader categories of treasure (e.g., play jewels, animals, or cars).

Suggest that children feel each shape to discover its characteristics. Ask the children to describe the characteristics. Have them place the shapes on an incline board or light box to see them better.

Use sign language as you describe the shapes with children who have hearing impairments.

Use larger shapes that are easier to find and pick up. Use a brush with a large handle.

Pose questions that help advanced learners see the relationship between two-dimensional and three-dimensional shapes, for example, between a circle and a sphere, a triangle and a triangular pyramid, and a square and a cube.

Going Beyond

Have the "treasure hunter" describe a discovered shape before showing it to the other children. See if the other children can identify the shape on the basis of the verbal description. Take note of the attributes that the children talk about when they describe the shape.

Share a book about shapes, such as *Shapes, Shapes, Shapes* by Tana Hoban or *The Shape of Things* by Dayle Dodds. Take the children on a walk around the school or neighborhood to find everyday objects that are the same shapes discussed in the "Buried Treasure" activity.

Place an assortment of large cut-out shapes on the floor. Play music and let the children move to the music. When the music stops, give instructions such as "Stand on a triangle," or "Hop on a circle." Offer assistance when needed.

Add other two-dimensional shapes, such as a square (a special kind of rectangle), rhombus, or ellipse, or repeat the activity using three-dimensional shapes.

Begin a shape scrapbook in which children can place drawings or pictures of variously shaped objects that they find. Label the shapes as they are added. Place the scrapbook in the Library Area for the children to enjoy.

Individual	Small Groups	Large Group	Interest Area	Single Day	Multi-Day	Time
●	●		Sand and Water, Discovery	●		15–20 minutes

The Shape Song
(To the tune of "The Farmer in the Dell")

A circle has curved lines,
A circle has curved lines.
Round and round,
It never stops.
A circle has curved lines.

A rectangle has four sides,
A rectangle has four sides.
One, two,
Three, four,
A rectangle has four sides.

A triangle has three sides,
A triangle has three sides.
Up the hill,
Down and back,
A triangle has three sides.

I Spy With My Little Eye

Goal(s) & Objectives	**Objectives**
	22. *Observes objects and events with curiosity;* 32. *Shows awareness of position in space*
	Other Concepts
	• Identifies geometric shapes and their properties

Materials and Preparation

☐ Binoculars made from two cardboard rolls or a pair of silly glasses

Guiding Children's Learning

Explain how to play "I Spy With My Little Eye." Use the binoculars or glasses to look around the room. Then say something like this:

> *I spy with my little eye, something in the Toys and Games Area, on the top shelf, next to the puzzles.*

> *I spy with my little eye, something in the Dramatic Play Area. It's in a basket, next to the refrigerator. It's like a ball or a sphere, and it's green.*

Have the children give a thumbs-up sign when they think they have figured out what the object is. Let them whisper the answer to a neighbor. Choose one or more children to reveal their answers. Ask, "How do you know?"

Continue playing as long as children are interested. Invite children to take turns being the leader who spies something.

Note which children are able to use positional words and which children respond to them.

Closing

Tell children that you will put the binoculars or glasses in one or more interest areas so they can play "I Spy With My Little Eye" with their friends.

Developmental Progression

Simple ▼ Complex	Play the game, using one or two familiar positional words (e.g., *in, on top of,* or *under*) or give simple directions (e.g., "I spy with my little eye, something in the Library Area under the rocking chair.").
	Play the game, using less familiar positional words (e.g., *between, behind,* or *beside*) or more complex directions.
	Let children assume the role of leader in the game.

Meeting the Needs of Diverse Learners

To include a child who cannot see objects in the room, whisper directions to the child to hide an object *in* a basket, *under* a chair, *on top of* a shelf, or *inside* a box.

Provide photos or drawings of the different room areas and positional words to help children locate objects and understand the different positions.

Say the positional words in a child's primary language, along with the English words.

Use visual supports that help children understand positional concepts.

Let advanced learners give clues or directions to other children to help them locate an object that is spied.

Going Beyond

Use this as a transitional activity. For example, *I spy with my little eye, something next to the sink, under a rock. Yes, (child's name); the sponge is next to the sink and under the rock. You may choose an interest area to work in."*

Individual	Small Groups	Large Group	Interest Area	Single Day	Multi-Day	Time
●	●	●	All	●		10–15 minutes

I'm Thinking of a Shape

Goal(s) & Objectives

Objectives

22. *Observes objects and events with curiosity*

Other Concepts

- Names three-dimensional shapes and describes their properties
- Defines relationships among shapes by analyzing, comparing, and sorting
- Makes connections among shapes and everyday objects
- Analyzes and organizes data

Materials and Preparation

☐ Geometric solids: rectangular prism and/or cube, cylinder, sphere, cone, and pyramid

☐ Empty containers of different sizes similar in shape to the geometric solids (e.g., cans, oatmeal cartons, spools, cardboard paper towel tubes, assorted boxes, balls, cone cups, party hats)

Guiding Children's Learning

Gather a small group of children and let them examine and explore the geometric solids. Introduce the children to the names of the shapes and discuss their attributes. For example, a rectangular prism and cube are *like a box*, a cylinder is *like a can*, and a sphere is *like a ball*. Invite the children to talk about how the shapes are alike and different. Introduce terms like *points, edges, corners,* or *faces* as appropriate.

Place two (or three) shapes at a time in front of the children. Describe one shape and see if they can guess which one you are describing. Examples are below.

> *The shape I'm thinking of has two ends that are round and flat, and the face is smooth.* (cylinder)

> *This shape has flat faces that are all exactly the same and that have pointed corners.* (cube)

> *I'm thinking of a shape that is smooth and round all over.* (sphere)

> *I'm thinking of a shape that is flat and round on the bottom and pointed on the top. It's face is smooth.* (cone)

> *This shape has a flat, square base (bottom) with a pointed top, and its faces are triangles.* (square pyramid)

Next, display the collection of everyday objects. Continue playing "I'm Thinking of a Shape" and have the children take turns selecting objects of the appropriate shape. Ask them to describe or explain how they made their decisions.

Closing

Challenge children to bring objects from home that have the shapes you discussed. Explain that the shapes, boxes, and other materials will be in the Block Area for them to continue to explore and use in building.

Developmental Progression

Simple	Have children explore three-dimensional shapes to learn their attributes. Introduce children to descriptive terms related to each shape (e.g., *faces, edges, corners, rounded*).
	Offer one or more collections of everyday objects. Have the children match the objects to the appropriate three-dimensional shape.
	Modify "I'm Thinking of a Shape" so that children identify three-dimensional shapes by what they look like (i.e., like a box, ball, or can).
	Have children identify objects in the classroom or another environment having the attributes of a given three-dimensional shape.
Complex	Use "I'm Thinking of a Shape" so that children identify three-dimensional shapes by name.

Meeting the Needs of Diverse Learners

Introduce the three-dimensional shapes one at a time. Give children time to identify or find objects that resemble the shapes.

Introduce the names of geometric solids in an English language learner's primary language.

Have advanced learners create a book that includes drawings or pictures of three-dimensional shapes identified in the environment.

Going Beyond

Give each child a lump of modeling dough or clay and a paper plate. Introduce one of the three-dimensional shapes and talk about its attributes. Then have the children make it with their dough. Offer assistance as needed.

Ask family members to work with children at home to identify and collect everyday objects of a specific shape (e.g., those "like a can"). Set up an area of the classroom where children can share and explore these objects.

Have the children work with a partner or in a small group. Let each child choose one geometric solid; then take the children on a walk around the school, playground, or neighborhood to find objects of the same shape. Take pictures of the objects and use them to make a book. Use a sentence pattern such as (*child's name*) *saw a* (*object*). *It has the shape of a* (*geometric solid*). Let the children come up with a title for the book and sign their names as authors. Share the book at group time and then place it in the Library, Block, or Toys and Games Area.

Give children a collection of everyday objects that are shaped like the geometric solids you have discussed. Have the children sort the materials and then describe their sorting rule.

Use a floor graphing mat with several columns. In the first row of each column, place one of the geometric solids. Have the children place the objects they found in the classroom in the appropriate column. Lead a discussion, using the following questions as a guide:

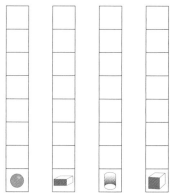

Do you agree with the placement of the objects? Should any be moved?

How are the objects in a column alike? How are they different?

Are the objects in any two columns similar? Which ones? How?

Which shape did we find the most? Which shape did we find the least?

Reinforce the use of the terms *sphere, rectangular prism, cylinder,* and *cube* and continue to talk about the attributes of each.

Set up a ramp in the Block Area. Display a collection of commercial geometric solids and everyday objects and have the children predict which objects will roll (slide) down the ramp and which will not roll (slide) down the ramp. Allow the children to test their predictions. Then sort the objects. Have the children represent what they learned through drawing or graphing.

Display a collection of commercial geometric solids and everyday objects having the same shape. Choose a criterion for sorting the objects (one that will call attention to the attributes of the shapes). Have the children guess the sorting rule, for example, spheres and not spheres; objects that roll and objects that do not roll; objects with points or corners and objects without points or corners.

Individual	Small Groups	Large Group	Interest Area	Single Day	Multi-Day	Time
	●		Blocks	●		10–15 minutes

My Shadow and I

<table>
<tr>
<td>

Goal(s) & Objectives

</td>
<td>

Objectives

22. Observes objects and events with curiosity; 23. Approaches problems flexibly; 24. Shows persistence in approaching tasks; 25. Explores cause and effect; 32. Shows awareness of position in space

Other Concepts

- Describes and names shapes
- Uses comparative words related to size

</td>
</tr>
</table>

Materials and Preparation

☐ Overhead projector or flashlights

☐ Construction paper or colored transparencies

☐ Shape

Use the patterns in the Appendix to cut shapes from construction paper or make shape cards using colored transparency film.

Position the overhead projector on the floor so that the projected shape will be the same size as the children.

Guiding Children's Learning

Lead a discussion about shadows. Take the children outside to explore their shadows or use a flashlight to create shadows on a blank wall. Ask questions such as these:

How do you think shadows are made?

Do you think you can you touch someone's shadow without touching the person?

If someone stepped on your shadow, would it hurt? Why or why not?

How can you make your shadow tall/long? Short?

How or what could you do to make your shadow disappear?

Teach the children how to play "Follow the Leader." Then play "Shadow Follow the Leader." Use directional words as you give instructions about ways for children to move their bodies. For example,

Put your right hand high up in the air.

Bend your body toward the left.

Pat the top of your head.

Make a shadow that bends or curves.

Return to the classroom and invite the children to share what they learned about shadows. Children might say, "You need light to form a shadow... Shadows take the form of an object... You can make a shadow move or change shape."

Review the names of two-dimensional shapes, using the construction paper shapes. Place a paper shape on the projector to create a shape shadow on the wall.

Talk about the shape's characteristics and then have the children suggest ways to use their bodies to outline or fill in the shape shadow. Invite one or more children to try a suggestion while others participate by giving directions about ways in which to move. For example, a child might stand with his legs apart and his hands in a triangle over his head. Another child might form the base of the triangle by lying on the floor between the first child's legs.

Encourage children to experiment and try other ways of making the shapes. Continue as long as they are enjoying the activity. Afterwards, ask,

Which shapes were easy to make?

Which shapes were difficult to make?

Which shapes need two people?

Can anyone make this shape alone?

Closing

Show the children how to work the overhead projector. Tell them that they will be able to use it with the shapes to make shape shadows at choice time.

Developmental Progression

Simple → Complex	
	Have the children make and explore shadows.
	Have the children move their own shadows in response to instructions.
	Have children make basic shadow shapes by using their hands.
	Have children make basic shapes by moving their bodies to fill a shape projected on the wall.
	Have children work with partners to make more complex shadow shapes.

Meeting the Needs of Diverse Learners

Children can make shadows of shapes by using their hands.

Have children work with a partner. One child can suggest a movement, and the other can make it. One child can make a movement, and the other can guess what they are doing to make the shape.

Use pin art or a shallow pan of damp sand to make imprints of children's hands and other objects so that children can better understand the concept of shadow shapes. Children can feel the shapes.

Place the different forms and shapes on a light box, a few at a time. This makes it easier to see the forms of the shapes.

Take pictures of buildings or objects, outdoors or in the classroom. Have advanced learners predict and then draw a picture of what an object's shadow might look like at a particular time of day. Take them outside to check their predictions.

Going Beyond

Gather children together. Ask,

Do you think you can make shape shadows? How?

Using the overhead projector, have children take turns or work together to try making differently shaped shadows. Model or provide assistance when necessary. For example,

Remember, a circle is round and has curved lines. How can you make a circle with two fingers? Your hands? Your arms? Your body? How can you work with a friend to form a circle?

Repeat the process with other shapes.

Individual	Small Groups	Large Group	Interest Area	Single Day	Multi-Day	Time
	●	●	Outdoors, Music and Movement	●	●	15–20 minutes

Straw Shapes

Goal(s) & Objectives

Objectives

22. Observes objects and events with curiosity; 26. Applies knowledge or experience to a new context

Other Concepts

- Identifies basic geometric shapes and their properties
- Describes, classifies, and sorts basic geometric shapes
- Uses comparative words related to size

Materials and Preparation

- ☐ Geometric shapes
- ☐ Drinking straws
- ☐ Pipe cleaners (optional)
- ☐ Sandwich-size baggies
- ☐ Writing materials (math journals or clip boards)

Cut the straws into 3-inch, 5-inch, and 7-inch lengths and place numerous pieces in a baggie. Prepare one baggie for every two children.

Guiding Children's Learning

Lead a discussion about various geometric shapes. Call attention to the attributes of each.

Have the children form pairs. Give each pair a bag of straws. Explain that they are to work together and use the straws to make as many different shapes as they can. Model the activity, thinking aloud as you work. If children have difficulty keeping the shapes together, provide pipe cleaners and demonstrate how to thread them through the straws and connect the ends.

As children work, move about to observe, provide assistance, and ask open-ended questions such as these:

If you took away this straw, would it still be a rectangle? Why or why not?

Can you make a triangle with one really long side?

You made a very large rectangle. How many straws did it take to make it?

After a reasonable time period, stop the work. Demonstrate how the children can document their work by drawing the shapes they made. Then give each pair of children writing materials. Provide assistance as needed.

Closing

Share some of your observations. Invite several of the children to share the results of their work. Have children place the straws back into the bags and place them in the Toys and Games Area or Art Area. Explain that the straws will be available to use at choice time.

Developmental Progression

Simple ▼ **Complex**	Give children a bag of straws and have them explore and experiment with them.
	Have children work with straws of only two lengths and/or have them focus on creating one shape at a time (e.g., square).
	Have children create shapes using three different lengths of straws.
	Have children document their work by gluing the straws on paper or by drawing or writing.

Meeting the Needs of Diverse Learners

If drinking straws are difficult to grasp, use chunkier materials such as paper towel or wrapping paper tubes, or PVC pipes.

Use a light box to manipulate the straws into different shapes. This helps children to see the forms of the shapes.

Translate the names of the shapes into the children's home languages and use them as you interact with children.

Challenge advanced learners to build three-dimensional shapes using straws and modeling clay. (Clay is used as a connector.)

Going Beyond

Have the children focus on one shape at a time, such as the triangle. Remind them that a triangle has three sides and three corners and that the sides can be the same or different lengths.

Rather than recording their work through drawing and writing, provide glue for children to create a model of their work.

Individual	Small Groups	Large Group	Interest Area	Single Day	Multi-Day	Time
	●		Art, Toys and Games	●		15–20 minutes

The Bear Went Over the Mountain

Goal(s) & Objectives	Objectives
	32. *Shows awareness of position in space*
	Other Concepts
	• Uses measurement vocabulary

Materials and Preparation

☐ Prepare an obstacle course outdoors or indoors. Below is a suggested list of objects to use as obstacles.

Box or overturned waste basket – mountain

Sheet or long piece of cloth – river

Table – bridge

Stool – large boulder

Large cardboard box, open on two ends – tunnel

Large plant or barrel – tree

Large cardboard box, placed on side – cave

Familiarize yourself with the song "The Bear Went Over the Mountain." (See the end of this activity.)

Gather photographs of items that might be unfamiliar to the children (e.g., mountain, cave, boulder, or tunnel).

Guiding Children's Learning

Sing the first verse of the song "The Bear Went Over the Mountain." Invite the children to share their ideas about what the bear might see.

Explain to the children that they are going to pretend that they are bears going out for a walk to explore and see what they can find. Tell them to watch carefully because there might be some *obstacles* (things that get in the way) on their journey. Use the photographs to introduce the children to items that might be unfamiliar. Introduce measurement vocabulary as you talk about the size and shape of the items (e.g., *large* boulders, *small* mountains, *long* tunnels, or *deep* river).

Lead the children to the obstacle course. Sing the song or make up a story of your own as you make your way through the course. When you get to each obstacle, pose open-ended questions such as these:

What should we do?

How can we bears get beyond this mountain?

Who can show us how?

Choose a child to demonstrate each action (e.g., going *over* the mountain or *through* the tunnel) then sing the related verse of the song as each child performs the appropriate action.

Closing

Lead a discussion about the imaginary walk. Have children recall what they did each time they encountered an *obstacle*, emphasizing the positional words. Invite the children to name some other things that might have gotten in their way on their adventure and how they might have gotten beyond each.

Developmental Progression

Simple ▼ Complex	Focus on one or two positional words at a time such as *over* and *under,* and have children say the words as they move *over* and *under* a variety of obstacles.
	Add obstacles to the course and introduce new or less familiar positional words to the children. Observe to see who follows instructions and understands the positional words.
	Invite children to give instructions to peers to navigate the obstacle course.

Meeting the Needs of Diverse Learners

Modify the obstacle course or the story so that all children are able to perform the actions.

Have the children work in pairs. One child can give instructions to the other child for navigating the obstacle course or give a stop signal when an obstacle occurs.

Teach positional words in a child's primary language, along with the English words.

Use sign language for children with hearing impairments.

Have advanced learners construct an obstacle course and then draw a representation of it.

Going Beyond

Take the children on a walk around the playground, leading them *through* a gate, *inside* a fenced area, *up* and *down* the slide, and so forth. Emphasize the positional words as you go. Invite children to take turns being the leader.

Share books that highlight positional words and spatial concepts. Have the children reenact stories when appropriate.

The Three Billy Goats Gruff by Paul Galdone

Rosie's Walk by Pat Hutchins

We're Going on a Bear Hunt by Helen Oxenbury

Apollo by Caroline Gregoire

Over, Under, Through by Tana Hoban

Where is the Green Sheep? by Mem Fox

Elephants Aloft by Kathi Appelt

Have children work in pairs or groups of three to build an obstacle course in the Block Area. Let them take turns moving small block figures through the course as one child gives directions. Make note of the positional words the children use.

Individual	Small Groups	Large Group	Interest Area	Single Day	Multi-Day	Time
	●	●	Outdoors	●		20–30 minutes

The Bear Went Over the Mountain
(sung to the tune of "He's a Jolly Good Fellow")

The bear went over the mountain,
The bear went over the mountain,
The bear went over the mountain,
To see what he could see.

And all that he could see,
And all that he could see
Was a cold and raging river,
So what do you think he did?

He walked beside the river,
He walked beside the river,
He walked beside the river,
To see what he could see.

And all that he could see,
And all that he could see
Was an old, rickety bridge,
So what do you think he did?

He walked across the bridge,
He walked across the bridge,
He walked across the bridge,
To see what he could see.

And all that he could see,
And all that he could see
Was a great, big boulder,
So what do you think he did?

He climbed on top of the boulder,
He climbed on top of the boulder,
He climbed on top of the boulder,
To see what he could see.

And all that he could see,
And all that he could see
Was a long, dark tunnel,
So what do you think he did?

He went right through the tunnel,
He went right through the tunnel,
He went right through the tunnel,
To see what he could see.

And all that he could see,
And all that he could see
Was a mighty oak tree
So what do you think he did?

He went around the tree,
He went around the tree,
He went around the tree,
To see what he could see.

And all that he could see,
And all that he could see
Was a cold, dark cave,
So what do you think he did?

He went inside the cave,
He went inside the cave,
He went inside the cave,
To see what he could see.

And all that he could see,
And all that he could see
Was his bear friend sleeping,
So what do you think he did?

He woke his bear friend up,
He woke his bear friend up,
He woke his bear friend up,
And what do you think they did?

They ran outside to play,
They ran outside to play,
They ran outside to play,
Then started their long walk home.

The Farmer Builds a Fence

Goal(s) & Objectives	Objectives 22. *Observes objects and events with curiosity* Other Concepts • Visualizes, describes, and represents geometric shapes • Identifies geometric shapes and their properties • Uses measurement vocabulary

Materials and Preparation

☐ Elastic band with ends attached (about 8 feet)

☐ Two-dimensional shapes (plastic or paper triangle, circle, rectangle, and square)

Guiding Children's Learning

Gather a small group of children. Tell a story about a farmer who likes to build fancy fences for his farm animals. Explain to the children that they will pretend that they are the farmer's helpers and build fences in four different shapes.

Hold up each shape as you name it and then display it for the children to see. Discuss the attributes of each shape. Tell them to listen carefully as you sing "The Farmer Builds a Fence," so they will know the shape of the first fence the farmer wants them to build. To the tune of "The Farmer in the Dell," sing,

> *The farmer builds a fence,*
> *The farmer builds a fence,*
> *Hi-ho the derry-o,*
> *The farmer builds a fence.*
>
> *Make the fence a triangle,*
> *Make the fence a triangle,*
> *Hi-ho the derry-o,*
> *Make the fence a triangle.*

Ask the children to name the shape of the first fence they are to build. Have a child locate the triangle on display. Discuss the characteristics of a triangle and ask the children to suggest ways to make a triangle by using the elastic band.

Have the children stand, holding on to the elastic band to form a triangle. Offer assistance as needed. After they have successfully made the triangular fence, you might sing,

> *You made the fence a triangle*
> *You made the fence a triangle*
> *Hi-ho the derry-o*
> *You made the fence a triangle.*

Challenge children with these questions and prompts:

> *If you make one side of this triangle longer, will it still be a triangle? How do you know?*
>
> *Show me how to make a triangle with one really long side.*
>
> *Can you make a triangle with two long sides?*
>
> *Can you turn your triangle around? Is it still a triangle?*

Repeat the process with other shapes, such as a circle, rectangle, or square. Remind the children that the square is a special kind of rectangle that has four sides that are exactly the same.

Invite the children to suggest other types of fences to make.

Closing

Comment on how well the children worked together to build the farmer's fences in the shapes that he wanted. Explain that the elastic band will be in the Music and Movement Area or Outdoors for them to use.

Developmental Progression

Simple	Give children one of each of the four shapes. Have them listen to "The Farmer Builds a Fence" and then point to the shape named in the song.
	Have the children work together to make the shapes by using an elastic band. Provide assistance by helping them recall the attributes of each shape.
	Have the children move, to make the fences a different size while maintaining the same shape.
Complex	Have children adjust the shape and determine if the name for the shape still applies. For example, make one side of triangle longer but keep the other sides the same as they were originally. Children might also move to make a circle longer (forming an ellipse) or make only one side of a rectangle shorter (forming a trapezoid). Invite children to explain their answers.

| | **Meeting the Needs of Diverse Learners** | Have a child who cannot hold the band securely give instructions for making the shapes to the other children. |

Meeting the Needs of Diverse Learners

Have a child who cannot hold the band securely give instructions for making the shapes to the other children.

If standard geoboards are difficult for some children to handle, offer simplified geoboards.

Have additional shapes ready for children who will benefit from feeling them as you describe them.

Going Beyond

Introduce geoboards to the children. Play alongside them, modeling ways to make different shapes with rubber bands. Talk aloud about the attributes of each shape as you make it. Place the geoboards in the Toys and Games Area for children to explore at choice time.

Encourage the children to draw or construct fences that are different shapes. They may do so during choice time, in the Art and Block Areas.

During the activity, pose a challenge such as this:

Show me how you can make this circle (triangle, rectangle, square) larger (smaller), wider (more narrow), or taller (shorter).

Challenge children to make fences of different sizes, using a given number of blocks of the same size (e.g., using only ten blocks). Offer drawing materials so they can represent the differently shaped fences they make with the same number of blocks.

Individual	Small Groups	Large Group	Interest Area	Single Day	Multi-Day	Time
	●		Music and Movement, Outdoors		●	15–20 minutes

Where's the Beanbag?

Goal(s) & Objectives

Objectives

32. *Shows awareness of position in space;* 34. *Uses numbers and counting*

Other Concepts

- Describes and names relative positions

Materials and Preparation

- ☐ Beanbags
- ☐ Basket or tub
- ☐ Masking tape
- ☐ Chart paper
- ☐ Marker

Place the basket (tub) on the floor. Measure 4 feet from the basket and then make a line on the floor with the masking tape.

Draw a basket or large circle in the middle of the chart paper to represent the basket. Place the poster on the floor to the side of the basket and use it to indicate where a beanbag lands when tossed.

Guiding Children's Learning

Tell the children that they will be playing a beanbag game. Demonstrate how to play as you give these instructions:

Stand behind the line on the floor.

Try to toss the beanbag into the basket.

Tell where the beanbag landed (e.g., inside the basket, behind the basket, beside the basket, etc.)

Draw the children's attention to the chart. Explain that you will use it to show where the beanbag lands each time. Demonstrate by making an X or a tally mark on the chart to represent where the beanbag you tossed landed. Think aloud as you make the mark on the chart (e.g., "I tossed the beanbag behind the basket, so I will make a mark behind the circle on the chart.")

Let the children take turns tossing the beanbags as long as they are interested. Have them tell and show you where you should mark the chart.

Closing

Invite the children to share their thoughts about the activity. Draw their attention to the chart, and talk about the areas in relation to the basket. Count the number of marks on the chart that show how many beanbags landed in each area. Emphasize positional words such as *inside, near, far, behind, in front of, next to* or *beside*.

Tell the children that the beanbags and basket will be available in the Music and Movement Area or outside so children can play "Where's the Beanbag?" as a choice activity. Remind them that paper and pencil are available in interest areas to record their tosses.

Developmental Progression

Simple ↓ **Complex**	Have children toss the beanbag and tell if it lands *inside* or *outside* the basket.
	Introduce a simple tally sheet. Record a tally mark to indicate whether the bag landed *inside* or *outside* the basket. Count the tally marks for each position and have the children tell whether more beanbags landed *inside* the basket or *outside* the basket.
	Introduce more positional words or introduce positional words that are less familiar to children (e.g., *in front of, behind, near, far, beneath, beyond, left, right*). Have children use them to tell where the beanbag is in relation to the basket. Make a mark on a chart to show where each beanbag lands.
	Give children their own record sheets to mark where the beanbags land when they are tossed.

Meeting the Needs of Diverse Learners

Pair a child who has difficulty tossing the beanbag with a child who does not have difficulty. Have him tell where the beanbag lands or have him give instructions to the other child.

For a child who cannot see the basket, place a beeping ball or other sound maker in the basket to help the child know where to toss the beanbag.

Use photos or line drawings to help children understand positional words when you talk about the chart.

Teach positional words in a child's home language, along with the English words.

Going Beyond

Give each child a paper with a basket or a circle drawn in the middle of it. Have them make marks on their papers to indicate where each beanbag lands after it is tossed. At the end of the game, have the children count the marks and tell where the most and fewest beanbags landed.

Have the children toss the beanbags in a variety of ways:

- above their heads
- below a bar
- between their (or a friend's) legs
- behind their backs
- backwards
- through a hoop
- underneath a table
- beyond a designated spot

Offer children standard and nonstandard measuring tools (e.g., chain links) to measure the distance from a beanbag to the basket or target. Introduce or reinforce words such as *near, far, farther, close, closer,* and *closest.*

Offer children a variety of things to toss, such as pompoms, balls, or sock balls. Have them compare their experience with tossing beanbags. Ask questions such as these:

What do you think will happen when you toss the ball (pompom, sock ball)?

Will you need to throw it harder or more softly to get it in the basket?

Individual	Small Groups	Large Group	Interest Area	Single Day	Multi-Day	Time
	●	●	Music and Movement, Outdoors	●		20–30 minutes

Balancing Act

Goal(s) & Objectives

Objectives

28. *Compares and Measures*

Other Concepts

- Uses measurement vocabulary related to weight
- Understands that weight and size are different attributes (e.g., small objects may weigh more than large objects)
- Understands the concept of equal (same) weight

Materials and Preparation

☐ Plastic bags that zip (e.g., sandwich, quart, or gallon)

☐ Various fill materials (e.g., sand, cornstarch, marbles, potting soil, coins, counters, cotton balls, feathers, Styrofoam® peanuts, nuts and bolts)

☐ Balance scale

Use two bags of the same size and put different amounts of a single material into each bag (e.g., 1/4 full, 1/2 full, completely full). Make sure that there is an obvious difference in the weights of the bags. Secure the openings with sturdy tape if necessary. Repeat the process using other fill materials, but be mindful that the bags of feathers and Styrofoam® peanuts will vary little in weight regardless of how full they are.

Note: A material will weigh more when the quantity of the *same* material is larger (e.g., one cup of sand will weigh more than ½ cup of sand.) However, relative weight cannot always be determined by visually comparing the volume of *different* materials (e.g., a bag full of feathers will not weigh the same as a bag full of sand; a bag with a small volume of sand might weigh more than a bag with a large volume of feathers).

Guiding Children's Learning

Display two of the bags containing one of the heavier materials such as sand. Have a child examine each bag and tell how they are different. Observations might include that one has *more* or *less* than another. Introduce the terms *heavy/heavier* and *light/lighter*. Pass the bags around so that each child can feel the difference in weight. Explain that *weight* is the way you measure or tell how heavy something is.

Introduce the other fill materials one at a time. Ask,

Which bag do you think is heavier (lighter)? What makes you think so? How can you find out?

Is the bag that is most (least) full heavier (lighter)? Why do you think that is so?

After all the materials are introduced, display two bags having different materials. The bags should contain approximately the same volume of material but vary in weight (e.g., a full bag of feathers and a full bag of potting soil). Lead a discussion, using these questions as a guide:

Do you think these bags are heavy or light? Why do you think so?

Do you think one of these bags is heavier (lighter) than the other? Why? Which bag is heavier (lighter)?

If the bag is completely full, does that mean it will be heavy?

Continue having the children compare materials of different volumes and weights. Have the children make and check their predictions about the weights of the materials. Ask,

Can you think of any other ways to compare the weight of things?

Introduce the balance scale. Have the children choose two bags of the materials they have been exploring. Ask them to tell what they think will happen when the bags are placed on both ends of the scale. Let the children test their predictions and share their observations. Explain that the object that makes the arm of the scale go down weighs more, or is heavier, while the other object weighs less, or is lighter.

Continue to let the children explore the balance scale. Reinforce the terms *heavier* and *lighter*, and introduce the terms *level, balanced, equal,* and *flat* to describe what happens to the scale when things are the same weight.

Closing

Review these points with the children:

- *Weight* tells how heavy something is.

- An object that weighs more than another object is said to be *heavier.*

- An object that weighs less than another object is said to be *lighter.*

- When two objects weigh the same, they are said to be *equal.*

- When two objects of equal weight are placed on a scale, the scale is *level* or *balanced.*

Tell the children that the balance scale will be in the Discovery Area along with different things to weigh and compare.

Developmental Progression

Simple ↓ **Complex**	Have children hold and compare two different volumes of a single material, to determine which is heavier or lighter.
	Have children hold and compare similar volumes of two different materials, to determine if one is heavier, lighter, or the same in weight.
	Have children hold and compare the same volume of three different materials and place them in order from lightest to heaviest.
	Have children use a simple balance scale to compare the weights of the same volume of two materials.

Meeting the Needs of Diverse Learners

Have children who learn by moving act as the balance scale, using outstretched arms. Ask them to predict which of two items is heavier before placing them in their hands. (This is a great activity for helping all children learn to compare weights.)

Offer very heavy and very light objects, so it will be very easy for children to tell the difference.

Introduce the words *heavy* and *light* in the children's home languages (e.g., *ligero* [*light*] and *pesado* [*heavy*]).

Use hand gestures to show the meaning of new words.

Prepare a third bag of each fill material. Then have children place the bags in order from lightest to heaviest, if you think they are ready for the challenge.

Going Beyond

Provide a variety of materials for the children to use with the balance scale. When one object is heavier (lighter) than another, ask the children to suggest ways to level, or balance, the scale. Let them test their suggestions.

Place an assortment of items in the Discovery and Toys and Games Areas. Let the children weigh them and then place them in order according to weight.

Have the children explore weight and volume by using a variety of substances and the balance scale. For example, put salt on one side of the scale. Then have children try to balance the scale using another substance, such as cornstarch. When the scale is balanced, measure the two substances to see whether there is more, less, or the same volume of each. Another idea is for children to place equal volumes of two substances on each end of the scale, to see if it balances.

Duplicate the balance scale patterns in the Appendix. Place them in the Discovery and/or the Toys and Games Areas along with stickers, a balance scale, and counters. Have children place different numbers of counters on each side of the scale to see the effects. Then show children how to use the stickers to represent their discoveries. For example, if two counters are placed on the left arm of the scale and one counter on the right arm of the scale, the scale would tilt to the left, meaning that two counters weigh more than one. To document this, place two stickers on the drawing of the scale with the left arm tilted downward and one sticker on the right arm.

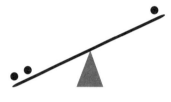

Use objects of different sizes and weights for children who need a greater challenge. For example,

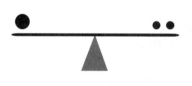

Individual	Small Groups	Large Group	Interest Area	Single Day	Multi-Day	Time
•	•		Discovery, Toys and Games	•		20 minutes

Cover Up

Goal(s) & Objectives	Objectives
	28. *Compares and measures*

Objectives

28. *Compares and measures*

Other Concepts

- Learns and uses measurement language related to area
- Explores the concept of area
- Understands more/fewer or less

Materials and Preparation

☐ Masking tape

☐ Pictures of various floor coverings

☐ Floor covering samples, such as carpet squares, tiles, or wooden products (blocks may also be used)

Use the masking tape to mark off a section of the Block Area or Dramatic Play Area.

Guiding Children's Learning

Explain that, when a building is made, its floor is usually covered with carpet, wood, or tile. Point out the floor coverings in the classroom and invite the children to talk about the types of floor coverings they have in their homes. Show them the pictures of floor coverings you have collected. Discuss any patterns in the tiles or the ways in which the floor coverings are laid.

Explain that they are going to pretend that they are covering a floor that is designated by the masking tape. Show them the various floor coverings that they may use. Ask,

> *Do you think it will take more carpet squares or tiles to cover the area? Why do you think that? How can you find out?*

> *How many tiles (blocks, carpet squares, wooden planks) do you think it will take to cover this space, or area?*

Record the children's predictions.

Let the children select one of the materials to cover the defined area. Refer back to their predictions and then ask,

> *Did it take you more or fewer tiles than you predicted to cover the area? Why do you think that was?*

How big of an area could you cover if you used only the number of tiles you predicted? Tell me why you think that. How could you test your prediction?

If the area were smaller (larger), would it take more or fewer tiles to cover it? Why?

How could we represent, or show others, what we have learned?

If time permits and the children are interested, let them repeat the measuring process using another material. Again, record their ideas. Afterwards, ask,

Why do you think it took more (fewer) tiles than carpet squares to cover this area?

What do you think would happen if you used smaller blocks to cover this area? Would you use more, fewer, or the same number of blocks? What makes you think so?

Closing

Have the children suggest other materials to use to cover or measure the floor area. Encourage them to continue to experiment on their own at choice time. Remind the children that drawing and writing materials are available for them to record their findings.

Developmental Progression

Simple	Have children explore and experiment with the carpet squares, tiles, and other floor coverings to compare the materials.
	Have children compare materials to determine which single unit has the greater area (e.g., 4-inch, 8-inch, and 12-inch tiles).
	Have children cover an area by placing a material, such as tiles, adjacent to each other.
	Have children estimate the number of units of a floor covering (e.g., carpet squares) it would take to cover a defined area. Let them test their estimations. Repeat the process using different coverings.
Complex	Pose problems that encourage children to think about measuring area. For example, ask, *If you want to cover this area with tiles, how will you figure out how many you will need? Show me.*

Meeting the Needs of Diverse Learners

Provide a tray or table surface on which to arrange similar shapes for children who have difficulty moving the squares around the floor.

Have children work in pairs, with one child making the prediction and another child testing the prediction.

Going Beyond

Cut construction paper or poster board in a variety of shapes and/or sizes. Challenge the children to find out which shape or size takes the most unit blocks to cover and which shape or size takes the least.

Give children a defined area (e.g., 1/2 sheet of construction paper or a piece of cardboard) and two sizes of blocks. Have the children predict which blocks they will use more of (fewer of) to cover the area. Ask them to explain their reasoning. Then have them check their answers by covering the area with each set of blocks and counting the blocks.

Cut construction paper in a variety of sizes. Let each child explore to see how many 1-inch tiles or blocks it will take to cover each paper. Have them describe their discoveries.

Give children half a sheet of paper and a variety of pattern blocks. Challenge them to cover the area completely with the blocks. Invite them to share their observations and strategies for solving any problems.

Have children predict how many canned goods or cereal boxes would fit on a shelf in the Dramatic Play Area. Have them test their predictions.

Offer other experiences, such as covering a table with sheets of art paper and with index cards, a sheet of paper with two differently sized Post-its®, the floor of a wagon with large blocks and LEGO®, and a shoebox with adult shoes and baby shoes.

Individual	Small Groups	Large Group	Interest Area	Single Day	Multi-Day	Time
	●		Blocks, Dramatic Play	●		20–25 minutes

Morning, Noon, and Night

Goal(s) & Objectives

Objectives

31. Shows awareness of time concepts and sequence

Other Concepts

- Uses measurement vocabulary related to time and sequence
- Notices patterns in daily routines

Materials and Preparation

- ☐ *Jesse Bear, What Will You Wear?* by Nancy White Carlstrom
- ☐ Magazines, newspapers, catalogs, advertisements
- ☐ Chart paper or poster board
- ☐ Markers
- ☐ Scissors
- ☐ Glue sticks

Make a chart with three columns. Label column one *Morning*, column two *Noon*, and column three *Night*. Pictures may be added to the labels (e.g., partial sun for morning, full sun for noon, and moon and stars for night).

Cut several magazine pictures that show activities children and family members might do during each period of the day.

Guiding Children's Learning

Read the story *Jesse Bear, What Will You Wear?* Lead a brief discussion.

What kinds of things did Jesse do in the morning?...at noon?...at night?

In what ways are your days similar to Jesse's day?

How are your days different?

Next, give each child a magazine. Have the children look through the magazine to find one or two pictures of activities that occur during the morning, at noon, and/or at night. Show and discuss the sample pictures.

Give each child a pair of scissors to cut out their pictures. Provide assistance with cutting as needed.

After the children have completed their task, collect the magazines and scissors. Review the chart headings. Use the glue stick to demonstrate how to place the sample pictures in the appropriate columns. Next, have the children take turns showing their pictures and telling during which time of day the activity most likely occurs. Let the children glue their pictures in the appropriate columns on the chart.

When finished, summarize the activity with comments and questions such as these:

These are the things you do first, in the morning, or at the beginning of your day.

Second are the things you do at noon, or in the middle part of the day.

Third are the things you do at night, or the last part of the day.

Setsuko, what did you put in the first column?...in the second column?...in the third column?

Who can point to a picture that shows one of the last things you do during the day, at night?

Closing

Talk about the sequence of the school day. Refer to the daily schedule and explain how it is used to tell what will happen first, second, third, and so forth during the school day. Again, use terms like *beginning, middle*, and *end*; *first* and *last*; *first, second*, and *third*.

Developmental Progression

Simple ▼ Complex	
	Focus on only one period of the day (e.g., morning, noon, or night). Have children find pictures of events that happen during that period.
	Focus on two periods of the day (e.g., day and night.)
	Have the children place three pictures depicting particular events of the day in sequential order. For example, in the morning children might enter the classroom, put their belongings away, and then join circle time; around noon children wash hands, serve and eat lunch, and then put dishes away; at night, children might bathe, put on pajamas, and then go to bed.

Meeting the Needs of Diverse Learners

Include cultural activities of the children's families. For example, some may play special games, sing particular songs, or have favorite foods.

Children may have routines that are different from other children's. Be sure to have pictures available (for example, putting in hearing aids or removing supports) that enable all children fully to participate in the activity.

For children who have trouble cutting, place pre-cut pictures in a photo album, one on each cardboard page. Add foam pieces to separate each page, thereby making it easier to turn them. Give the child Post-its® to mark the pages he wants to use for the chart.

Children can work in pairs to look through the magazines. Give each child a separate color of Post-its® to mark individual selections. Loop scissors can make cutting possible for some children. Be sure to rip the page out first.

For children who are unable to identify pictures in magazines, ask them what they do when they get up, after lunch, and before bed. Write their answers down to use during the activity. This will help them to understand time concepts.

Advanced learners may be interested in telling time. If so, provide clocks or timers and let them time how long they or the class participates in a specific activity (e.g., at the computer, at circle time, or outdoors).

Going Beyond

Give each child a blank chart like the one used in the activity and a collection of pictures. Have them glue the pictures in the correct section on the basis of their own experiences.

Read other stories that are related to time or the sequence of events during the day or week. For example,

Rise and Shine, Mariko-chan! by Chiyoko Tomioka

Today Is Monday by Eric Carle

The Best Time of the Day by Eileen Spinelli

On Monday When It Rained by Cherryl Kachenmeister

One Monday Morning by Uri Shulevitz

Today I Feel Silly by Jamie Lee Curtis

The Grouchy Ladybug by Eric Carle

It's About Time, Jesse Bear by Nancy White Carlstrom

Now It's Morning by Candace Whitman

Display a blank calendar. At the end of each day, have the children tell about one important event of the day. Record it on the calendar. You can also use the blank calendar to record upcoming activities or events, such as a trip to the pizza restaurant or Grandparent's Day. Review the calendar with the children. Use terms like *yesterday*, *tomorrow*, *last week*, and *next week*.

Use a digital camera to take pictures of the children participating in activities and daily routines. Print one picture on each page and then have the children sort the pictures by time of day (e.g., early morning, lunch time, afternoon) or put them in the sequence in which they occurred. Let the children tell about what is happening in each picture while you take dictation or provide a sentence pattern such as "In the morning, we...," "Around lunch, we...," or "In the afternoon, we...." Combine the pages to form a book and then read it at group time. Place the book in the Library Area for the children to read at choice time.

Prior to the activity, draw a poster-size picture of a house to represent the children's homes and another picture to represent your school. Laminate the pictures.

Follow these procedures:

- Gather the children and ask a question such as "In the morning, do you eat breakfast at home or at school?"

- Have the children keep their answers to themselves or turn to their neighbors and whisper their answers.

- Show the children the pictures, explaining what each represents. Place them on the floor in separate areas of the classroom.

- Have the children who eat breakfast at home form a group by the house, and have the children who eat breakfast at school form a group by the school.

- Ask, "Which group has more people?" When children indicate the answer by pointing to the group, ask, "How do you know that group has more people? How could we check, or make sure?" Try the children's suggestions.

- Have the children in each group form a line (beginning at the same point) so that they are standing across from a child in the other group. Ask again, "Which group has more? How do you know?"

- Have the children shake hands with the person standing opposite them. Then ask, "How many people do not have a hand to shake? What does that mean? Are there more people who eat breakfast at home or more who eat breakfast at school? How many more?"

Individual	Small Groups	Large Group	Interest Area	Single Day	Multi-Day	Time
	●		Library, Dramatic Play, Art	●		20 minutes

The Long and Short of It

Goal(s) & Objectives

Objectives

28. Compares and measures; 29. Arranges objects in a series

Other Concepts

- Develops an understanding that the length of an object does not change when the position or shape of the object changes (conservation)
- Notices the similarities and differences of objects

Materials and Preparation

☐ Pieces of ribbon (or yarn) of the same width

Cut the ribbon into pieces that are noticeably different in length. Also cut a few that are the same in length.

Guiding Children's Learning

Have a small group of children sit in a circle. Pass the container of ribbon around the circle and have each child to select a piece. Ask them to lay their ribbons on the floor in front of them.

Have two children with ribbons of noticeably different lengths place their ribbons in the center of the circle for all to see. Ask the children to tell how the ribbons are alike and different. Their comments might be related to the color, pattern, texture, or size of the ribbons. During the discussion, use the words *short-shorter* and *long-longer*. Introduce the word *length* and explain that length is a way to measure or tell how long something is. Ask,

How could you find out which piece of ribbon is longer than the other?

Allow the children to demonstrate and explain their reasoning. Next, show them how to line one end of each ribbon up evenly. Explain that the ribbon extending farther than the other ribbon is said to be *longer*.

Continue inviting children to compare their ribbons, two by two, until everyone in the group has had a turn. Allow the children to compare their ribbons with others in the group. Use questions and comments such as these:

Sonya's ribbon is the same length as Dallas's ribbon.

Leo, can you find someone who has a ribbon shorter than yours?

Your two ribbons are equal, or the same, in length.

Derrek's ribbon is as long as Tasheen's ribbon but shorter than Crystal's ribbon.

Next, change the position of the ribbons by lining them up at the opposite ends or by holding them so that one end of each ribbon touches the floor. Then ask this question:

If I move the ribbon or change its position, does the length of the ribbon change?

Children's comments may include words such as *smaller, bigger, shorter,* or *taller.* Explain that the words to describe the positions change, but the length does not change. Introduce the word *height* and explain that height is a way to tell how tall something is.

Have the children compare their ribbons to various objects in the classroom. Pose problems by asking,

I wonder if your ribbon is longer than the ramp in the Block Area. How could you find out?

Can you find something that is shorter (longer or taller) than your ribbon?

Closing

Explain to the children that the ribbons will be available to use at choice time. Encourage them to use the ribbons to measure the length of other things in the classroom.

Help the children make the transition to the next activity by dismissing the child with the longest ribbon, the shortest, etc.

Developmental Progression

Simple ▼ Complex	
	Have children describe the attributes of the ribbons.
	Have children compare two ribbons and describe one as longer than, taller than, or shorter than the other.
	Have children compare three ribbons and place them in order from shortest to longest or tallest.
	Have children arrange a group (more than three) of ribbons in order from shortest to longest or tallest.

Meeting the Needs of Diverse Learners

Provide wider, heavier ribbons (e.g., 1-inch grosgrain) in contrasting colors to make them easier to see and use.

Give a child in a wheelchair some ribbons to use on the tray. Use a strip of double-faced tape to hold one end of each ribbon in place for measuring.

Use pictures, sign language and other body language to indicate the meaning of *long*, *tall*, and *short*.

Introduce measurement vocabulary in the children's home languages (e.g., in Spanish, *largo* for *long* and *corto* or *bajo* for *short*). Use sign language for children with hearing impairments.

Going Beyond

Repeat the activity using other objects such as straws, dowels, yarn, PVC pipes, or paper tubes.

After the children easily describe the relationship between two objects, introduce a third object of a different length. Have the children determine where it fits in relation to other two.

As a group, have the children place all of their ribbons in order from shortest to longest.

Have children compare and sort the ribbons according to another attribute, such as texture or pattern. Invite them to represent their learning by writing, drawing, graphing, or some other means.

Group the students by pairs. Have them take turns lying on the floor and measuring each other with yarn. Cut the yarn to be the length of each child. Use a marker and masking tape to attach the child's name or attach a small photograph of the child to the yarn. Compare the heights of each pair of children by having them stand next to each other and by having them compare their yarn pieces. Attach the yarn to the classroom wall or hallway. Remind the children that each piece of yarn must touch the floor, just as everyone's feet touch the floor. Invite the children to dictate sentences telling who is shorter or taller. (If you have a child who is unusually short or tall, you may choose not to do this activity.)

Repeat the activity several months later and have the children compare their first measurements. Record their observations.

If appropriate, have the children place all of the ribbons in order from shortest to tallest.

Give each child an envelope with straws of varying lengths. Have the child put them in order by length. Next, give each child a paper plate and a lump of clay. Have the child roll the clay into the shape of a snake. Ask each child to place the straws in the clay in length order. Use the words *height, tall, taller,* and *tallest*. This activity will help children understand that, when the spatial orientation or position of an object changes, the positional words change but the measurement remains the same.

Individual	Small Groups	Large Group	Interest Area	Single Day	Multi-Day	Time
	●		Toys and Games, Dramatic Play	●		20 minutes

The Queen's New Bed

Goal(s) & Objectives	Objectives 28. *Compares and measures* Other Concepts • Uses numbers and counting

Materials and Preparation

☐ *How Big Is a Foot?* by Rolf Myller

☐ Construction paper

☐ Foot patterns

Use the patterns in the Appendix to cut at least nine large feet and nine small feet out of heavy construction paper. Laminate them for durability.

Familiarize yourself with the story *How Big is a Foot?* so that you can tell the story in your own words.

Guiding Children's Learning

Gather a small group of children. Then tell the story *How Big Is a Foot?*, using the foot story props as you go. Remember to introduce any new vocabulary such as *carpente*r, *apprentice*, *Prime Minister*. Ask questions such as these:

> *How will the king figure out how big to make the bed? What would you do?*
>
> *What happened when the queen lay down in the bed?*
>
> *Why do you think the bed was too small for the queen?*
>
> *What should the apprentice do? How do you think he can solve this problem?*
>
> *How did the story end?*

Have the children take turns measuring items in the classroom (e.g., table, shelf, block, sink, or book) by using the foot shapes. Pose problems such as these:

> *If you measured the length of the shelf using the apprentice's foot, how many do you think it would take? Show me how you would find out.*
>
> *How many feet long will the shelf be if you measure it with the king's foot? Did it take more or fewer than the apprentice's feet? Why?*

Find something that is as long as three of the apprentice's feet. Now find something that is as long as three of the king's feet. How are the items different?

Of the things you measured with the apprentice's foot, which is the shortest (longest)?

If you wanted to measure something really, really long, would you use the king's foot or the apprentice's foot? Why?

Record children's findings on chart paper. Invite them to share their observations.

Closing

Encourage the children to continue measuring things indoors and outdoors by using the foot patterns.

Developmental Progression

Simple → Complex	
	Have children compare the lengths of two objects and say which is longer and which is shorter.
	Have children compare lengths of more than two objects and say which is longest and which is shortest.
	Have children locate an object that is longer than/shorter than a given nonstandard unit (e.g., an object the same length or longer than the king's foot.)
	Have children compare lengths of objects using equal, nonstandard units (e.g., tell which is longer: an object that is as long as three of the apprentice's feet or six of the apprentice's feet.)
	Have children measure objects to determine length, placing duplicates of a nonstandard unit end to end.
	Have children estimate the length of an object with a nonstandard unit. Let them test their estimations. Repeat the process using different units.
	Have children use a 1-foot (12-inch) ruler to determine whether objects are larger than or smaller than a foot.

Meeting the Needs of Diverse Learners

Cut the footprint out of textured paper or glue a strip of sandpaper from toe to heel for children to feel how long a foot is.

To make measuring easier, use three-dimensional objects such as a 12-inch dowel or music/rain stick. Provide a secure starting point when measuring any object.

Translate the words *long* and *short* into the child's home language and use them as necessary.

Use sign language for children with hearing impairments.

Going Beyond

Have children measure items using other body parts, such as their hands. Ask them to measure objects by using the length of their hands (fingertip to wrist) and the width of their hands. Invite them to share their observations.

Have children use yarn, paper clip chains, or interlocking links to find the length of their arms. Then ask them to measure items to find out how many arm's lengths an object is.

Read the story *Inch by Inch* by Leo Lionni. Cut green yarn or ribbon to represent worms. Let the children use them to measure various items. Commercial models of inchworms can be used as well.

Place foot patterns in interest areas so children can measure things at choice time. Make sure writing and drawing materials are available for them to record their findings.

Individual	Small Groups	Large Group	Interest Area	Single Day	Multi-Day	Time
	●	●	All		●	15–20 minutes

Wash Day

Goal(s) & Objectives	Objectives
	28. *Compares and measures;* 29. *Arranges objects in a series*
	Other Concepts
	• Sorts and classifies

Materials and Preparation

☐ *Mrs. McNosh Hangs Up Her Wash* by Sarah Weeks

☐ Collection of socks in varying lengths

☐ Clothesline

☐ Clothespins

Hang the clothesline.

Guiding Children's Learning

Read the story *Mrs. McNosh Hangs Up Her Wash*. Lead a brief discussion.

What can you tell me about Mrs. McNosh?

Who can tell about a time when you helped with laundry?

Why do you think Mrs. McNosh hung her clothes and everything else outside?

Do you think Mrs. McNosh needs help? Why?

Next, spread out the collection of socks so that the children can see them easily. Lead a discussion about the similarities and differences among the socks. Talk about different ways the socks could be sorted and organized.

Point the clothesline out to the children and explain that they are going to pretend to be Mrs. McNosh's helpers. Explain that Mrs. McNosh has given instructions to hang the socks on the clothesline in order from shortest to longest. Demonstrate how to work the clothespins to hang a sock. Invite the children to take turns hanging the rest of the socks. Ask,

Which is the shortest sock? Who do you think wore that sock? Why do you think that?

Which sock do you think should go next? How do you know?

Is that sock shorter or longer than the last one on the clothesline? Where should you hang it?

Did we follow Mrs. McNosh's instructions? Are the socks arranged from the shortest to the longest? How can you tell?

Closing

Tell the children that you will place the clothesline, clothespins, and socks in the Dramatic Play Area, where they may pretend to hang the wash.

Invite the children to name and bring other pieces of clothing to use on wash day.

Developmental Progression

Simple ⟶ Complex	
Simple	Hang two socks on the clothesline. Ask which is longer or shorter.
	Hang two socks of different lengths on the clothesline. Give children a sock of another length and have them place it in the appropriate place so that the socks are ordered from shortest to longest.
	Make several collections of socks, each with three distinct lengths. Have the children order each collection from shortest to longest.
Complex	Have children hang collections of more than three socks in order from shortest to longest.

Meeting the Needs of Diverse Learners

Use photos, drawings, gestures and other body language to indicate the meaning of long/longer/longest, tall/taller/tallest, short/shorter/shortest and so forth.

Introduce measurement vocabulary in the children's primary language (e.g., in Spanish, *largo* for *long* and *corto* or *bajo* for *short*).

Use sign language for children with hearing impairments.

Offer other ways for children to hang the socks. For example, have the children fasten the socks onto a strip of Velcro® on a chalkboard tray.

Working in pairs, one child can describe where the next sock should go while the other fastens it.

Children can hold two socks in one hand and identify the longer/shorter one.

Going Beyond

Repeat the activity, using other articles of clothing such as shirts, shorts, skirts, pants, hats, or scarves. Ask, *What did you have to do first? Next? Then what?*

Fill a laundry basket with clothing that children can sort by type and size or arrange in order from largest to smallest.

Give the children other collections. Have them figure out a way in which to order the objects. For example, they might choose softest to hardest, holds most to holds least, lightest to darkest, shortest to tallest, youngest to oldest, smallest to largest, smoothest to roughest, slowest to fastest, or heaviest to lightest.

Give children an object such as a block. Have them search for two other objects, one that is larger than the first item and one that is smaller. Have them arrange their group of objects in order and describe their arrangement (e.g., largest to smallest or smallest to largest.)

Individual	Small Groups	Large Group	Interest Area	Single Day	Multi-Day	Time
	●	●	Dramatic Play, Library	●		20 minutes

Which Holds More?

Goal(s) & Objectives

Objectives

28. *Compares and measures*

Other Concepts

- Explores capacity
- Uses measurement vocabulary related to capacity
- Uses numbers and counting
- Describes data

Materials and Preparation

☐ Sand table or tubs of sand

☐ Various sizes of clean, clear plastic containers with smooth edges (e.g., ketchup bottle, peanut butter or mayonnaise jar, juice bottle, water bottle, boxes)

☐ A common container (e.g., a paper cup, a measuring cup, a can)

☐ Funnel

☐ Writing materials

Before this activity, allow time for children independently to explore and experiment with the materials in the Sand and Water Area during choice time. Observe the children to see if they are making comparisons related to capacity (how much something holds).

Guiding Children's Learning

Lead a discussion about the containers in the sand table. Discuss their size and shape (e.g., *slender*, *wide-mouthed*, *long-necked*) and what they might have contained. Ask,

> *Which container do you think will hold the most sand? Why do you think so?*

> *How could you find out which container will hold more?*

Let the children test their predictions. Introduce the funnel when appropriate. Use words such as *more*, *less*, *too much*, *too little*, and *same*.

Next, show the cup (can) and one of the containers the children thought would hold the most sand. Pose the following problem:

> *I want to fill this large container with sand, but I only have one cup. How many cupfuls of sand do you think it will take to fill it?*

Record the children's predictions on paper. Then let them take turns filling the cup and pouring the sand into the container. Make a tally mark to represent each cup of sand poured into the container. Ask,

What does our chart tell you?

Did it take more (fewer) cups than you predicted to fill the container? How do you know? How can we find out?

Repeat the process with one of the other containers the children thought would hold the most sand. Invite them to share their observations and conclusions.

Closing

Encourage the children to continue to explore and experiment with the containers and sand during choice time. Show them how to record their observations by using the writing materials in the area.

Invite the children to bring other containers from home to use in their explorations.

Developmental Progression

Simple ↓ **Complex**	Provide a variety of containers in the Sand and Water Area so that children can explore concepts related to capacity.
	Have children make comparisons related to capacity (which holds more or less), using a small selection of containers (1–3).
	Have children make comparisons related to capacity (which holds more or less), using a larger variety of containers.
	Have children measure the capacity of various containers by using a nonstandard unit (e.g., caps, cans, spoons, margarine tubs, scoops, or shovels).
	Have children estimate and measure the capacity of various containers by using standard units (e.g., cup, pint, gallon).
	Have children measure the capacity of two or more containers using a standard unit. Have them tell which holds more or less.

Meeting the Needs of Diverse Learners

Introduce words related to capacity in the children's primary language.

Use sign language as you say the words for children with hearing impairments.

Have children work in pairs or small groups to make comparisons related to capacity. Make sure to identify a role for each child.

Children who cannot see the level of sand or water in a container can feel when the container is full with their hands. Use words to describe the various levels.

Use pictures of cups on the chart instead of tally marks, to help children better understand the tallying process.

Going Beyond

Provide other materials for the children to explore capacity, such as sawdust, potting soil, birdseed, pea gravel, aquarium gravel, or Styrofoam® peanuts. Pose questions such as these:

Do you think it will take more cups of birdseed or sand to fill this jar? Why do you think that? How can you find out? How many more (fewer) cups did it take?

Vary the types of containers used (e.g., short and wide; tall and slender).

Individual	Small Groups	Large Group	Interest Area	Single Day	Multi-Day	Time
●	●		Sand and Water	●		15–20 minutes

Action Patterns

Goal(s) & Objectives	Objectives
	30. *Recognizes patterns and can repeat them*

Materials and Preparation

☐ Action cards

☐ Pocket chart

Use the action card master in the Appendix to create action cards on card stock. Laminate them for durability.

Hang the pocket chart at the children's eye level.

Guiding Children's Learning

Explain to the children that they will move their bodies to create patterns. Act out a simple pattern, such as *clap, stamp, raise arms up; clap, stamp, raise arms up;* and so on. Invite the children to join in whenever they like. Have the children suggest and perform other action patterns.

Introduce the action cards. Explain that each card illustrates a movement (for example, clapping, pointing to nose, patting head, or touching knees). Select the cards that illustrate one of the movement patterns you performed. Insert them into the pocket chart, sequencing them from left to right. Name each illustrated action as you insert the card into the chart. Then read the entire pattern several times, sweeping your fingers under each card as you read. For example, read *clap, stamp, raise arms up; clap, stamp, raise arms up* while pointing to the related cards.

Next, have the children act out the pattern as you point to and name each action. Use positive comments to describe the way the children listened, read, and performed the pattern.

Invite a child to choose other action cards to create a pattern. Then have the rest of the children act the pattern out. Continue as long as the children are interested and engaged.

Closing

Explain that patterns are all around, for example, on clothes, buildings, and walls; in artwork and jewelry; and in dances and music. Tell the children that the action cards and the pocket chart will be in the Music and Movement Area so they can create their own action patterns at choice time.

Developmental Progression

Simple ↓ Complex	Perform a simple action pattern. Have the children identify or describe the actions.
	Perform a simple action pattern and invite the children to join in.
	Use the action cards to illustrate the pattern you created. Have the children read the pattern as you point to each card. Then have them perform the pattern as you point to each card and name the action aloud.
	Let children take turns choosing action cards to create a simple pattern. Lead the children in acting it out.
	Let children take turns choosing action cards to create a simple pattern. Have each child lead the rest of the children in acting it out as the pattern develops.
	Have the children identify, copy, or create new and perhaps more complex patterns using actions. Ask children to describe or represent the patterns using the action cards.

Meeting the Needs of Diverse Learners

Adapt movements so that all children can participate, e.g., raising hands instead of standing.

Have advanced learners translate patterns they created in interest areas into words and actions. For example, a pattern made from alternating red and blue sponge prints could be translated as *snap, stamp, snap, stamp*. Let them choose the corresponding action cards, place them in the pocket chart, and then read the pattern aloud.

Going Beyond

Create your own action cards by taking photographs of children performing particular actions (for example, jumping, squatting, stamping). Use them to create patterns that the children can read and perform.

Sing songs that use patterns and involve children physically. Examples include these songs:

"Head, Shoulders, Knees, and Toes"

"Hokey Pokey"

"Did You Ever See a Lassie?"

Create action patterns that call attention to positional words such as *step right, step left, turn around; step right, step left, turn around;* and so on.

Individual	Small Groups	Large Group	Interest Area	Single Day	Multi-Day	Time
	●	●	Music and Movement, Outdoors	●		15–20 minutes

Cube Trains

Goal(s) & Objectives	Objectives
	30. *Recognizes patterns and can repeat them*
	Other Concepts
	• Describes geometric shapes
	• Understands and uses positional words

Materials and Preparation

☐ Interlocking cubes

☐ *Freight Train* by Donald Crews or another book about trains

Guiding Children's Learning

Read *Freight Train*. Lead a brief discussion about the book and invite children to share personal experiences they have had with trains. Use these questions as a guide:

Who would like to tell about a time when you went for a ride on a train or when you watched as a train traveled down the track? What did it look like? What sounds do you remember?

Why do you think trains are important? What do they do?

How would you describe the train in the book?

Who can name each train car or tell what it looks like? What shapes do they remind you of?

What is a train engineer? What do you think the train engineer's job is?

Can you make the sound of the train whistle or the train moving down the track?

Where did the train in the story travel?

Tell the children that you are going to pretend that each cube is one car of a train. Show the children how to connect the cubes. Then let them make their own trains.

Next, ask them to watch carefully so they can make a train just like yours. Recite the following rhyme as you construct a train out of the cubes.

What kind of train will it be?

Red and blue, come and see.

See the pattern when I'm done.

Red and blue trains are lots of fun.

Invite the children to read the pattern with you as you touch each block.

Red, blue; red, blue; red, blue.

Toot! Toot!

Explain that making a pattern is like taking turns. Ask,

If the last car on the train is blue, what color would you put next to continue this train pattern? Red, blue, red, blue, red, blue, _____.

Then demonstrate how to extend the pattern.

Continue making trains, allowing a different child to choose the colors each time. Insert the new color words into the rhyme and invite the children to chant it with you.

Again, engage the children in extending the pattern by having them tell or add the next colored cube in the sequence.

For a change of pace or to close the activity, tell the children to pretend that they are train engineers who like to make different motions and sounds. Have the children watch, listen to, and act out the simple pattern of this rhyme:

What kind of pattern will it be?

Stomp and clap; come and see;

Hear the pattern when I'm done.

Stomp and clap is lots of fun.

Stomp, clap; stomp, clap; stomp, clap.

Toot! Toot!

Closing

Challenge the children to make pattern trains at choice time, with unit blocks in the Block Area or with the interlocking cubes in the Toys and Games Area.

One by one, help the children make the transition to the next activity by having them perform a simple action pattern.

Developmental Progression

Simple ↓ **Complex**	Children identify and read simple patterns (trains) created by alternating two colors of interlocking cubes (e.g., red, blue; red, blue or green, green, orange; green, green, orange). Have children read the pattern.
	With guidance, have children extend a simple pattern.
	Have children copy a simple pattern using objects, motions, or sounds.
	Have children create a simple pattern of their own by using concrete materials such as interlocking cubes. Then encourage them to describe their patterns aloud.
	Have children create a simple pattern by using pictures or represent a pattern of concrete objects by using pictures.
	Repeat the process above, using more complex patterns such as red, blue, yellow, blue, yellow; red, blue, yellow, blue, yellow.

Meeting the Needs of Diverse Learners

Use larger cubes or interlocking materials for children who have trouble using small objects. Use cubes that connect with magnets or Velcro® if necessary. Software programs such as *Millie's Math House* offer several pattern activities. Adapt the computer to meet individual needs (e.g. touch screen, single key use, larger keyboard).

Make sure that all children can either see and/or hear the various train patterns that you make with the group. Provide objects of different sizes, shapes, and function, so that children who cannot see color can make train patterns based on how objects feel.

Translate color words and the word *train* into the child's primary language.

Use sign language for children with hearing impairments.

Going Beyond

Cut colored construction paper into squares to represent interlocking cubes. Have children use the paper squares to copy a simple pattern created with cubes. You might also duplicate the cube train by using the master in the Appendix. Have the children color the squares to match a pattern of interlocking cubes.

Create other train stories that also engage children in patterning activities.

Have the children represent the train going up a hill, down a hill, up a hill, down a hill by crouching, standing, crouching, standing.

Have the children imitate a pattern of train sounds, such as *chug, chug, choo, choo; chug, chug, choo, choo.*

Have the children use motions, such as brushing their hands together and stamping their feet, to represent the way a train moves along the track (e.g., brush, brush, brush, stamp; brush, brush, brush, stamp). Begin slowly, increasing speed as a train does when pulling out of the station.

Integrate more mathematics into the activity by asking questions such as these:

How many red cubes did you use? How many blue ones? How many altogether?

Show me how to make a pattern train using ten cubes. How many of each color will you need?

Who has the longest train? Who has the shortest?

Make a pattern train as long as your arm. How many cubes of each color did it take?

Can you make your train go under the chair (over the bridge, through the tunnel)?

Provide cutouts or stencils of different types of train cars (e.g., engine, caboose, boxcars, tank car, hopper, and cattle car). Challenge the children to create trains with different patterns of cars.

Individual	Small Groups	Large Group	Interest Area	Single Day	Multi-Day	Time
●	●	●	Toys and Games	●		15–20 minutes

My Little Sister

Goal(s) & Objectives

Objectives

30. Recognizes patterns and can repeat them; 34. Uses numbers and counting

Materials and Preparation

☐ *My Little Sister Ate One Hare* by Bill Grossman

☐ Story strips (see Appendix)

Hang the pocket chart in an area where children can see and reach it.

Familiarize yourself with the book *My Little Sister Ate One Hare* by Bill Grossman

Guiding Children's Learning

Have the children sit facing the pocket chart. Introduce the book and then lead a brief discussion about "yucky" or unpleasant things siblings do or about things the children like and dislike eating.

Read or tell the story, *My Little Sister Ate One Hare.* As you do so, place the corresponding story strips in the pocket chart. Align the pictures one below the other so that the children can see the growing pattern (plus one) as it emerges (e.g., one hare, two snakes, three ants). Use questions and comments such as these:

> *What do you think the storyteller's sister ate next? I wonder how many she ate. What makes you think so?*

> *If the storyteller's sister ate one hare, two snakes, three ants, and four shrews, how many bats do you think she will eat? How many of the next creature?*

> *How many creatures do you think the little sister ate altogether? How could you find out?*

> *If the little sister had not thrown up, how many creatures would she have eaten next? Then how many would she eat? Why do you think so?*

> *Do you see a pattern in the story? Tell me about it.*

Closing

Place the story strips and book in the Library Area. Tell the children that they may retell the story by remembering the pattern and using the story strips.

Developmental Progression

Simple ↓ **Complex**	Read or tell the story, and display the story props as you do so. Use questions and comments to draw children's attention to the simple growing pattern.
	Invite the children to find the appropriate prop and display it as you read or retell the story.
	Have children continue, or add on to, the growing pattern of the story.
	Using a familiar story that has a growing pattern, have children create new text. Let them illustrate the text. Share the new story at story time and place the book in the Library Area.

Meeting the Needs of Diverse Learners

Give children who can't see well a set of story strips with raised dots to feel. Give them one strip at a time. Have them put them in a box top on the floor to feel the emerging pattern with their fingers.

Learn key words from the story in the languages of the children in your class. Use them as you preview the story with children who have few English language skills.

Learn the sign language for the key words for children with hearing impairments.

Going Beyond

Give each child drawing paper. Write a numeral at the top of the page. Encourage the children to draw the related number of new creatures on the page. Combine the pages to make a class counting book and have the children title the book.

Have the children follow recipes for animal-shaped snacks and count a specified number of creatures. For example, they might make "Ants on a Log," by using celery, cream cheese, and raisins, or make snakes out of edible dough.

Read other books with growing patterns, such as

The Napping House by Audrey Wood

A Frog in the Bog by Karma Wilson

Rooster's Off to See the World by Eric Carle

The Hungry Caterpillar by Eric Carle

One Monday Morning by Uri Shulevitz

Jump, Frog, Jump! by Robert Kalan

The Enormous Turnip by Kathy Parkinson

The Grouchy Ladybug by Eric Carle

The Gingerbread Boy by Paul Galdone

I Know an Old Lady Who Swallowed a Fly by various authors

Shoes From Grandpa by Mem Fox

The House That Jack Built illustrated by Pam Adams

The Cake That Mack Ate by Rose Robart

The Farm by Marie Aubinais

Mrs. McTats and Her Houseful of Cats by Alyssa Satin Capucilli

Sing songs that have growing patterns, such as

"BINGO"

"The Ants Go Marching"

"There's a Hole in the Bottom of the Sea"

"The Green Grass Grows All Around"

Individual	Small Groups	Large Group	Interest Area	Single Day	Multi-Day	Time
●	●	●	Library	●		15–20 minutes

Patterns Under Cover

Goal(s) & Objectives	Objectives
	30. Recognizes patterns and can repeat them

Materials and Preparation

☐ Counters

☐ Paper cup

Guiding Children's Learning

Explain to the children that they are going to play a pattern game in which they are detectives. Ask,

> *What is a detective?*
>
> *What kinds of things does a detective do?*
>
> *Do you know anyone who is a detective?*
>
> *How does a detective solve a problem? What does he do?*

Make a simple repeating pattern with the counters (e.g., yellow, green, yellow, green, etc.). Have the children read the pattern as you construct it. Explain that you are going to cover one counter with the cup and, as detectives, they will figure out which counter is under the cup.

Have the children close their eyes. Cover a counter and ask,

> *What's under the cup? How do you know?*

Lift the cup to confirm the children's answer.

Change the pattern and repeat the activity. Invite the children to take turns creating a pattern while the other children act as detectives.

Closing

Tell the children the materials will be in the Toys and Games Area. Encourage them to play the pattern game at choice time.

Developmental Progression

Simple ↓ **Complex**	Have children read simple repeating patterns with two alternating colors of counters.
	Have children continue a simple pattern with two alternating colors of counters.
	Have the children predict the color of the hidden last item in patterned row.
	Have children identify any hidden item in a simple color-pattern sequence.
	Have children use counters to create simple patterns of their own. Then let them cover a counter in the sequence.
	Repeat the process above, creating simple patterns of other attributes, such as shape, size, texture, etc.
	Repeat the process above, using more complex patterns such as red, blue, yellow, blue, yellow; red, blue, yellow, blue yellow.

Meeting the Needs of Diverse Learners

Use large counters or objects (e.g., red blocks and blue beads) for children to see and feel the differences more easily.

Translate color words into an English language learner's home language or allow them to play the role of pattern-maker. Use sign language for children with hearing impairments.

Offer pictures, colored paper, or additional counters and let the child point to the object or color of the object he thinks is covered with the cup.

With advanced learners, cover the first two or three objects and have the children figure out how the pattern started.

Going Beyond

Have children predict the color of the covered counter and draw the pattern.

Cover more than one counter and have the children identify what is hidden.

Individual	Small Groups	Large Group	Interest Area	Single Day	Multi-Day	Time
	●		Toys and Games		●	15–20 minutes

People Patterns

Goal(s) & Objectives	Objectives
	30. *Recognizes patterns and can repeat them;* 32. *Shows awareness of position in space*
	Other Concepts
	• Represents and translates patterns

Materials and Preparation

☐ Unit blocks and half-unit (square) blocks

☐ Art supplies

☐ Interlocking cubes

Guiding Children's Learning

Explain to the children that they will use their bodies to create patterns and then describe them. Have 6–8 volunteers come to the front of the room and form a line facing the other children. Pose this question:

How could you use your bodies to show high *and* low?

After the children have decided on the two positions to represent high and low, guide the volunteers in creating a simple pattern such as high, low, low; high, low, low; and so forth. Invite the other children to describe the pattern as it is created and to become a part of the extended pattern. When the last child is placed in the pattern, return to the beginning and have the children say the positional word of the pattern as you touch each child's head.

Next, lead a discussion with children about ways they might represent the high-low pattern they made with their bodies in a different way. Offer the collections of materials and invite them to explore ways to translate the pattern.

Closing

Encourage children to explore other ways to create patterns by using their bodies (e.g., using a variety of positions such as front and back, bent and straight, or eyes open and eyes closed). Also encourage them to represent their ideas.

Developmental Progression

Simple ↓ **Complex**	Have children identify patterns depicted in a book and elsewhere in their environment (e.g., clothing, classroom, school or center).
	Show examples of simple patterns and have children identify and describe them.
	With guidance, have children use their bodies to make simple patterns and then describe the pattern.
	Have the children form two groups. Have one group create a simple people pattern. Then have the other group copy the pattern.
	Have the children become a part of extending an existing people pattern.
	Have children identify, copy, and create new and perhaps more complex patterns using their bodies (e.g., stand, sit, stand, stand, kneel; stand, sit, stand, stand, kneel). Ask children to describe the patterns.
	Have children translate a pattern they created in one medium by using another medium.

Meeting the Needs of Diverse Learners

Adjust the actions to movements that all children can perform. (e.g., nod your head, clap your hands).

Be sure to name the actions as children do them.

Going Beyond

Sing songs that use patterns and involve children physically, such as these:

"Head, Shoulders, Knees, and Toes"

"Hokey Pokey"

"Did You Ever See a Lassie?"

Have children copy and/or create patterns using different motions (e.g., raise right arm, raise left arm, turn around; raise right arm, raise left arm, turn around or stamp, clap, clap; stamp, clap, clap)

Have children represent their patterns through drawings or other media (e.g., children use straws of two different lengths to represent the high-low pattern or pipe cleaners to represent the straight-bent pattern)

Take children on a walk to look for patterns in nature. Take photos of patterns or collect samples of items to place in the Discovery Area.

Duplicate the action cards in the Appendix. Laminate them for durability. Let children use the cards at choice time to create their own action patterns. They can place the selected cards in a pocket chart and refer to them as they perform or have their friends perform the action pattern (e.g., arms up, tap head, tap head; arms up, tap head, tap head).

Individual	Small Groups	Large Group	Interest Area	Single Day	Multi-Day	Time
	●	●	Music and Movement, Outdoors	●		15–20 minutes

Picture Patterns

Goal(s) & Objectives

Objectives

30. Recognizes patterns and can repeat them

Other Concepts

- Represents patterns through writing

Materials and Preparation

☐ A book or collection of photos of objects and animals that have patterns (e.g., flag, bee, butterfly, building, clothing, fence, bridge)

☐ Camera

☐ Paper and writing materials

Guiding Children's Learning

Explain that you have some photographs of animals and other objects that have patterns. Invite the children to select a photo from the collection or book and describe the pattern. Continue discussing patterns in the other photos.

Take the children on a pattern hunt around the school, playground, or neighborhood. Use the digital camera to take photographs of patterns identified by the children. Print the pictures, along with a caption such as this:

> (*Child's name*) *found a pattern on a* (*name of object*).
> *It was* _____, _____, _____, _____, _____, _____.

Have each child complete the sentences that describe what he found. For example,

> *Leo found a pattern on a gate. It was circle, rectangle; circle, rectangle; circle, rectangle.*

Combine the pages to form a book. Share it at group time, making sure to point out the different kinds of patterns, including color, shape, size, position, and others. Place copies of the book in one or more of the interest areas.

Closing

Encourage children to continue to look for patterns on objects or animals. Invite them to represent the pattern by drawing or through some other medium, or continue to take photographs of their pattern discoveries.

Developmental Progression

Simple ▼ Complex	Have children identify and describe simple patterns on objects or animals in the environment.
	Have children copy patterns using a variety of media (e.g., drawing, construction).
	Have children verbally extend patterns they have identified in objects or animals.
	Have children create an object, structure, or model of a creature with a unique pattern.

Meeting the Needs of Diverse Learners

Have children describe a pattern using objects found at school and home. Make drawings of their descriptions and add them to the book.

Use highly contrasting picture patterns to make them easier to see. Red, yellow, and orange on a dark background are the easiest colors to see.

Going Beyond

Invite children to make patterned frames for the photos taken on the pattern walk. You can begin a pattern on the frames by using stamps and ink or sponges and tempera paint. Then let the children extend the pattern to complete the frame or let children create their own patterns.

Post some of the photos in classroom interest areas (e.g., bridges and walkways in the Block Area) and encourage the children to represent them.

Invite children to design and create a uniquely patterned structure or article of clothing by using blocks or art materials. Let the children take turns identifying and reading one another's patterns.

Have children create a "Zany Zoo" with animals or make-believe creatures having unique, zany patterns.

Have children use pattern blocks to build patterned fences for the animals in the Block Area.

Individual	Small Groups	Large Group	Interest Area	Single Day	Multi-Day	Time
	●		Library, Outdoors, Discovery		●	20–30 minutes

When I Was Little

Goal(s) & Objectives	Objectives
	22. *Observes objects and events with curiosity*; 28. *Compares and measures*; 31. *Shows awareness of time concepts and sequence*
	Other Concepts
	• Describes change over time

Materials and Preparation

☐ *When I Was Little: A Four-Year-Old's Memoirs of Her Youth* by Jamie Lee Curtis or another book about children growing and changing, such as *Another Important Book* by Margaret Wise Brown, *Now I'm Big* by Margaret Miller, or *When Frank was Four* by Allison Lester

☐ Chart paper and marker

☐ Writing and drawing materials

Guiding Children's Learning

Introduce the book, *When I Was Little: A Four-Year-Old's Memoirs of Her Youth*. Invite the children to tell what they think the book will be about. Ask,

> *Have you ever heard the word* memoir? *What do you think it means? What about the word* youth?

Read the story and then discuss the questions. Explain or clarify the meanings of the words *memoir* and *youth*.

Next, draw a line down the middle of the chart paper to form two columns. At the top of the left column, write *Baby*. At the top of the right column, write *4-Year-Old*. Have the children name some of the things the girl in the story could *not* do when she was a baby but can do now that she is 4 years old. Record them on the chart in the appropriate column. Invite the children to tell how and why they think things changed.

Lead a discussion with the children about how they have changed and grown since they were babies. Explain that they will make a book similar to the one you read. It will show and tell what they were like as a babies and what they are like now. Offer some examples, using the following sentence pattern and some of the children's comments. For example, on blank drawing paper, write,

> *Crystal said, "When I was little, I <u>was bald</u>. Now I am big, and I <u>have curly red hair</u>."*

Explain that Crystal should then draw two pictures, one of herself as a baby without hair and one as a girl with curly red hair.

Place the drawing materials in the Library Area and explain that you will be available to take dictation during choice time. Explain that the pages will be combined to form a book that they will be able to read in the Library Area. Take dictation if children have difficulty drawing and send the papers home for families to help children select photos that illustrate their sentences.

Closing

Ask the children if they are interested in exploring other ways that they grow and change. Encourage them to create their own memoir over the next several days, weeks, or months to share with friends and family members.

Developmental Progression

Simple → Complex
Create an environment where children have opportunities to observe growth and change (e.g., add plants and animals to the classroom).
Engage children in firsthand activities that focus on growth and change (e.g., measure and document their heights periodically throughout the year; call attention to when a child has grown enough to reach the pedals on a tricycle; celebrate other new accomplishments; create a class garden and observe it over time).
Share books and other visuals about the ways in which children, animals, or plants grow and change. Engage children in related follow-up activities that help them focus on patterns of growth and change (e.g., have the children name things characters could not do at one age but could do as they aged).
Have children document, or create representations, that demonstrate growth or change (e.g., draw pictures that show the rapid growth of the class gerbil population; create their own memoir using pictures or stories about themselves as infants, toddlers, 2-year-olds, and preschoolers).

Meeting the Needs of Diverse Learners

Learn key words from the story in the home languages of the children in your class. Use them as you preview the story with children who have few English language skills.

Learn the sign language for key story words, for children with hearing impairments. Always say the word as you make the sign.

Label the chart with pictures or drawings of a baby and preschool child to help children understand the meaning of each column.

Phrase your questions to encourage yes-no responses, for children with limited language skills. For example, you might say, "Did you have red curly hair when you were a baby?"

Offer an alternative to drawing. Cut pictures from magazines of things babies and preschoolers do. Include glue sticks on the table with the drawing materials.

Going Beyond

Create a "Then and Now" display where children can share and compare photos of themselves as infants, toddlers, 2-year-olds, and preschoolers.

Have children bring pictures of themselves at various ages and put them in order from youngest to oldest.

Choose a specific attribute for children to focus their attention on (e.g., their weight, height, or shoe size as an infant and as a preschooler). Then involve them in making comparisons. For example, have children bring copies of their footprints as infants. Then make their footprints as preschoolers and compare the two. You might also have families tell you their child's height (length) when they were born. Then measure their heights as a preschoolers. Cut yarn to illustrate both heights and have the children make comparisons.

Read other books about growth and change, such as *A Frog in the Bog* by Karma Wilson, *Andrew's Bright Blue T-Shirt* by Jessica Wollman, *Before You Were Big* by Jennifer Davis, *I Love You Just the Same* by Erica Wolf, *It's Hard to Be Five* by Jamie Lee Curtis, *Once I Was...* by Niki Clark Leopold, *The Hungry Caterpillar* by Eric Carle, *The Enormous Turnip* by Kathy Parkinson, and *When I Get Bigger* by Mercer Mayer.

Have children observe and document the growth and change of such things as plants in the class garden or the class pet.

Individual	Small Groups	Large Group	Interest Area	Single Day	Multi-Day	Time
●	●		Library		●	20 minutes

I Want to Know

<table>
<tr>
<td>Goal(s) &
Objectives</td>
<td>

Objectives

26. *Applies knowledge or experience to a new context;*
28. *Compares/measures;* 33. *Uses one-to-one correspondence;*
34. *Uses numbers and counting*

Other Concepts

- Asks questions
- Learns various ways to gather data
- Describes and compares data

</td>
</tr>
</table>

Materials

- ☐ "Question of the Day" forms
- ☐ Clipboard
- ☐ Pencils, crayons, or other materials for recording data

Preparation

The Appendix includes three "Question of the Day" forms from which to choose.

- Form 1: Children answer a simple yes-no question (e.g., "Would you let a caterpillar crawl on your arm?") by signing their names or placing a check mark in the appropriate column.

- Form 2: Children respond to a question that has up to three response options. For example,

  What is your favorite flavor of ice cream? (chocolate, vanilla, strawberry)

  How did you get to school? (walked, rode bus, rode in car)

  Children place a tally mark or check mark in the row that indicates their response. The "surveyor" totals the marks in each row and records the total in the box at the end of the row.

- Form 3: Children respond to a question that has four response options. The response choices are placed in the bottom row of each column of the graph. Children answer the question by writing their names in a rectangle in the appropriate column. Responses are recorded from bottom to top so that they can be read as a bar graph.

Listen to and observe the children to determine what they are curious about or interested in. They may have a question related to a topic of study, an upcoming event, or a life experience. They may simply want to know about their friends' preferences (e.g., "What kind of toothpaste do you like?"). Choose the "Question of the Day" form that is appropriate for collecting data about the question. Duplicate the form and attach it to a clipboard.

Guiding Children's Learning

At a group meeting, lead a discussion about a topic of interest, an upcoming event, or something the children want to know more about. Use open-ended questions and comments such as these:

I noticed some of you talking about....

What can you tell me about...?

What else would you like to know about...?

I wonder how or why...?

How could we find out who (how many of you)...?

Help the children figure out a question about a topic that was discussed during the group meeting. Introduce the appropriate "Question of the Day" form to the children and explain that it can be used to collect information that will help them answer one of their questions. Discuss or demonstrate how the form is similar to some of the real graphs they have made.

Record the question at the top of the "Question of the Day" form. Then demonstrate how the children are to record their responses on the form. Emphasize that each person responds to the question only once.

Invite the children to predict what the results will show. Then continue collecting responses to the question. After everyone has responded, have the children look at the data on the graph. Ask questions such as these:

What does the survey or graph tell?

How many of you...?

How many of you do not...?

How many more (fewer) of you...?

Which row (column) has the least (most)? Are any the same?

Was your prediction correct?

Why do you think most children in our class...?

Record children's responses on a chart or sentence strips.

Closing

Explain to the children that they will take turns collecting data as other questions arise.

Developmental Progression

Simple ↓ **Complex**	Have children create graphs by using concrete objects to compare two groups (e.g., children physically represent their responses by standing on a large floor graph; each child places a real object, such as his shoe, on a graph).
	Have children create graphs by using concrete objects to compare three groups.
	Have children create picture graphs comparing two groups of objects or choices (e.g., children place their photos to indicate a preference or respond to a question; children draw pictures to represent their responses and then place them on a graph).
	Have children create picture graphs comparing three groups of objects or choices.
	Have children create symbolic graphs comparing two groups of objects or choices (e.g., children sign their names to indicate a preference or respond to a question).
	Have children create symbolic graphs comparing three groups of objects or choices.

Meeting the Needs of Diverse Learners

Include questions that involve senses other than sight, such as

Which sound do you prefer to use to make music? Do you like to whistle, hum, or buzz?

Which texture do you prefer, fur, silk, or corduroy?

Offer three-dimensional response markers (e.g., foam board shapes with an adhesive back, keyboard locator dots) for better understanding of the graph's meaning.

Going Beyond

Have children survey teachers and other school staff members or family members. Then combine their data to create a class graph.

Create a question box or jar. Encourage children to write or dictate questions they would like answered. Draw a question from the box and let the children decide how they will collect and organize data related to the question.

Mount photos of each child on a block or cube (for example, a pint carton). Have the children create and then interpret picture graphs by using the photo blocks. For example, ask,

What would you like for snack today?

On three 3" x 5" cards, draw a picture of an apple, orange, or banana and lay them side by side on the floor. Have the children indicate their snack preferences by stacking their photo blocks on top of the appropriate card. After everyone has made his or her selection, ask questions that encourage the children to count, compare, add, subtract, and so on.

Individual	Small Groups	Large Group	Interest Area	Single Day	Multi-Day	Time
		●	All	●		15–20 minutes

I Have a Secret

<table>
<tr>
<td>Goal(s) &
Objectives</td>
<td>

Objectives

22. Observes objects and events with curiosity; 27. Classifies objects

Other Concepts

- Develops reasoning skills
- Describes and compares data

</td>
</tr>
</table>

Materials and Preparation

☐ Two pieces of heavy string or rope that are approximately 8 feet long

☐ Two large signs, one labeled *Yes* and the other *No*

Guiding Children's Learning

Use the string to form two circles on the floor. Make them large enough for several children to stand inside. Place the *Yes* sign next to one circle and the *No* sign by the other.

Lead a discussion with the children.

> *What is a secret?* or *What does it means to have a secret?*
>
> *Have you ever told anyone a secret?*
>
> *Who can tell us what a rule is?*

Explain to the children that they are going to play a game called "I Have a Secret." Give the following instructions:

> *I'm going to put you into two groups, but I'm not going to tell you how I decide in which group to put you. You will have to guess my secret sorting rule. Some of you will fit the rule, but some of you will not. If you fit the secret rule, you will stand in the circle that is labeled* Yes. *If you do not fit the secret rule, you will stand in the circle labeled* No.
>
> *Your job is to see if you can figure out my secret sorting rule. Don't say anything until you think you know the secret sorting rule. When you think you know it, show me a "thumbs-up." If you need more clues, show me a "thumbs-down."*

Decide upon a sorting rule (e.g., children wearing long pants, children wearing short sleeves, or children with curly hair), but do not use a child's disability or home language as a sorting criterion. Call several children forward one at a time and place them in the appropriate circle. Have children indicate their readiness to state your sorting rule by using the thumb signals. Offer comments such as these:

All the children in the Yes *circle are alike in one way. They all have something in common.*

Think about the way in which the children in the No *circle are different from the children in the* Yes *circle.*

Continue sorting the children one by one, or invite a child to come forward and ask the children to determine whether the child fits the rule. Then place the child in the correct circle.

When it appears that most of the children think that they have identified the rule, ask someone to state the rule or have the group state the rule together.

Lead a brief discussion, inviting children to share their strategies for figuring out the sorting rule. Ask questions such as these:

How did you figure out the secret sorting rule?

When did you figure out the secret rule?

Could there have been another sorting rule other than this one?

Were there more (fewer) children in the Yes *group? How do you know?*

Closing

Offer encouraging comments about the ways in which children were thinking and the ideas they generated. Explain that you will be offering more opportunities to play "I Have a Secret."

Developmental Progression

Simple	Sort the children (a collection) by one obvious or unique characteristic. Then have the children identify the secret rule.
	Use a less obvious rule to sort the children (a collection) or begin by sorting children who have more than one thing in common.
	Sort the children (a collection) into more than two sets (e.g., children with no sleeves, children with short sleeves, children with long sleeves).
	Have a child or a small group of children decide upon a sorting rule and sort a collection for others to guess.
Complex	Sort by two or more attributes (e.g., children wearing lace-up/ not lace-up shoes)

Meeting the Needs of Diverse Learners

Provide a *Yes* and *No* sign (e.g., pictures of thumbs-up/down) to hold as an option to moving to a circle.

Be sure verbally to describe how the children are the same. Use sorting rules that involve attributes that can be felt by children who cannot see (e.g., curly hair, long pants).

Write the words *Yes* and *No* in different colors in the children's home languages (e.g., in Spanish, *sí* and *no*).

Going Beyond

Create an "I Have a Secret" game with two sorting hoops and collections of materials such as bottle caps, keys, buttons, or geometric shapes. Place it in the Toys and Games Area. Encourage children to work in pairs or small groups, taking turns creating their own sorting rules.

Have the children in each group line up across from one another to create a graph with their bodies. Have them determine whether there are more or fewer children in the group that fits the sorting rule or in the group that does not fit the rule.

Individual	Small Groups	Large Group	Interest Area	Single Day	Multi-Day	Time
	●	●	Toys and Games, Outdoors	●		15–20 minutes

Shoe Sort

Goal(s) & Objectives

Objectives

22. Observes objects and events with curiosity; 27. Classifies objects;
28. Compares/measures; 33. Uses one-to-one correspondence;
34. Uses numbers and counting

Other Concepts

- Describes and compares data

Materials and Preparation

☐ Book about shoes, such as

Shoes by Elizabeth Winthrop

Shoes, Shoes, Shoes by Ann Morris

The Foot Book by Dr. Seuss

☐ Two or more large hoops or pieces of yarn to make circles

Guiding Children's Learning

Read a book about shoes or feet. Call attention to the attributes of the shoes or feet pictured in the book. Use these questions and comments below as a guide:

Tell me about your favorite pair of shoes.

Why do you think there are so many different kinds of shoes?

How many feet do you have? How many feet do you and a friend have altogether?

Can you find someone in class who has shoes like this?
(Point to an illustration in the book.)

Can you find someone in class who has shoes like yours?
Tell me how they are the same.

Next, have the children take off their shoes and look at them carefully. Invite the children to describe their shoes. Place the hoops or yarn on the floor, choose a criteria for sorting them, and then begin sorting. Give directions such as these:

If your shoes have laces, put them in this circle.

If your shoes do not have laces, put them in the other circle.

Once the shoes are sorted, ask questions like these:

How are the shoes in this circle the same? (Point to each circle.)

Which group has more (fewer) shoes? How do you know? How could you find out?

Can you name any other ways that the shoes with laces (without laces) are alike (different)?

In the group of shoes that do have (do not have) laces, which shoe is the largest (smallest)?

What other ways can you sort your shoes?

As long as the children are interested, continue sorting their shoes as they suggest.

Closing

Comment on the many ways the shoes were sorted. List the children's sorting rules on chart paper as they state them. Encourage the children to continue to think of even more ways to sort the shoes.

Explain that shoe collections will be in the Toys and Games, Discovery, and Dramatic Play Areas and that they may be explored and sorted at choice time.

Developmental Progression

Simple ↓ **Complex**	Have children show shoes with a particular attribute.
	Have children explore a collection of shoes freely and share what they discover.
	Have children identify or describe one characteristic of the shoes and then sort the collection into two groups (e.g., those that have the characteristic and those that do not have the characteristic). Ask the children to recall the sorting rule.
	After shoes have been sorted by one characteristic, have the children establish a new sorting rule and then resort the shoes.
	Have the children sort shoes into groups with subgroups (e.g., sort shoes with laces into running shoes with laces and not running shoes with laces)

Meeting the Needs of Diverse Learners

Simplify the steps. If children have trouble arranging four shoes into groups, begin with two shoes. Then ask them to tell what is the same (or different) about the shoes. Next, have a child find a third shoe that fits the same description and place that shoe in the appropriate group. Continue with individual shoes.

Use a supply of extra shoes so that children do not have to remove and use their own shoes. Provide shoes with characteristics that can be identified by touch, such as those with laces or straps.

An investigation of shoes is also a wonderful opportunity to introduce counting by twos to advanced learners. Have a small group of children take off their shoes and arrange the pairs vertically. Place numeral cards to the left and right of the shoes so that the odd numbers are on the left and the even numbers are on the right. Highlight the even numbers by counting alternately in a whisper (odd numbers) and then a shout (even numbers).

Going Beyond

Ask a question such as this:

Do you think more children have shoes with laces, or do more children have shoes that do not have laces?

After discussing the question, introduce a large graphing mat (floor graph) and have the children sit facing the mat. Create two labels to describe the shoe characteristic being discussed. Have the children take turns placing their shoes in the appropriate column on the graph. Guide children's observations and interpretations of the data on the graph. For example, ask,

Why were these shoes put in this column? How are they alike?

What can you tell me about the column for shoes without laces? Compared with the shoes with laces, are there more, fewer, or the same number of shoes with no laces? How do you know?

How many more (fewer) shoes are there with laces?

If we want to have the same number of shoes in each column, how many more shoes with (without) laces will we need?

For each child, prepare a bag with identical collections of items. For example, each bag has red bears, blue bears, red tiles, and blue tiles. Have the children sort their collections individually. Then let them take turns describing the way in which they sorted. After a child shares, ask,

Did anyone else sort the materials in the same way?

Do you have the same items in your groups? Why? Why not?

Emphasize that there are many ways to arrange materials and many reasons for grouping items in certain ways.

Use other concept books as a springboard for sorting and graphing activities. Useful books include

Is it Larger? Is it Smaller? By Tana Hoban

Of Colors of Things by Tana Hoban

Bread, Bread, Bread by Ann Morris

Hats, Hats, Hats by Ann Morris

Tools by Ann Morris

On the Go by Ann Morris

Individual	Small Groups	Large Group	Interest Area	Single Day	Multi-Day	Time
		●	Dramatic Play	●		15–20 minutes

What Do You See?

Goal(s) & Objectives	Objectives 27. *Classifies objects* Data Analysis Concepts • Describes and compares data

Materials and Preparation

☐ Collection of objects that can be sorted in a variety of ways (e.g., color, shape, size, texture, weight, height, taste, smell, or function)

☐ A hoop or tray

Guiding Children's Learning

Have the children sit in a circle. Place a hoop in the center of the circle along with the collection of objects. Choose one of the items and ask questions like these:

What do you see that is like me? What do you see that's <u>blue</u>?

Place the object inside the hoop. Have the children identify the objects in the collection that have the specified attribute and place each inside the hoop. Use questions and comments such as these:

Tell me about the objects in the hoop. How are they the same? How are they different?

Why does (doesn't) this item belong inside the hoop?

Who can tell the sorting rule?

How would you describe the things inside (not inside, or outside) the hoop?

Are more items blue or more that are not blue? How can you find out?

What other ways could we sort these objects?

Continue sorting the objects using different criteria. Invite the children to find other things in the classroom that fit the sorting rule and add them to the set.

Closing

Comment on how many different ways the collection of objects was sorted. Tell the children that the objects and hoop will be in the Toys and Games Area for them to use at choice time.

Developmental Progression

Simple ▼ **Complex**	Have children separate a set with a similar characteristic from a collection of objects.
	Have children sort a collection of objects on the basis of a given attribute such as color, shape, or size.
	Have children sort a collection and then resort it using a different attribute.
	Have children sort a collection and state the sorting rule.
	Have children sort a collection into groups and sort those groups into subgroups.

Meeting the Needs of Diverse Learners

Include objects with characteristics that can be determined with senses other than sight. These can include texture, shape, or size. Have duplicates for children to feel as objects on the tray are discussed.

Start with fewer objects and offer objects with obvious similarities and differences.

Have advanced learners sort a collection of objects into two groups (e.g., shoes with laces, shoes with Velcro®) by placing each object in a separate hoop. Be sure to include some objects that have both of the sorting attributes (e.g., shoes with laces and Velcro®). Invite the children to suggest ways for sorting these objects and representing their thinking. If necessary, demonstrate how the two hoops might be overlapped so that some objects are in both hoops (as in a Venn diagram).

Going Beyond

Plan sorting experiences in other interest areas or with collections related to a study topic (e.g., rocks or leaves in the Discovery Area, foods in the Cooking Area, or clothing in the Dramatic Play Area).

Place two or more hoops and a collection of objects on the floor or table. Without stating the rule, begin sorting the collection by putting at least two or three objects in each hoop.

Invite the children to take turns sorting, and recite this rhyme:

Here's the collection. (Point to the collection.)

Here are the hoops. (Point to the hoops.)

Please help me put these into two (three, four) groups.
(Point to the collection again.)

Tap your nose, 1, 2, 3, (Tap nose.)

If you'd like to sort these objects with me.

Each time, ask the children to tell why an object belongs in a particular group. If hoops are not available, use yarn to form a circle.

Provide materials for children to represent the ways in which they sorted collections. Have the children discuss their representations with one or more friend(s).

After sorting a collection, create a graph with the children and have them interpret the data. Begin by having the children compare two groups, then three groups, and then four groups. Create graphs with concrete objects, picture graphs, and symbolic graphs.

Individual	Small Groups	Large Group	Interest Area	Single Day	Multi-Day	Time
	●	●	All	●		15–20 minutes

Appendix

Numeral Cards (0–5)

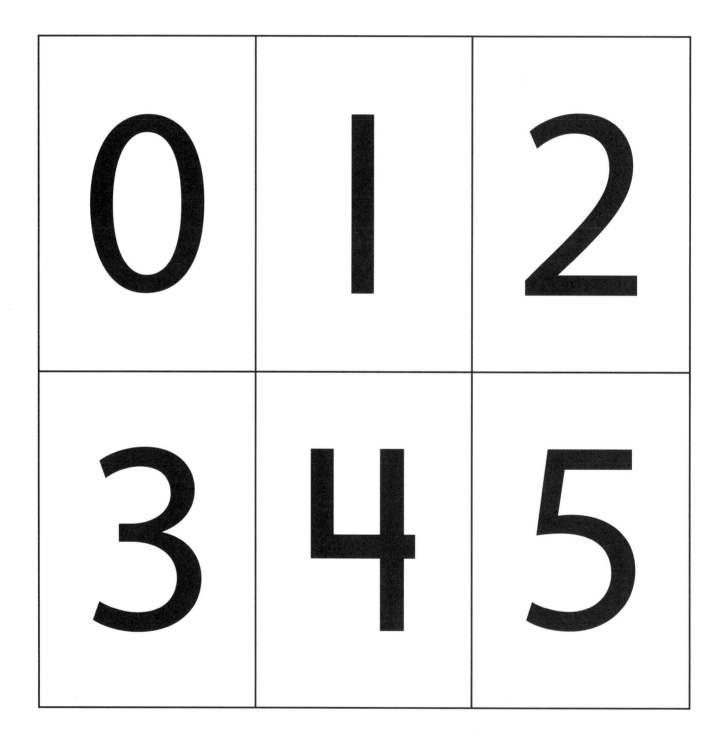

Numeral Cards (6–10)

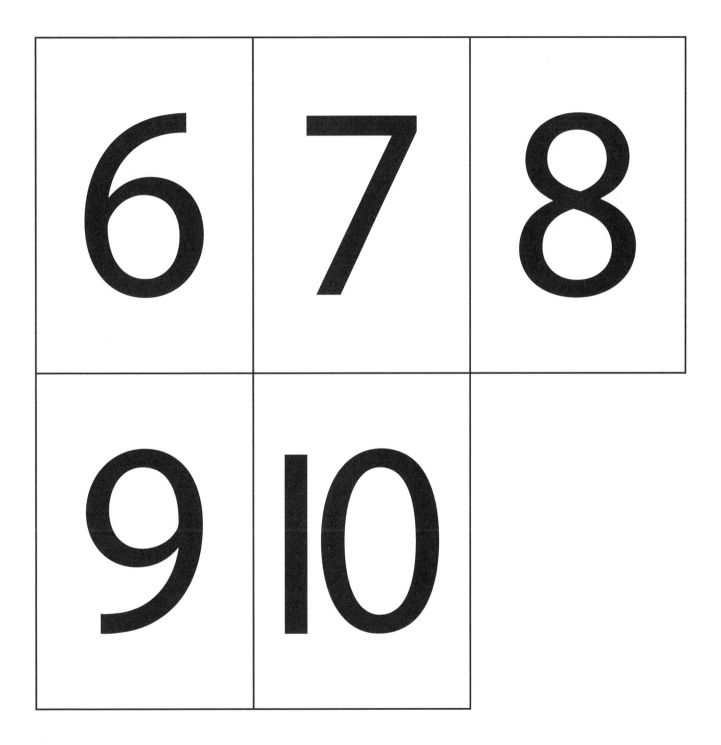

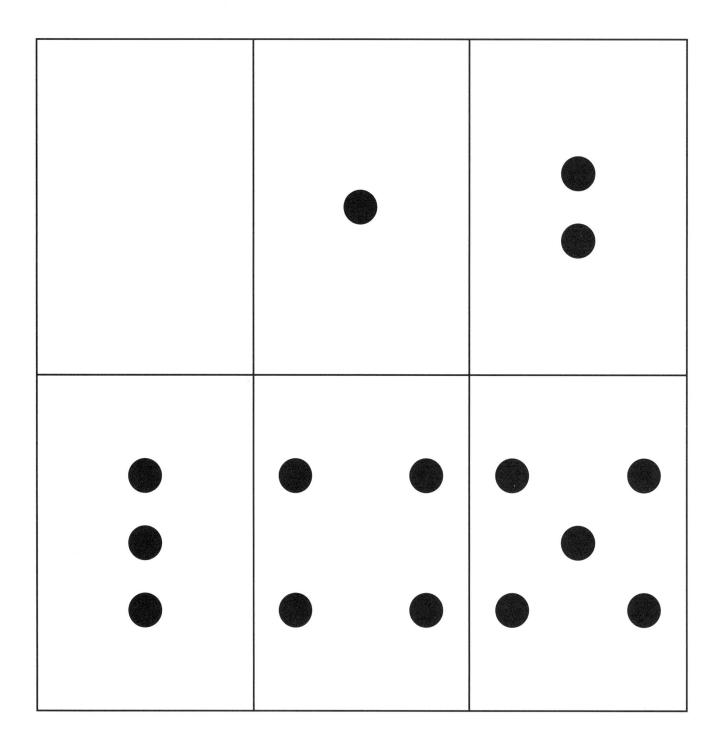

Quantity Cards (6–10)

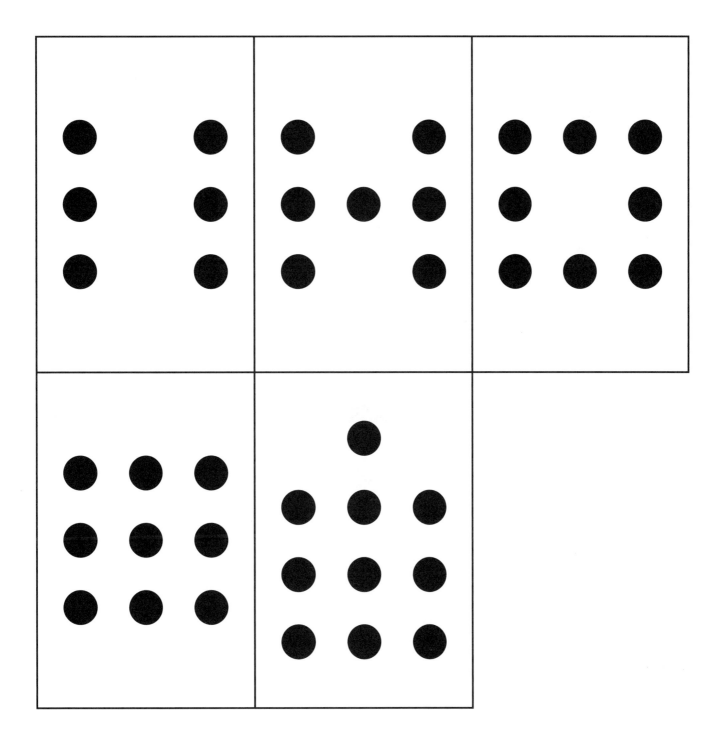

Numeral/Quantity Cards (1–5)

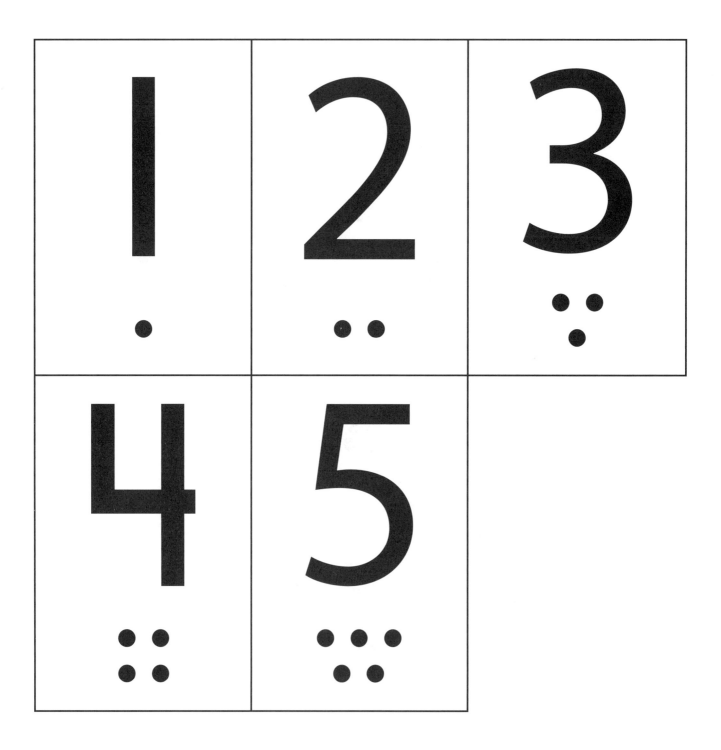

Numeral/Quantity Cards (6–10)

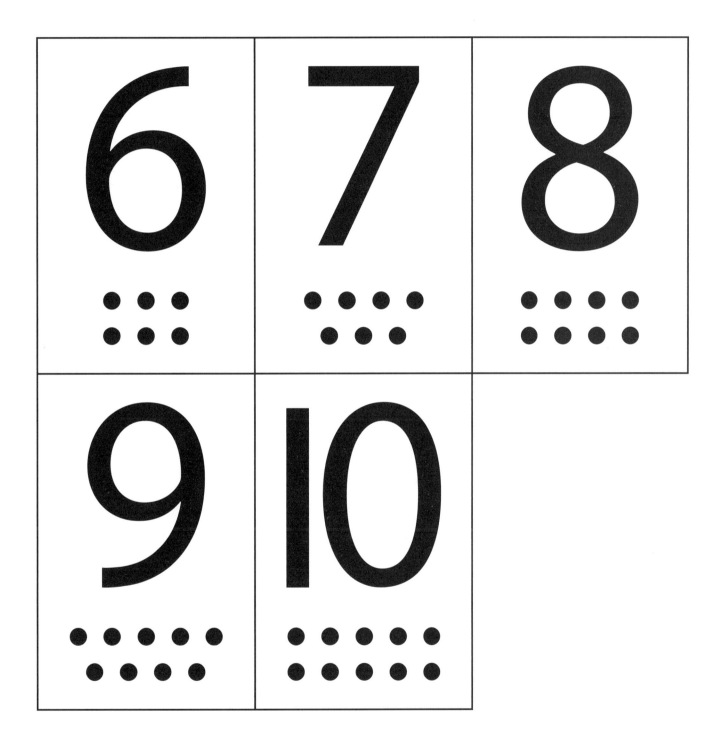

Fish Cards

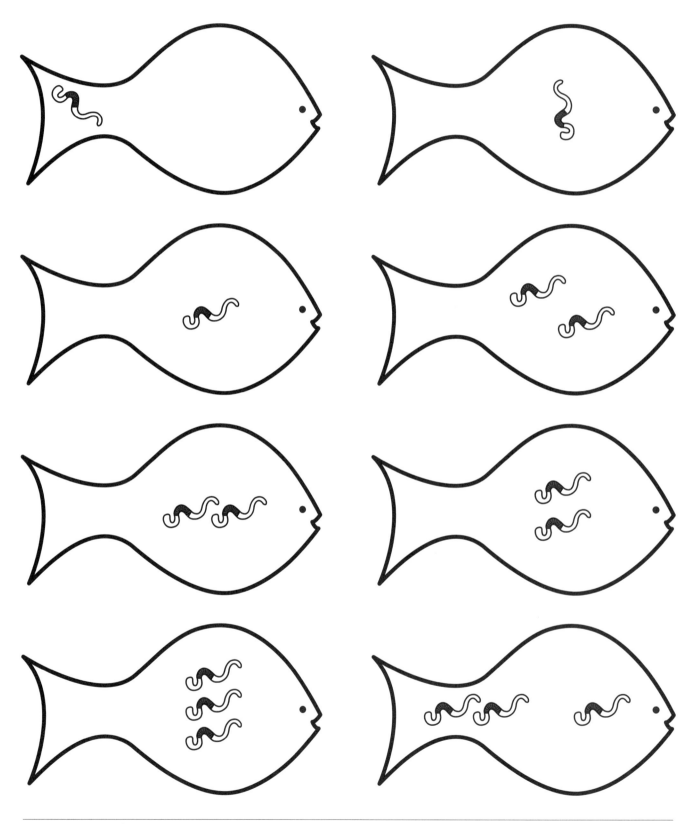

Fish Cards, *continued*

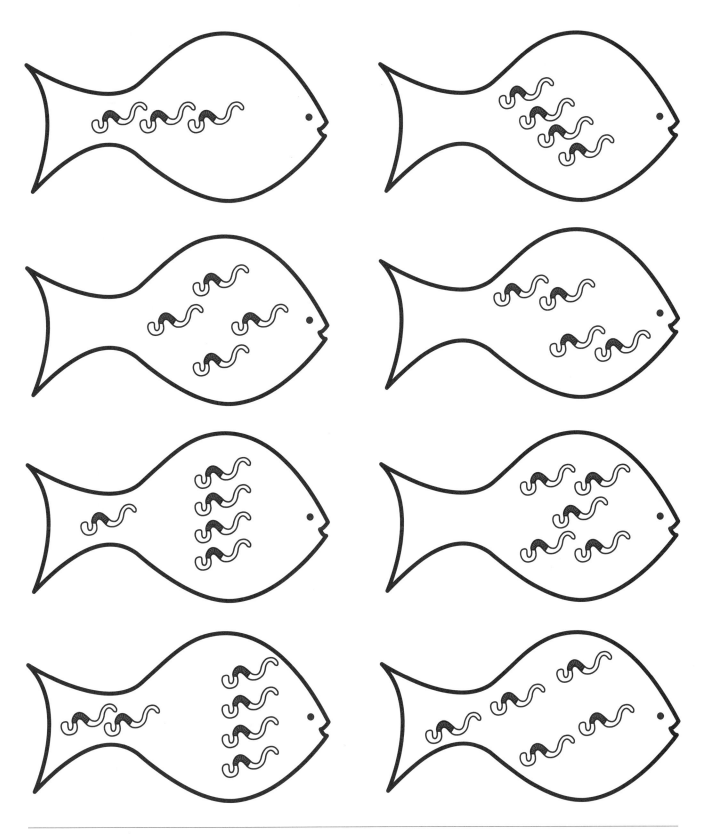

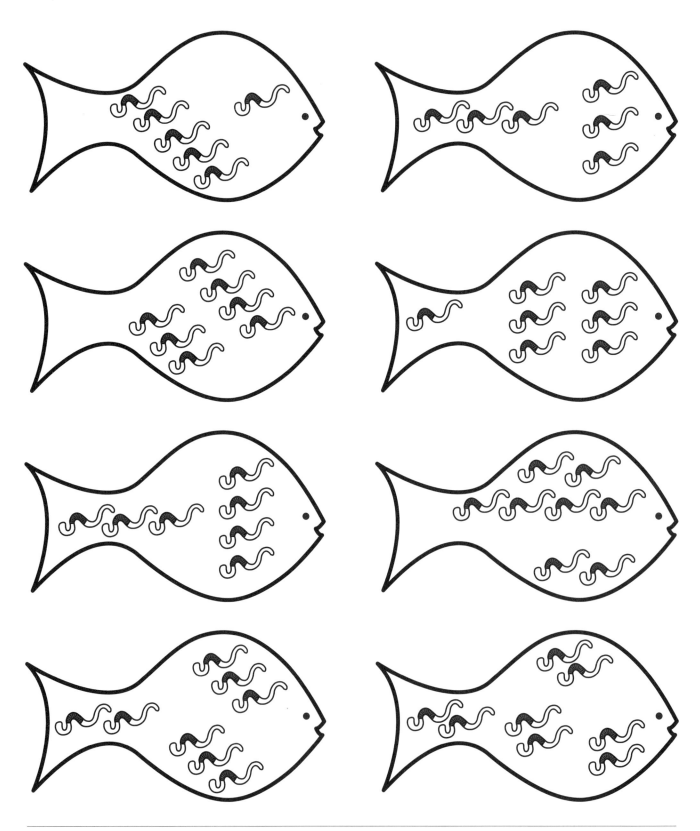

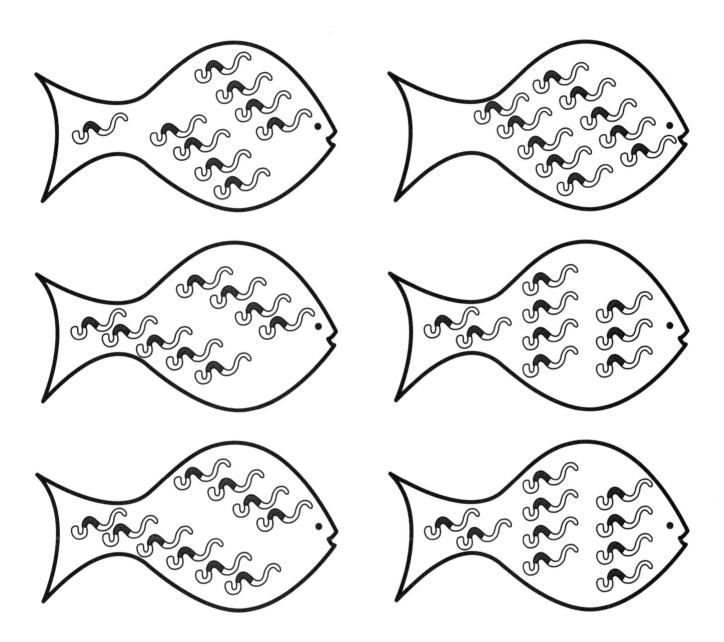

Merry Monkey Cards (1–5)

Merry Monkey Cards (6–10)

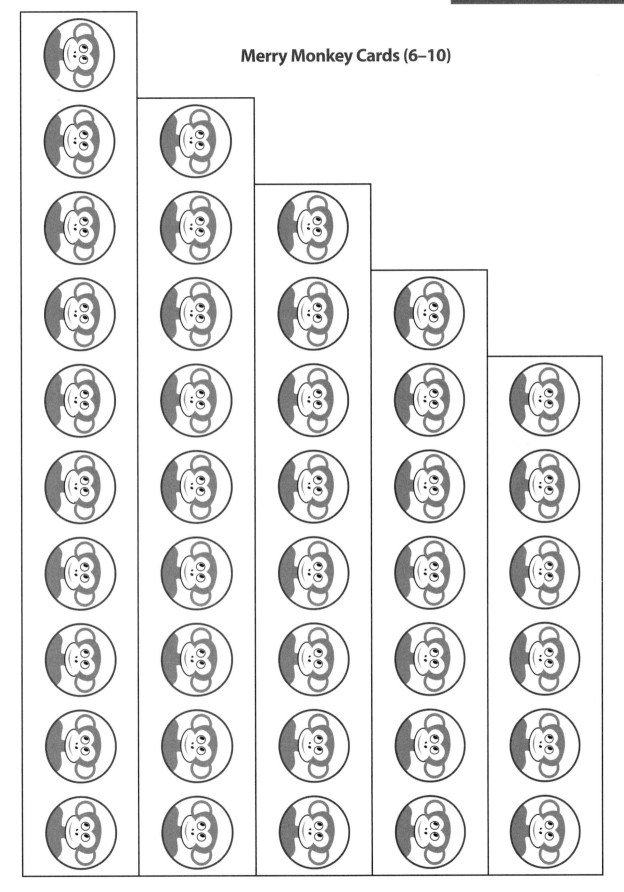

More/Fewer Spinner

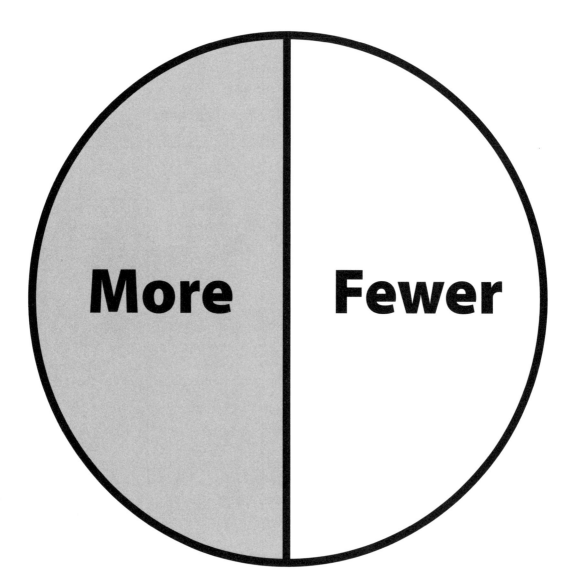

Shape Patterns

Balance Scale Patterns

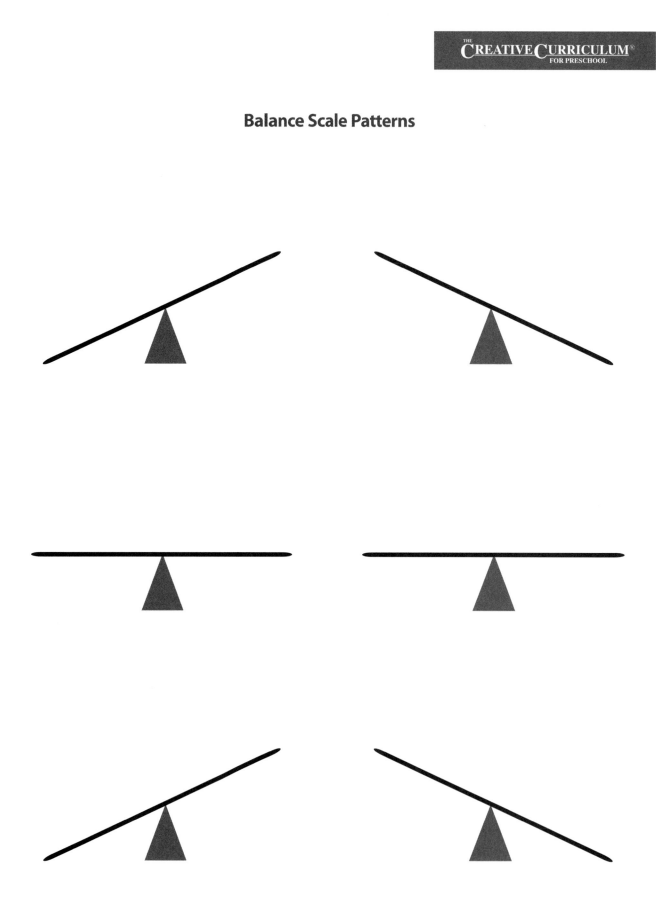

Foot Patterns

Action Cards

shoulders

nose

chin

clap

Action Cards, *continued*

hop

knee

nod

pat

Action Cards, *continued*

snap

stamp

up

legs

Cube Trains

My Little Sister (1–5)

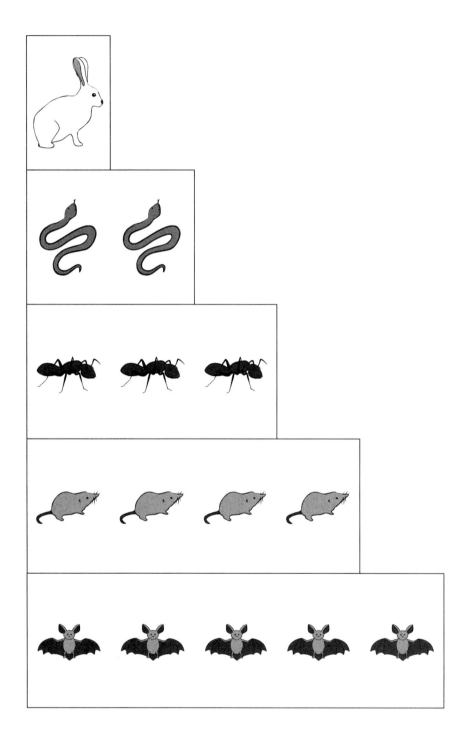

My Little Sister (6–10)

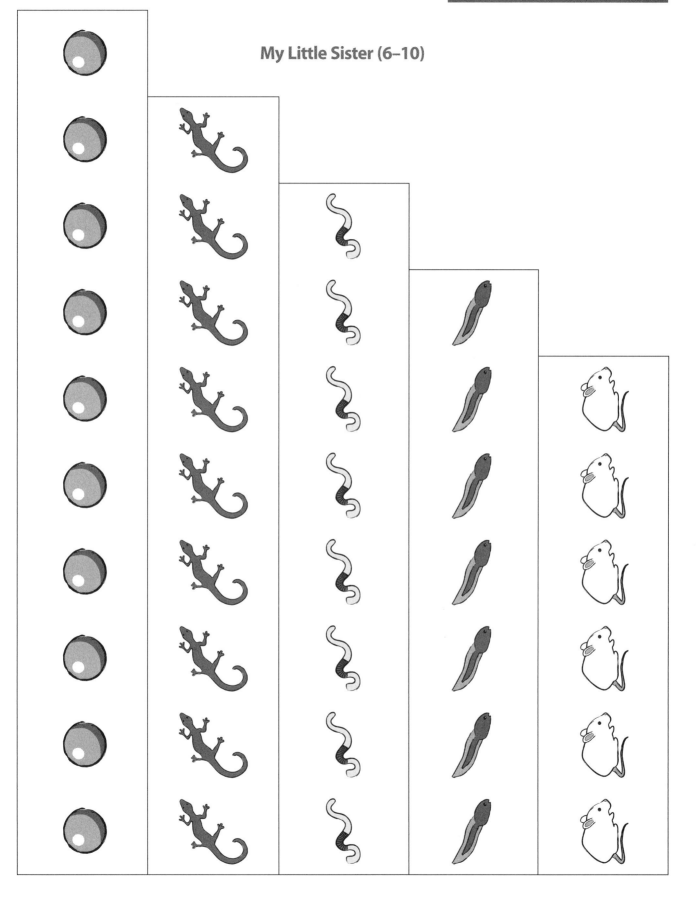

Question of the Day

Question of the Day

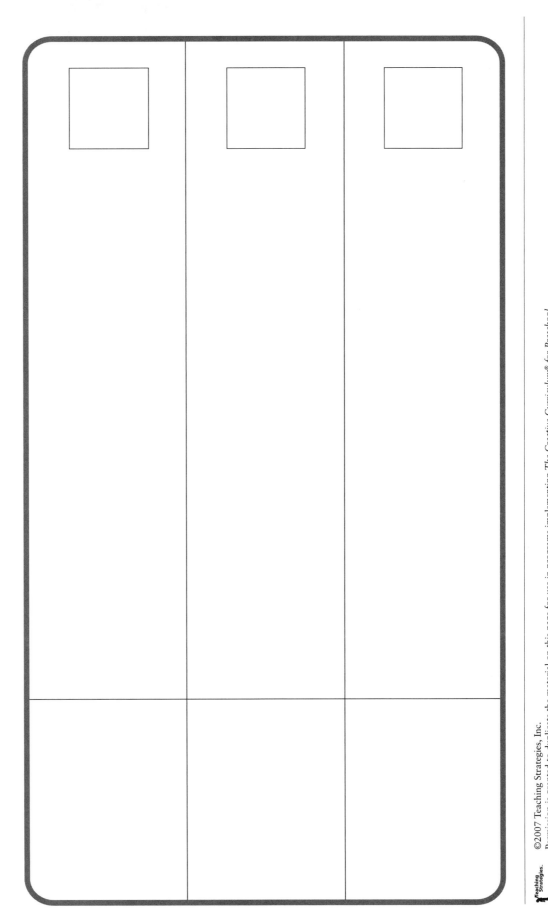

Teaching Strategies.

Question of the Day

Interest Areas | **Components**

Activities	Blocks	Dramatic Play	Toys and Games	Art	Library	Discovery	Sand and Water	Music and Movement	Cooking	Computer	Outdoors		Number and Operations	Geometry	Measurement	Patterns	Data Analysis
Number and Operations																	
Compare It		•											•		•		•
Counting Calisthenics (Aerobics)								•			•		•	•	•	•	
Dinner Time		•							•				•	•			
Learning About Numerals			•	•	•								•				
Let's Go Fishing		•	•							•			•				
Merry Monkeys					•			•					•		•		
More or Fewer Towers			•										•		•		
Nursery Rhyme Count			•					•					•				
Secret Numbers			•					•		•			•				
Shake, Rattle, and Roll			•										•	•		•	
Show Me Five			•										•				
The Fishing Trip			•						•				•				
Oh Where, Oh Where			•					•		•			•				
Geometry																	
Buried Treasure						•	•							•	•		•
I Spy With My Little Eye	•	•	•	•	•	•	•	•	•	•	•			•			
I'm Thinking of a Shape	•													•			•
My Shadow and I								•			•			•	•		
Straw Shapes			•	•										•	•		
The Bear Went Over the Mountain											•			•	•		
The Farmer Builds a Fence								•			•			•	•		
Where's the Beanbag?								•			•			•			
Measurement																	
Balancing Act			•			•								•			
Cover Up	•	•											•	•			
Morning, Noon, and Night		•		•	•										•	•	
The Long and Short of It			•	•											•		
The Queen's New Bed	•	•	•	•	•	•		•	•	•	•				•		
Wash Day		•			•										•		•
Which Holds More?							•						•		•		•
Patterns (Algebra)																	
Action Patterns								•			•					•	
Cube Trains			•											•		•	
My Little Sister					•								•			•	
Patterns Under Cover			•													•	
People Patterns								•			•			•		•	
Picture Patterns					•	•					•			•		•	
When I Was Little					•											•	•
Data Analysis																	
I Want to Know…	•	•	•	•	•	•	•	•	•	•	•		•				•
I Have a Secret			•								•						•
Shoe Sort		•											•		•		•
What Do You See?	•	•	•	•	•	•	•	•	•	•	•						•

Scope of Instruction

This section shows teachers at a glance the full range of mathematical concepts and skills to be taught. Children learn some skills in a straightforward fashion, so the way skills are built upon each other is fairly easy to see. For example, a child usually learns to count accurately to 10 before counting accurately to 20. Learning other mathematical skills and concepts depends upon previous skills and understandings in more complex ways. The components of mathematics and particular skills and concepts are connected and intertwined. For example, counting to determine a quantity also requires an understanding of one-to-one correspondence. Counting four sides and four corners of a square applies an understanding of number concepts to geometry.

While mathematics learning is embedded throughout the day, it should not be left to chance. This Scope of Instruction helps teachers thoughtfully and intentionally plan math experiences based on each child's current level of understanding. Children gain mathematical knowledge by exploring materials and ideas as an adult guides them in understanding and applying a variety of interrelated concepts skills.

After each of the five component areas, there is a list of instructional strategies and the activities and materials that link to that component.

Number and Operations

Teaching Focus

Skills and Concepts

Counting in sequence up to 20

Using one-to-one correspondence
- Matches pairs of objects in one-to-one correspondence
- Places objects in one-to-one correspondence with another set of objects
- Uses one-to-one correspondence as a way to compare sets

Counting to determine quantity
- Imitates counting behavior using number names (may not always say one number per item or get the sequence right)
- Counts or creates sets of 1–10 objects using one number for each object
- Keeps track of what has or has not been counted
- Knows that the last number counted describes the total number of objects in a set
- Counts or creates sets of 11–20 objects connecting number words spoken to the objects

Understanding quantity
- Compares two sets to determine which has more, fewer/less, or the same number.
- Understands the concept of two, three, and four
- Describes the parts of a set having 3–6 objects
- Makes sets up to 10 using two different types of objects then describes the parts

Using numerals 1–10
- Recognizes numerals (e.g., points to the correct numeral when named)
- Names numerals (names a numeral when pointed to)

Using the ordinal numbers first and second

Understanding part/whole relationships
- Describes the parts in sets with up to six objects (e.g., describes a set of four apples as having two red apples and two green apples)
- Describes the parts in sets with up to eight objects (e.g., says, "I tossed eight bean bags. Five went in the basket and three landed on the floor.")

Working with sets
- Tells how many are in a set without counting when one more object is added to a set
- Joins two sets of objects, then counts to find out how many in all (quantities to 10)
- Separates small sets (e.g., 1–5) by taking away one or more objects, then telling how many are left
- Shares or divides a collection equally (e.g., while playing in the Dramatic Play Area, gives each child three strawberries)
- Engages in set-making activities (e.g., places two mini muffins on each child's snack plate)

Instructional Strategies

- Create a numerically-rich environment.

- Count using a variety of learning styles and representations (e.g., using rhymes and verses; in ways that involve children physically).

- On occasion, point to numerals when counting aloud.

- Call attention to patterns in numbers (e.g., twenty-one, thirty-one, forty-one).

- Provide a variety of materials to help children develop an understanding of quantity (e.g., call attention to number representations such as the pips on a domino or number cube; have children create sets using concrete objects).

- Model counting strategies (e.g., how to keep track of objects you have counted; labeling the quantity of a set verbally or using numerals).

- Model different ways of comparing two sets of objects.

- Use ordinal numbers during everyday situations (e.g., "Leo will be the first to choose an interest area today.")

- Offer a variety of problem-solving opportunities that involve combining, separating, sharing, or set-making.

- Pose story problems for children to act out.

- Use books to encourage numerical reasoning.

- Ask questions or tell stories that encourage children to say how many.

- Share number books and have children create their own number books.

Activities & Materials

Compare It, Counting Calisthenics, Dinner Time, Learning About Numerals, Let's Go Fishing, Merry Monkeys, More or Fewer Towers, Nursery Rhyme Count, Secret Numbers, Shake, Rattle, and Roll, Show Me Five, The Fishing Trip, Where, Oh Where

Kit 1: Number, Geometry, and Data

Geometry and Spatial Sense

Teaching Focus

Skills and Concepts

Working with two- and three-dimensional shapes

- Recognizes two- and three-dimensional shapes by their appearance (e.g., points to a cube when asked to find a shape that looks *like a box*)

- Describes and names two- and three-dimensional shapes by a property (e.g., says, "It's a ball because it rolls." Or, "This triangle has three points and three lines."

- Describes and names shapes by properties (e.g., says, "This triangle has three points and three lines." Or, "This can rolls sometimes and slides when you put it on its side.")

Understanding positional words

- Responds to instructions involving basic positional words (e.g., puts an object *in, on, under, on top of, next to* another object)

- Uses positional words correctly (e.g., tells where an object is located)

Transforming shapes or materials (e.g., sliding, flipping, or turning shapes over to work a puzzle; molding clay into a three-dimensional shape; creating a symmetrical block picture)

Visualizing and representing shapes (e.g., looking at a model of a block structure, then recreating the same structure from memory when the structure is removed)

Instructional Strategies

- Make the Block Area available as a daily choice for all children.

- Label shapes with the correct names as children use them.

- Provide a rich variety of shapes for children to investigate including two- and three-dimensional shapes.

- Introduce three-dimensional shapes first.

- Introduce activities that require children to investigate and predict what will happen when shapes are combined.

- Model and describe how to make two- and three-dimensional shapes.

- Have children act out stories that involve position and space words.

- Plan activities that invite children to visualize and represent particular shapes (e.g., show photos, models, or sketches of shapes, have children look at them then recreate them using their own set of shapes.)

- Provide children access to computer programs that allow them to manipulate shapes.

- Provide many opportunities for children to sort shapes into two groups.

- Frequently use the word *not* to introduce non-examples of specific shapes.

- Make and use maps with children (e.g., to find hidden shapes; to draw attention to positional words).

- Provide materials and supplies so children can represent their constructions or discoveries with blocks (e.g., sketches or blueprints).

- Encourage discovery of attributes of shapes.

- Use transformational language, such as *turn*, *flip*, *slide*, as children work puzzles.

- Make cleanup time an opportunity for children to sort and match geometric shapes.

Activities & Materials

Buried Treasure, I Spy, I'm Thinking of a Shape, Me and My Shadow, Straw Shapes, The Bear Went Over the Mountain, The Farmer Builds a Fence, Where's the Bean Bag

Kit 1: Number, Geometry, and Data

Measurement

Teaching Focus

Skills and Concepts

Exploring the attributes of objects

- Describes objects by length, capacity, weight, and area

- Notices similarities and differences in length, area, weight, and volume of objects

Making comparisons

- Measures two objects by directly comparing them

- Uses comparative words related to number, size, area, texture, weight, speed, or volume to compare and describe two objects (e.g., more, bigger, covers more, softer, heavier, faster, holds more)

- Uses comparative words to compare and describe three objects (e.g., most, biggest, covers most, softest, heaviest, fastest, holds the most)

Modeling measuring behaviors (e.g., using a plastic cup and counting the number of cups it takes to fill a bottle; pretending to measure a friend's foot)

Experimenting with nonstandard measurement tools (e.g., says, "My arm is 12 chains long.")

Arranging three or more objects in a series using one or more physical attributes (e.g., lines up rods of different lengths from shortest to longest or shortest to tallest)

Showing an awareness of time concepts and sequence (e.g., says, "We have story time after lunch." Or, "Today is pizza day.")

Instructional Strategies

- Offer many standard and nonstandard measuring tools.

- Model measuring behaviors often and in a variety of meaningful contexts (e.g., determining the size of paper needed to cover a table for a messy activity).

- Talk aloud about what you are doing as you measure. Use measurement vocabulary.

- Pose problems to children that involve measurement.

- Intentionally discuss or introduce measurement concepts during various events of the day (e.g., "Let's see how much time we have before lunch.")

- Use estimation vocabulary such as about, close to, and almost.

- Plan for experiences that allow children to explore measurement involving length, area, weight, capacity, and time.

Activities & Materials

Balancing Act, Cover Up, The Queen's New Bed, Morning, Noon, and Night, The Long and Short of It, Wash Day, When I Was Little, Which Holds More

Kit 2: Measurement and Patterns

Patterns (Algebra)

Teaching Focus

Skills and Concepts

Recognizing and reading simple repeating patterns

- Recognizes and reads patterns involving color, shape, then size

- Recognizes and reads patterns involving position, texture, or number

- Reads a simple repeating pattern in an alternate way using own words

Copying simple repeating patterns

Extending or adding to simple patterns created or discovered by others

Creating simple patterns of own design

Working with simple growing patterns

- Recognizes simple growing patterns (e.g., notices the plus one pattern when singing "The Ants Go Marching" and predicting that three ants go marching, then four, then five, and so on)

- Extends simple growing patterns

- Creates a simple growing pattern of own design

Analyzing and describing changes that occur in the everyday environment (e.g., says, "I'm bigger than my brother 'cause I growed.")

Instructional Strategies

- Call attention to patterns that occur naturally during the day such as in the daily schedule and routines.

- Model and encourage pattern talk (e.g., "Look, I see a pattern on the gate.")

- Call attention to patterns in a variety of contexts (e.g., in nature or in numbers).

- Focus children's attention first on patterns involving color. Then progress to shape and then size.

- Introduce children to position patterns (e.g., up, down, up, down).

- Read books that have patterned language.

- Sing songs and recite rhymes that have patterned and repetitive language.

- Have the children create pattern books or take dictation about topics that involve change (e.g., "When I was little, I could… Now that I am bigger, I can…")

- Create an environment that allows children to observe change (e.g., plant and animal growth).

- Use sounds, words, movements, and objects to describe patterns rather than letters of the alphabet.

- Provide opportunities for children to identify, copy, extend, and create a variety of patterns (e.g., visual, auditory, movement, stories, and verse).

Activities & Materials

Action Patterns, Cube Trains, My Little Sister, Patterns Under Cover, People Patterns, Picture Patterns

Kit 2: Measurement and Patterns

Skills and Concepts

Separating a group of objects from a larger collection (e.g., child finds all the shiny buttons and puts them together because they are "the prettiest")

Sorting and classifying objects

- Sorts and classifies objects by one property, such as color, size, shape, texture, sound, or function

- Sorts and classifies objects by one property then resorts using a different property

- Sorts and classifies objects into groups with subgroups (e.g., sorting animals into a group of cats and dogs, then sorting each of the two groups into those with spots and those with no spots)

Using data

- Organizes and represents data in a variety of ways (e.g., creating real, pictorial, or symbolic graphs; using pictures and/or words; using symbols such as tally marks)

- Describes data using vocabulary such as more, fewer, the same number as, larger than, smaller than, and not.

Instructional Strategies

- Use routine experiences as opportunities for children to sort, classify, and graph (e.g., attendance or snack choices)

- Focus first on sorting objects into only two groups.

- Encourage children to sort or organize objects according to their own rules.

- Have children explain or describe how and why they organized object in a particular way.

- Model a number of ways a collection could be organized.

- Describe collections in multiple ways.

- Create many graphs using the children or concrete objects as indicators of a particular attribute (e.g., have the children form two lines: one with those wearing shoes that tie and one with those wearing shoes that do not tie).

- Introduce pictorial and then symbolic graphs.

- Play sorting games in which the children must guess the sorting rule.

- Label graphs and other representations using symbols that are easily understood by the children (e.g., writing objects sorted by color using the respective colored marker).

- Provide materials and supplies in all interest areas so children can sort, classify, and represent data in a variety of ways.

Activities & Materials

I Want to Know…, I've Got a Secret, Shoe Sort, What Do You See

Kit 1: Number, Geometry, and Data

COGNITIVE DEVELOPMENT

Learning and Problem Solving

Curriculum Objectives	Developmental Continuum for Ages 3–5			
		I	II	III
22. **Observes objects and events with curiosity**	**Forerunners** Looks at and touches object presented by an adult or another child Explores materials in the environment *e.g., touching, looking, smelling, mouthing, listening, playing*	Examines with attention to detail, noticing attributes of objects *e.g., points out stripes on caterpillar; notices it gets darker when the sun goes behind a cloud; points out changes in animals or plants in room*	Notices and/or asks questions about similarities and differences *e.g., points out that two trucks are the same size; asks why the leaves fall off the trees*	Observes attentively and seeks relevant information *e.g., describes key features of different models of cars (such as logos, number of doors, type of license plate); investigates which objects will sink and which will float*
23. **Approaches problems flexibly**	**Forerunners** Imitates adult or peer in solving problems Repeats and persists in trial and error approach	Finds multiple uses for classroom objects *e.g., uses wooden blocks as musical instruments; strings wooden beads into necklace for dress-up*	Experiments with materials in new ways when first way doesn't work *e.g., when playdough recipe produces sticky dough, asks for more flour; fills plastic bottle with water to make it sink*	Finds alternative solutions to problems *e.g., suggests using block as doorstop when classroom doorstop disappears; offers to swap trike for riding toy she wants and then adds fire-fighter hat to the bargain*
24. **Shows persistence in approaching tasks**	**Forerunners** Remains engaged in a task for short periods with assistance Stays involved in self-selected activity such as playing with playdough for short periods	Sees simple tasks through to completion *e.g., puts toys away before going on to next activity; completes 5-piece puzzle*	Continues to work on task even when encountering difficulties *e.g., rebuilds block tower when it tumbles; keeps trying different puzzle pieces when pieces aren't fitting together*	Works on task over time, leaving and returning to complete it *e.g., continues to work on LEGO® structure over 3-day period; creates grocery store out of hollow blocks, adding more detail each day, and involves other children in playing grocery*
25. **Explores cause and effect**	**Forerunners** Notices an effect *e.g., shows pleasure in turning light switch on and off, wants to do it again; repeatedly stacks blocks and watches them fall* Looks for something when it is out of sight	Notices and comments on effect *e.g., while shaking a jar of water says, "Look at the bubbles when I do this"; after spinning around and stopping says, "Spinning makes the room look like it's moving up and down"*	Wonders "what will happen if" and tests out possibilities *e.g., blows into cardboard tubes of different sizes to hear if different sounds are made; changes the incline of a board to make cars slide down faster*	Explains plans for testing cause and effect, and tries out ideas *e.g., places pennies one by one in 2 floating boats ("I'm seeing which boat sinks first"); mixes gray paint to match another batch ("Let's put in one drop of white at a time 'til it's right")*

Learning and Problem Solving (continued)

Curriculum Objectives	Developmental Continuum for Ages 3–5			
		I	II	III
26. **Applies knowledge or experience to a new context**	**Forerunners** Follows familiar self-help routines at school (toileting, eating)—may need assistance	Draws on everyday experiences and applies this knowledge to similar situations *e.g., washes hands after playing at sand table; rocks baby doll in arms*	Applies new information or vocabulary to an activity or interaction *e.g., comments, "We're bouncing like Tigger" when jumping up and down with peer; uses traffic-directing signals after seeing a police officer demonstrate them*	Generates a rule, strategy, or idea from one learning experience and applies it in a new context *e.g., after learning to access one computer program by clicking on icons, uses similar procedures to access others; suggests voting to resolve a classroom issue*

Logical Thinking

Developmental Continuum for Ages 3–5

Curriculum Objectives	Forerunners	I	II	III
27. **Classifies objects**	Finds two objects that are the same and comments or puts them together Groups similar kinds of toys together such as cars, blocks, or dolls	Sorts objects by one property such as size, shape, color, or use *e.g., sorts pebbles into three buckets by color; puts square block with other square blocks*	Sorts a group of objects by one property and then by another *e.g., collects leaves and sorts by size and then by color; puts self in group wearing shoes that tie and then in group with blue shoes*	Sorts objects into groups/subgroups and can state reason *e.g., sorts stickers into four piles ("Here are the stars that are silver and gold, and here are circles, silver and gold"); piles animals and then divides them into zoo and farm animals*
28. **Compares/ measures**	Notices something new or different *e.g., a new classmate or a new toy on the shelf* Notices similarities of objects *e.g., "We have the same shoes"*	Notices similarities and differences *e.g., states, "The rose is the only flower in our garden that smells"; "I can run fast in my new shoes"*	Uses comparative words related to number, size, shape, texture, weight, color, speed, volume *e.g., "This bucket is heavier than that one"; "Now the music is going faster"*	Understands/uses measurement words and some standard measurement tools *e.g., uses unit blocks to measure length of rug; "We need 2 cups of flour and 1 cup of salt to make dough"*
29. **Arranges objects in a series**	Uses self-correcting toys such as form boards and graduated stacking rings Sorts by one attribute *e.g., big blocks and little blocks*	Notices when one object in a series is out of place *e.g., removes the one measuring spoon out of place in a line and tries to put it in right place*	Figures out a logical order for a group of objects *e.g., makes necklace of graduated wooden beads; arranges magazine pictures of faces from nicest expression to meanest*	Through trial and error, arranges objects along a continuum according to two or more physical features *e.g., lines up bottle caps by height and width; sorts playdough cookies by size, color, and shape*
30. **Recognizes patterns and can repeat them**	Completes a sentence that repeats in a familiar story Hums, sings, or responds to a chorus that repeats in a familiar song Completes a simple form board	Notices and recreates simple patterns with objects *e.g., makes a row of blocks alternating in size (big-small-big-small); strings beads in repeating patterns of 2 colors*	Extends patterns or creates simple patterns of own design *e.g., makes necklace of beads in which a sequence of 2 or more colors is repeated; continues block pattern of 2 colors*	Creates complex patterns of own design or by copying *e.g., imitates hand-clapping pattern (long clap followed by 3 short claps); designs a 3-color pattern using colored inch cubes and repeats it across the table*

Logical Thinking (continued)

Developmental Continuum for Ages 3–5

Curriculum Objectives	Forerunners	I	II	III
31. **Shows awareness of time concepts and sequence**	**Forerunners** Follows steps in simple routine such as in dressing or at naptime Demonstrates understanding of what comes next in daily schedule *e.g., goes to the table anticipating mealtime*	Demonstrates understanding of the present and may refer to past and future *e.g., responds appropriately when asked, "What did you do this morning?"; talks about, "Later, when Mom comes to pick me up"*	Uses past and future tenses and time words appropriately *e.g., talks about tomorrow, yesterday, last week; says, "After work time, we go outside"*	Associates events with time-related concepts *e.g., "Tomorrow is Saturday so there's no school"; "My birthday was last week"; "I go to bed at night"*
32. **Shows awareness of position in space**	**Forerunners** Moves objects from one container to another Follows simple positional directions with assistance *e.g., puts paper in trash can*	Shows comprehension of basic positional words and concepts *e.g., puts object in, on, under, on top of, or next to another object as requested*	Understands and uses positional words correctly *e.g., "Come sit near me"; "The fish food goes on the top shelf"*	Shows understanding that positional relationships vary with one's perspective *e.g., turns lotto card around so player opposite him can see it right side up; "I can reach the ring when I'm on the top step, but from here it's too far"*
33. **Uses one-to-one correspondence**	**Forerunners** Places an object in each designated space *e.g., puts a peg doll in each hole in a toy bus*	Matches pairs of objects in one-to-one correspondence *e.g., searches through dress-ups to find two shoes for her feet*	Places objects in one-to-one correspondence with another set *e.g., lines up brushes to make sure there is one for each jar of paint; goes around the table placing one cup at each child's place*	Uses one-to-one correspondence as a way to compare two sets *e.g., lines up cubes across from a friend's row to determine who has more; puts one rider next to each horse saying, "Are there enough horses for all the cowboys?"*
34. **Uses numbers and counting**	**Forerunners** Understands the concept of "one" *e.g., picks up one object when asked* Understands the concept of more *e.g., picks up more of something when directed, or asks for more cheese*	Imitates counting behavior using number names (may not always say one number per item or get the sequence right) *e.g., says the numbers from 1 to 5 while moving finger along a row of 8 items (not realizing that counting means one number per item)*	Counts correctly up to 5 or so using one number for each object (may not always keep track of what has or has not been counted) *e.g., counts out 5 pretzels taking one at a time from bowl; counts a collection of objects but may count an object more than one time*	Counts to 10 or so connecting number words and symbols to the objects counted and knows that the last number describes the total *e.g., counts 8 bottle caps and says, "I have 8"; spins dial, then moves board game piece 6 spaces; draws 5 figures to show members of family*

Representation and Symbolic Thinking

Developmental Continuum for Ages 3–5

Curriculum Objectives	Forerunners	I	II	III
35. **Takes on pretend roles and situations**	**Forerunners** Imitates simple action *e.g., picks up phone; rocks baby* With adult or peer support, imitates routines *e.g., pretends to feed doll; pours coffee; pretends to sleep*	Performs and labels actions associated with a role *e.g., feeding the baby doll, says, "I'm the Mommy"; picks up phone and says, "Hello, is Suzie there?"*	Offers a play theme and scenario *e.g., "Let's play school"; while listening to doll's heartbeat with stethoscope announces that it's time to get the baby to the hospital*	Engages in elaborate and sustained role play *e.g., suggests a play theme and discusses who will do what; discusses with peer what to buy at grocery store, takes pocketbook and goes to grocery store*
36. **Makes believe with objects**	**Forerunners** Imitates adult's or another child's use of familiar objects *e.g., rocks doll; stirs the pot* Interacts appropriately with objects with adult or peer support *e.g., responds to pretend phone call by putting phone to ear and vocalizing*	Interacts appropriately with real objects or replicas in pretend play *e.g., uses a broken phone to make a pretend phone call; puts playdough cookies on little plastic plates*	Uses substitute object or gesture to represent real object *e.g., holds hand to ear and pretends to dial phone; builds a sand castle and puts shell on top for "satellite dish"*	Uses make-believe props in planned and sustained play *e.g., pretends with a peer to be garage mechanics working on cars made of blocks; sets up scene for playing school—students sit on pillows and teacher has a box for a desk*
37. **Makes and interprets representations**	**Forerunners** Labels scribbles as people or common objects Interacts and builds with blocks Begins to use descriptive labels in construction play *e.g., "house," "road"*	Draws or constructs and then names what it is *e.g., draws pictures with different shapes and says, "This is my house"; lines up unit blocks and says, "I'm making a road"*	Draws or builds a construction that represents something specific *e.g., makes a helicopter with Bristle Blocks; draws 6 legs on insect after looking at beetle*	Plans then creates increasingly elaborate representations *e.g., uses blocks to make a maze for the class gerbil; draws fire truck and includes many details*

Number and Operations Observation Form

Child's Name: _____

Directions: Use this form to record your observations about a child's knowledge of number and operations. You may choose to either check or date the appropriate lines as you observe the child demonstrate this knowledge.

Counts aloud in correct order

☐ to 5   ☐ to 10   ☐ to 15   ☐ to 20

Counts or creates groups of objects and says how many all together

☐ 1–5 objects   ☐ 6–10 objects

Recognizes numerals (e.g., when someone says five, points to the symbol 5)

☐ 1   ☐ 3   ☐ 5   ☐ 7   ☐ 9
☐ 2   ☐ 4   ☐ 6   ☐ 8   ☐ 10

Names numerals (e.g., when sees the symbol 5, can say the word *five*)

☐ 1   ☐ 3   ☐ 5   ☐ 7   ☐ 9
☐ 2   ☐ 4   ☐ 6   ☐ 8   ☐ 10

Describes parts of a small number of objects (e.g., "I have four cubes, two are red, and two are blue.")

☐ 3–5 objects   ☐ 6–10 objects

Joins sets of objects and tells how many (e.g., child counts out three objects; then counts out two objects. When asked how many all together, counts 1, 2, 3, 4, 5.)

☐ 1–5 objects   ☐ 6–10 objects

Geometry and Spatial Sense Observation Form

Child's Name: _____

Directions: Use this form to record your observations about a child's knowledge of geometry and spatial sense. Describe what the child did and said and date the appropriate line.

Explores and describes three-dimensional shapes by what they look like and what they can do (e.g., says, "This bead is round like a ball. It rolls." "This block has six sides and is like a box." "The marker is like a can and can roll.")

_____

_____

_____

Describes and names two-dimensional shapes by one or more attributes (e.g., a triangle has three points; a rectangle and square rectangle have four sides and four points; a circle…)

_____

_____

_____

Understands and uses positional words (e.g., *in, on, over, under, next to, on top of, near*)

_____

_____

_____

Mathematics Implementation Checklist: Mathematics in the Environment

For the purposes of this assessment, consider the total learning environment, including indoors and outdoors.

Do Teachers

		YES	NO
1. Provide a variety of materials (three or more) for exploring number concepts (e.g., counting bears, counting books, number puzzles, number lines)?		☐	☐
	1) _____		
	2) _____		
	3) _____		
2. Provide a variety of materials (three or more) for exploring geometry and developing spatial sense (e.g., shape puzzles and sorters, blocks, parquetry blocks, three-dimensional objects such as balls, boxes, cans)?		☐	☐
	1) _____		
	2) _____		
	3) _____		
3. Provide a variety of materials (three or more) for exploring measurement (e.g., measuring cups, spoons, balancing scales, rulers, string, scales, sand timers, play money)?		☐	☐
	1) _____		
	2) _____		
	3) _____		
4. Include a variety of materials that allow children to recognize, copy, create, and extend patterns (e.g., pattern blocks, unit blocks, colored wooden beads, collage materials)?		☐	☐
	1) _____		
	2) _____		
	3) _____		
5. Provide a variety of materials (three or more) for sorting and classifying objects (e.g., collections such as bottle caps, shells, leaves, buttons).		☐	☐
	1) _____		
	2) _____		
	3) _____		

Mathematics Implementation Checklist: Guiding Children's Mathematics Learning

Teachers guide children's learning during planned large- and small-group activities, as they interact with children in interest areas, and during routines and transitions throughout the day. This may happen outdoors as well as indoors.

Do Teachers	YES	NO
1. Talk with children about their work to extend **thinking** and build **vocabulary** (e.g., comment on or describe what they see, invite children to share ideas about their work, teach new language during play such as *cube* or *behind*)?	☐	☐
2. Ask open-ended questions that help children explain, predict, apply knowledge to **solve a problem**, evaluate, or consider consequences (e.g., "How did you decide…? What do you think will happen if …? How can you find out? Can you think of a way to…? What happened that time?")	☐	☐
3. Introduce mathematical ideas in planned, purposeful ways (e.g., read stories with mathematical concepts, teach counting rhymes, create graphs, explore math concepts in a cooking activity)?	☐	☐
4. Encourage children to **connect** mathematical ideas to everyday experiences (e.g., "We need to figure out a way to share the markers so everyone will have the same number.").	☐	☐
5. Encourage children to **communicate** and **represent** their mathematical thinking (e.g., create and talk about a graph of favorite cereals; explain how they sorted teddy bear counters; say, "This is how old I am" and share a drawing of a birthday cake with 4 candles)	☐	☐
6. Interact with children to support their understanding of **number and operations** (e.g., engage in counting, one-to-one correspondence, quantity, number recognition, comparison activities)?	☐	☐
7. Interact with children to support their understanding of **patterns** (e.g., identify, copy, extend, and create patterns)?	☐	☐
8. Interact with children to support their understanding of **geometry** and **spatial sense** (e.g., explore two- and three-dimensional shapes; engage in activities using spatial vocabulary such as *in, out, behind, beside, over, under, around, through, near, far*)?	☐	☐
9. Interact with children to promote their understanding of **measurement** (e.g., compare length, area, weight, capacity, time, temperature)?	☐	☐
10. Interact with children to promote their understanding of **data** collection, organization, and representation (e.g., sort, classify, represent data, create graphs, describe and compare findings)?	☐	☐

Glossary

area:

a measurement term describing how much space is covered

capacity:

a measurement term describing how much can be held

cardinal numbers:

numbers used to describe the amount or how many are present in a group; the last number said when counting (e.g., "There are four objects in the set.")

classifying:

putting objects into groups based on common attributes

conservation:

the ability of a child to understand that the amount of object (shape or size) remains the same even if the object is moved or subdivided

geometric shapes (two-dimensional figures):

circle: a collection of points on a plane where each point is the same distance from a fixed point called the center

These are *not* polygons.

 polygon: a closed figure made of line segments

 regular polygon: a polygon whose sides and angles are all the same length

 triangle: a three-sided polygon

 quadrilateral: a four-sided polygon

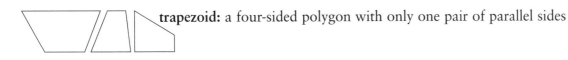 **trapezoid:** a four-sided polygon with only one pair of parallel sides

geometric shapes (two-dimensional figures), *continued*

 rectangle: a four-sided polygon with all right angles

 square rectangle: a special rectangle having equal length sides with all right angles

 **parallelogram:** a four-sided polygon with two pairs of parallel sides

 rhombus: a four-sided polygon with all four sides of equal length

pentagon: a five-sided polygon

hexagon: a six-sided polygon

growing pattern:

the unit in the pattern increases by at least plus one or more and continues to increase

length:

a measurement term describing how tall or long something is

ordinal numbers:

numbers used to describe position in an ordered sequence (e.g., first, second, third, etc.)

one-to-one correspondence:

counting giving one number name to one and only one object in the set being counted

position words:

words that describe the location in space of an object (e.g., on top of, near, under, far, next to, between)

repeating pattern:

a pattern where each unit appears again in a consistent, predictable way

rote counting:

reciting number names in proper order

solids (three-dimensional figures):

 sphere: a three-dimensional figure with all points equal distance from the center

 cube: a three-dimensional figure with six equal square faces

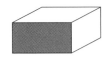 **triangular prism:** a three-dimensional figure with congruent triangular-shaped bases, that is, both bases are the same size and shape

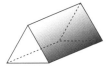 **rectangular prism:** a three-dimensional figure with congruent rectangular-shaped bases, that is, both bases are the same size and shape

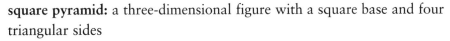 **cone:** a three-dimensional figure with a circular base and a single vertex

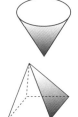 **square pyramid:** a three-dimensional figure with a square base and four triangular sides

 cylinder: a figure with two congruent circular parallel bases, that is, both bases are the same size and shape

 triangular pyramid: a three-dimensional figure with a triangular base and three triangular faces

subitize:

to accurately judge the number or quantity of a group of objects without counting

three-dimensional:

a figure that has width, height, and depth

transformations: moving a shape into a new position either by rotating, flipping, or translating

> **rotation or turning:** moving an object around a fixed point

> **flipping or reflection:** inverting an object to position it into its mirror image

> **translation or sliding:** moving every point of an object a fixed distance

transitivity:

a component of measurement that describes the comparison of the lengths of two objects by comparing their length to the length of a third object (e.g., if length A is less than length B, and length B is less than length C, then length A is less than length C.)

two-dimensional:

a figure that has width and height

weight:

a measurement term describing how heavy something is

Bibliography & References

Baroody, A. J. (2004). The developmental bases for early childhood number and operations standards. In D. H. Clements, J. Sarama, & A. Dibiase (Eds.), *Engaging young children in mathematics* (pp. 173–220). Mahwah, NJ: Lawrence Erlbaum Associates.

Carpenter, T. P., & Levi, L. (1999, April). *Developing conceptions of algebraic reasoning in the primary grades*. Paper presented at the meeting of the American Educational Research Association, Montreal, Canada.

Clements, D. H. (1999). Geometry and spatial thinking in young children. In J. V. Copley (Ed.), *Mathematics in the early years* (pp. 66–79). Reston, VA: National Council of Teachers of Mathematics.

Clements, D. H. (2003, September). *Good beginnings in mathematics: Linking a national vision to state action*. New York: Carnegie Corporation.

Clements, D. H. (2004). Geometric and spatial thinking in early childhood education. In D. H. Clements, J. Sarama, & A. Dibiase (Eds.), *Engaging young children in mathematics* (pp. 267–298). Mahwah, NJ: Lawrence Erlbaum Associates.

Clements, D. H., Battista, M. T., Sarama, J., & Swaminathan, S. (1997). Development of students' spatial thinking in a unit on geometric motions and area. *The Elementary School Journal, 98*(2), 171–186.

Clements, D. H., Swaminathan, S., Hannibal, M. A. Z., & Sarama, J. (1999). Young children's concepts of shape. *Journal for Research in Mathematics Education, 30*, 192–212.

Copley, J. V. (2000). *The young child and mathematics*. Washington D.C.: National Association for the Education of the Young Child and National Council of Teachers of Mathematics.

Copley, J. V. (2004). The early childhood collaborative: A professional development model to communicate and implement the standards. In D. H. Clements, J. Sarama, and A. Dibiase (Eds.), *Engaging young children in mathematics* (pp. 401–414). Mahwah, NJ: Lawrence Erbaum Associates.

Copley, J. V. (Ed.). (2004). *Showcasing mathematics for the young child: Activities for three-, four-, and five-year-olds*. Reston, VA: National Council of Teachers of Mathematics.

Copley, J. V. (2005). *Measuring with young children*. Paper presented at the International Conference for the Education of the Young Child, Madrid, Spain.

Copley, J. V., & Hawkins, J. (2005). *Interim report of C3 coaching grant: Mathematics professional development*.

Friel, S. N., Curcio, F. R., & Bright, G. W. (2001). Making sense of graphs: Critical factors influencing comprehension and instructional implications. *Journal for Research in Mathematics Education, 32*, 124–158.

Gelman, R., & Gallistel, C. R. (1978). *The child's understanding of number*. Cambridge, MA: Harvard University Press.

Kilpatrick, J., Swafford, J., & Findell, B. (2001). *Adding it up: Helping children learn mathematics*. Washington, DC: National Academy Press.

National Council of Teachers of Mathematics. (2006). *Curriculum focal points for prekindergarten through grade 8 mathematics: A quest for coherence.* Reston, VA: Author.

National Council of Teachers of Mathematics. (2000). *Principles and standards for school mathematics.* Reston, VA: Author.

Piaget, J., & Inhelder, B. (1967). *The child's conception of space* (F. J. Langdon & J. L. Lunzer, Trans.). New York: Norton.

Piaget, J., Inhelder, B., & Szeminska, A. (1952). *The child's conception of geometry.* London: Routledge & Kegan Paul.

Russell, S. J. (1991). Counting noses and scary things: Children construct their ideas about data. In D. Vere-Jones (Ed.), *Proceedings of the third international conference on teaching statistics* (pp. 158–164). Voorburg, Netherlands: International Statistical Institute.

Siegler, R. S., & Robinson, M. (1982). The development of numerical understanding. In H. W. Reese & L. P. Lipsitt (Eds.), *Advances in child development and behavior* (pp. 241–312). New York: Academic Press.

Starkey, P. (1992). The early development of numerical reasoning. *Cognition and Instruction, 43,* 93–126.

Steffe, L. P. & Cobb, P. (1988). *Construction of arithmetical meanings and strategies.* New York: Springer-Verlag.

Van Hiele, P. M. (1986). *Structure and insight: A theory of mathematics education.* Orlando, FL: Academic Press.

Teaching Strategies Inc.

Order Form

Please type or print clearly.

4 Ways to Order

Order online
www.TeachingStrategies.com
15% discount or more for online orders

Order by phone
800-637-3652
Washington, DC area:
202-362-7543
8 a.m.–7 p.m. Eastern Time, M–F

Order by fax
202-350-5940
24 hours a day

Order by mail
Teaching Strategies, Inc.
P.O. Box 42243
Washington, DC 20015

Ship to:

NAME	
ORGANIZATION	
ADDRESS	
CITY	STATE	ZIP
PHONE	FAX
E-MAIL	

Bill to:

Your Teaching Strategies Customer Number:
(If known)

NAME	
ORGANIZATION	
ADDRESS	
CITY	STATE	ZIP
PHONE	FAX

Order:

ITEM #	QTY	DESCRIPTION	UNIT PRICE	TOTAL
			$	$
			$	$
			$	$
			$	$
			$	$
			$	$
			$	$
			$	$
			$	$
			$	$

Please call for information on quantity discounts.

SUBTOTAL	$
SALES TAX CA, DC, IL: Add appropriate sales tax.	$
	$
TOTAL	$

Method of payment

All orders must be accompanied by payment, P.O. number, or credit card information. Customers with an established credit history are welcome to use P.O. numbers.
First-time customers must enclose pre-payment with order.

❏ Check (payable to Teaching Strategies)   ❏ Money order

❏ Purchase order (must include copy of P.O.)   ❏ Visa   ❏ MasterCard

❏ American Express   ❏ Discover

CREDIT CARD OR PURCHASE ORDER NUMBER   EXPIRATION DATE

SIGNATURE OF CARD HOLDER

❏ Yes, I would like to receive occasional e-mail notifications about new Teaching Strategies products and special offers. I understand that Teaching Strategies will not share or sell my e-mail address with any other individual, company, or organization.

SHIPPING
United States: Orders up to $60.00—$5.00;
Orders over $60.00—12% of total.
International/U.S. Territories: $20.00 (first book)
+ $7.00 for each additional book.
Rush Delivery: Call for shipping charges.
Method: ❏ Ground ❏ 2-day ❏ Next-day ❏ International

Guarantee: Teaching Strategies guarantees your complete satisfaction. If you are not thoroughly delighted with the printed materials you order, return the item(s) in sellable condition within 30 days for a refund (excluding shipping costs). We will gladly accept unopened CC-PORT software or Toolkits. However, we are unable to accept opened software or Toolkits (or components) with opened shrink-wrap. All video/DVD sales are final. Prices subject to change without notice. CC4M07

Thank you for your order.